DATE DUE

APR 2 3 1984			
	FEB 1 1 2003		

Also in this Series

THE RIGHTS OF MILITARY PERSONNEL	33365	$1.50
THE RIGHTS OF YOUNG PEOPLE	31963	$1.50
THE RIGHTS OF ALIENS	31534	$1.50
THE RIGHTS OF STUDENTS	32045	$1.50
THE RIGHTS OF MENTALLY RETARDED PERSONS	31351	$1.50
THE RIGHTS OF CANDIDATES AND VOTERS	28159	$1.50
THE RIGHTS OF GAY PEOPLE	24976	$1.75
THE RIGHTS OF HOSPITAL PATIENTS	22459	$1.50
THE RIGHTS OF THE POOR	28001	$1.25
THE RIGHTS OF SUSPECTS	28043	$1.25
THE RIGHTS OF TEACHERS	25049	$1.50
THE RIGHTS OF WOMEN	27953	$1.75

AN AMERICAN
CIVIL LIBERTIES
UNION HANDBOOK

THE RIGHTS OF REPORTERS
THE BASIC ACLU GUIDE TO A REPORTER'S RIGHTS

Joel M. Gora

General Editors of this series:
Norman Dorsen, *Chairperson*
Aryeh Neier, *Executive Director*

A DISCUS BOOK/PUBLISHED BY AVON BOOKS

AVON BOOKS
A division of
The Hearst Corporation
959 Eighth Avenue
New York, New York 10019

First Discus Printing, December, 1974.
Second Printing

DISCUS TRADEMARK REG. U.S. PAT. OFF. AND
FOREIGN COUNTRIES, REGISTERED TRADEMARK—
MARCA REGISTRADA, HECHO EN CHICAGO, U.S.A.

Printed in the U.S.A.

Acknowledgments

Thanks go to Les Whitten, who helped add his reporter's perspective to a lawyer's analysis, and most of all to Ann Ray, my favorite reporter and the best editor a lawyer ever had.

Contents

Preface

This guide sets forth your rights under present law and offers suggestions on how you can protect your rights. It is one of a series of guidebooks published in cooperation with the American Civil Liberties Union on the rights of mental patients, prisoners, servicemen, teachers, students, women, suspects, and the poor. Additional books, now in preparation, will include volumes on the rights of hospital patients, gay people, aliens, civil servants, veterans, and the aged.

The hope surrounding these publications is that Americans informed of their rights will be encouraged to exercise them. Through their exercise, rights are given life. If they are rarely used, they may be forgotten and violations may become routine.

This guide offers no assurances that your rights will be respected. The laws may change and, in some of the subjects covered in these pages, they change quite rapidly. An effort has been made to note those parts of the law where movement is taking place but it is not always possible to predict accurately when the law *will* change.

Even if the laws remain the same, interpretations of them by courts and administrative officials often vary. In a federal system such as ours, there is a built-in problem of the differences between state and federal law, not to speak of the confusion of the differences from state to state. In addition, there are wide variations in the ways in which particular courts and administrative officials will interpret the same law at any given moment.

If you encounter what you consider to be a specific abuse of your rights you should seek legal assistance. There are a number of agencies that may help you, among them ACLU affiliate offices, but bear in mind that the ACLU is a limited-purpose organization. In many communities, there are federally funded legal service offices which provide assistance to poor persons who cannot afford the costs of legal representation. In general, the rights that the ACLU defends are freedom of inquiry and expression; due process of law; equal protection of the laws; and privacy. The authors in this series have discussed other rights in these books (even though they sometimes fall outside the ACLU's usual concern) in order to provide as much guidance as possible.

These books have been planned as guides for the people directly affected: therefore the question and answer format. In some of these areas there are more detailed works available for "experts." These guides seek to raise the largest issues and inform the non-specialist of the basic law on the subject. The authors of the books are themselves specialists who understand the need for information at "street level."

No attorney can be an expert in every part of the law. If you encounter a specific legal problem in an area discussed in one of these guidebooks, show the book to your attorney. Of course, he will not be able to rely *exclusively* on the guidebook to provide you with adequate representation. But if he hasn't had a great deal of experience in the specific area, the guidebook can provide some helpful suggestions on how to proceed.

Norman Dorsen, General Counsel
American Civil Liberties Union

Aryeh Neier, Executive Director
American Civil Liberties Union

Introduction

In June, 1972, a narrow majority of the United States Supreme Court ruled that reporters called before grand juries did not have a general right under the First Amendment to refuse to answer questions in order to protect confidential news sources. A year and a half later, a Gallup Poll showed that sixty-two percent of the American public disagreed, expressing the opinion that reporters should not be required to reveal their sources. Applications for enrollment in journalism schools have increased dramatically. And it is probably safe to say that today, primarily because of the role of the press in uncovering Watergate and related scandals, a majority of Americans have a more favorable attitude toward reporters and their function than ever before.

In the ACLU experience, such developments are not unusual. Groups of individuals seeking to assert and establish their legal rights often lose individual court battles, yet ultimately win their particular wars—in other courts, or in the legislative arena, or, most importantly, in the forum of public opinion. In many ways the efforts to define and vindicate the rights of reporters reflect the same pattern. In recent years reporters have lost some important cases in the Supreme Court and elsewhere. Hundreds of reporters have been subpoenaed, dozens threatened with contempt-of-court citations, and some even arrested or jailed—all for attempting to do their job of keeping the public informed. But as a result of these various legal struggles, reporters have developed a heightened awareness of their legal rights and an increased determination to fight for them. New watchdog agencies have sprung up to monitor episodes of press censorship and mobilize resistance to them. As a consequence, whether the particular threat to press freedom comes from without—in the form of official

11

or legal pressures and sanctions—or from within—as a result of editorial caution in the face of such pressures, few
incidents of interference with the rights of reporters go
unnoticed or unattended for very long.

If this book helps to fuel that process—by telling reporters what their rights are and thereby strengthening their
determination to assert those rights—it will have achieved
its purpose.

I
General First Amendment Principles

Are reporters given protection by the Constitution?

Yes. The First Amendment to the United States Constitution provides:

> Congress shall make no law respecting an establishment of religion, or prohibiting the free exercise thereof; or abridging the freedom of speech, or of the press; or the right of the people peaceably to assemble and to petition the Government for a redress of grievances.

Though the provision speaks only in terms of the national Congress, its protection has been extended by judicial decision to encompass action by the executive branch,[1] state legislatures,[2] all municipal agencies,[3] and all public officials.[4] In short, the First Amendment applies to any action taken by any public official, agency, or body—from the Congress of the United States to a policeman on the beat—which has the effect of abridging freedom of the press.

Is the Constitution's protection limited to reporters for established journalistic institutions?

No. "Freedom of the press is a 'fundamental personal right' which is not confined to newspapers and periodicals.

It necessarily embraces pamphlets and leaflets. The press in its historic connotation comprehends every sort of publication which affords a vehicle of information and opinion."[5] Thus, as Justice Byron R. White observed, ". . . liberty of the press is the right of the lonely pamphleteer who uses carbon paper or a mimeograph just as much as of the large metropolitan publisher who utilizes the latest photo composition methods."[6] It is available to a reporter for an infrequently published underground newspaper no less than to the White House correspondent of *The New York Times*.

Does this constitutional protection apply only to reporting about political or governmental affairs?

No. The protections of the First Amendment "are not the preserve of political expression or comment upon public affairs"; they apply to writing and reporting about virtually everything.[7] "Freedom of discussion, if it would fulfill its historic function in this nation, must embrace all issues about which information is needed or appropriate to enable the members of society to cope with the exigencies of their period."[8] Nor is this protection limited to reporting which informs the members of the public; it applies as well to reporting which simply entertains.[9] Everything from the publication of the Pentagon Papers[10] to the review of a new play[11] is entitled to constitutional protection.

Does the Constitution envision that reporters will play a role in the functioning of democratic government?

Yes. The First Amendment was designed to give special protection to the press—one of the few callings singled out and afforded such constitutional status—because of the function which the press was expected to serve in the democratic process. In effect, the Fourth Estate was made an unofficial, yet vitally important, fourth branch of government.

And, time and again, the courts have reaffirmed the concept that the Fourth Estate's primary responsibility is to inform the public, about all issues in general and particularly about the conduct of government.

Thus, when a state imposed a special tax on newspapers, the Supreme Court observed:

The predominant purpose of the [First Amendment] was to preserve an untrammelled press as a vital source of public information. The newspapers, magazines and other journals of the country . . . have shed and continue to shed more light on the public and business affairs of the nation than any other instrumentality of publicity; and since informed public opinion is the most potent of all restraints upon misgovernment, the suppression or abridgment of the publicity afforded by a free press cannot be regarded otherwise than with grave concern. . . . A free press stands as one of the great interpreters between the government and the people. To allow it to be fettered is to fetter ourselves.[12]

When a newspaper editor was convicted for "electioneering" because he ran an editorial on election day, the Court said: ". . . the press serves and was designed to serve as a powerful antidote to any abuses of power by government officials and as a constitutionally chosen means for keeping officials elected by the people responsible to all the people whom they were elected to serve."[13]

And finally, when the government tried to suppress the publication of the Pentagon Papers, Justice Hugo L. Black said it all:

In the First Amendment the Founding Fathers gave the free press the protection it must have to fulfill its essential role in our democracy. The press was to serve the governed, not the governors. The Government's power to censor the press was abolished so that the press would remain forever free to censure the Government. The press was protected so that it could bare the secrets of government and inform the people.[14]

If the government attempts to infringe a reporter's rights, must there be a compelling reason to do so?

Yes. Because First Amendment rights have a preferred status, measures which infringe, even indirectly, on those rights require much greater justification than ordinary enactments or regulations. Accordingly, the courts have fashioned a number of doctrines to insure that First Amendment rights will generally not be interfered with unless it is absolutely necessary to do so. First, the government interest involved must be an "overriding and compelling" one; second, there must be a clear and necessary relationship between the infringement of such rights and the achievement of that governmental interest; finally, the government must demonstrate that there are no other methods with less harmful effects on First Amendment rights for accomplishing that public purpose.[15]

These principles are illustrated in a recent challenge to an Alabama law requiring reporters covering the legislature to file a statement of economic interest giving detailed information about their news organizations.[16] To justify the law, the state pointed to two interests: preventing biased reporting, and protecting legislators from "surreptitious lobbying newsmen." The court found the first justification not only not compelling, but totally improper. Regulation of lobbying, however, was found to be a valid governmental interest. But, the court concluded, requiring financial disclosure from all reporters was simply too broad and indiscriminate a method to achieve the otherwise valid purpose of regulating lobbyists.

Although the application of these principles has not always resulted in a victory for the press,[17] they are generally available as a restraint on official action and a guide to judicial decision.

Can the government stop a reporter from publishing a story?

Theoretically, no. The rule against prior governmental restraints or censorship of publication is a central feature of the First Amendment.[18] Any official attempt to prevent a story from being published bears a "heavy presumption against its constitutional validity."[19] And even in the Pentagon Papers case, where the government claimed that the censorship was vital to protect the national security, the Supreme Court ruled that the burden of proof had not been met.[20] This principle has also been applied to overturn orders against publishing defamatory articles,[21] stories about criminal cases,[22] or even pornographic material (unless there is a speedy judicial hearing).[23] Thus, under our First Amendment jurisprudence, publication can rarely, if ever, be restrained in advance.

Unfortunately, however, the ban on prior restraints has occasionally been disregarded. Indeed, publication of the Pentagon Papers, though ultimately allowed, was temporarily restrained for over two weeks, which many feel has set a regrettable precedent. Since then, a state judge in Indiana, in a trade libel suit brought by a manufacturer, granted an injunction against showing a portion of an ABC-TV documentary on flammable baby cribs; it took seven months for an appeals court to lift the injunction.[24] The New York courts have enjoined circulation of a book of anonymous psychiatric case histories at the request of a former patient claiming invasion of privacy; the injunction is now in its second year, and the matter will be resolved by the United States Supreme Court.[25] Finally, several judges have recently ordered the press not to publish prejudicial information relating to a criminal trial, and such restraints have remained in effect during often lengthy appeals.[26]

Can the government tell a reporter what to publish?

No. Any direct interference with journalistic discretion by telling a reporter what to publish presumably has the same constitutional infirmities as a directive telling him what not to publish. Thus, the Supreme Court recently ruled that television stations could not be compelled to sell commercial time for public-issue announcements.[27] In reaching that result, the majority placed great emphasis on the prerogatives of journalistic and editorial discretion. And, in another recent case, where a narrow majority of the Court upheld an order telling a newspaper to eliminate "male" and "female" designations from its classified ads, the Court was careful to limit the reach of the holding: "Nor . . . does our decision authorize any restriction whatever, whether of content or layout, on stories or commentary originated by Pittsburgh Press, its columnists, or its contributors. On the contrary, we reaffirm unequivocally the protection afforded to editorial judgment and to the free expression of views on these and other issues, however controversial."[28] The dissenters, however, were not so sanguine (one observed that "The camel's nose is in the tent.").[29] Such concerns were somewhat alleviated earlier this year when the Supreme Court unanimously invalidated a Florida law which required newspapers to publish replies from political candidates criticized by the paper.[30] Chief Justice Warren E. Burger ruled that such a law constituted improper government control of the press.

Can a reporter be punished for what he publishes?

Theoretically, yes. While the First Amendment bars prior restraints on publication, it does allow "subsequent punishment" based upon the content of what is published.[31] Thus, for example, where a story poses an immediate threat to the administration of justice in a criminal case, punishment theoretically can be imposed, although the Supreme Court has never in recent times upheld such a conviction.[32] Similarly, the publication of hard-core pornography can lead to criminal punishment.[33] And writing a story which contains defamatory statements about an individual or discloses material which invades his right of privacy can result in a civil lawsuit for monetary damages.[34] Some states also allow criminal prosecution for libel,[35] although the Supreme Court has cast serious doubt on such laws.[36] In another area, the editor of a Virginia underground newspaper was convicted for publishing an advertisement for legal abortion services in New York, but the Supreme Court may intervene.[37]

Finally, one unsettled question is whether a reporter can be punished for printing national security secrets. This key issue was left open in the Pentagon Papers case, and the applicable statutes almost defy understanding or interpretation.[38] What is clear is that some proposals to change the laws would make it criminal simply to publish classified government information—thus enacting the equivalent of the British Official Secrets Act.

Are reporters immune from criminal laws when covering a story?

Probably not. In general, while courts have invalidated most laws which punish reporters for what they publish, much less protection has been given to prepublication newsgathering activities. If a reporter violates a generally applicable law in the course of doing a story, he usually runs the same risk of punishment as any other citizen.[39] "It is clear that the First Amendment does not invalidate every incidental burdening of the press that may result from the enforcement of civil or criminal statutes of general applicability."[40]

Conversely, of course, reporters enjoy the same general constitutional protections against the police as any other citizen. Indeed, in some respects reporters have even greater protection. For example, the Fourth Amendment's prohibition of illegal searches and seizures was written against the historical background of raids on homes by agents of the King searching for the literature of dissent.[41] Thus, courts have ruled that searches directed against the press are governed by even stricter rules than normal.[42]

Can a reporter be denied direct access to the sources of news?

Not unless the restriction is necessary to achieve important governmental interests. Although the Supreme Court recently ruled 5 to 4 that reporters do not have a special right of access which entitles them to interview specific prisoners, the Court made it clear that reporters must be given the same right of access to news sources and information as members of the public generally.[43] Thus, for example, the press cannot be kept out of public meetings or open court proceedings,[44] and cannot be denied access to documents or materials generally available to the public.[45] And even in denying the right of reporters to interview named prisoners, the Supreme Court majority relied heavily on the fact that reporters were regularly allowed into the prisons to report on conditions and were also allowed to interview prisoners at random.

Similarly, once reporters are given special access to news or information, the public officials involved cannot give preferential treatment to some reporters but deny such advantages to others.[46]

If your exercise of any of these First Amendment rights is infringed, how can you fight back?

The first thing to do is put up a fuss and attempt to build support for your position, among your colleagues and the general public. Reporters are uniquely equipped to identify, describe, and focus attention on public issues and newsworthy matters. Make each infringement of press freedom such an issue, and employ your journalistic skills in that cause.

Fighting back pays off. Largely as a result of pressures from reporters, former Attorney General Eliot Richardson issued new Justice Department regulations requiring the personal approval of the Attorney General before any reporter can be questioned, subpoenaed, arrested, or indicted by any federal agency. And when former Vice President Agnew issued a flurry of press subpoenas, at least two of the most powerful publishers in the country pledged that they would go to jail rather than allow their reporters' confidential sources to be revealed. Such developments, prompted by an aroused press, can be as important as the most favorable court decision.

When reporters are in the mood to assert their rights, officials will think twice before undertaking to infringe those rights.

If legal assistance becomes necessary, the ACLU and its local offices throughout the country are ready to represent or support any reporter whose First Amendment rights are being infringed. The Reporters Committee for Freedom of the Press, operating out of Washington, D. C., is a vital clearinghouse for legal assistance and information. Its Press Censorship Newsletter is a valuable survey of current developments, judicial decisions, and legislative activity affecting reporters. Professional organizations such as the Newspaper Guild and Sigma Delta Chi can also be contacted. Such organizations have been increasingly active in seeking judicial vindication of the rights of reporters.

Footnotes to Chapter I

1. See, *e.g.*, *Schneider* v. *Smith*, 390 U.S. 17 (1968).
2. See, *e.g.*, *Gitlow* v. *New York*, 268 U.S. 652 (1925); *Thornhill* v. *Alabama*, 310 U.S. 88 (1940).
3. See, *e.g.*, *Lovell* v. *Griffin*, 303 U.S. 444 (1938).
4. See, *e.g.*, *Hague* v. *CIO*, 307 U.S. 496 (1939).
5. *Branzburg* v. *Hayes*, 408 U.S. 665, 704 (1972) [quoting from *Lovell* v. *Griffin*, 303 U.S. 444, 450, 452 (1938)].
6. *Ibid*; see also *Mills* v. *Alabama*, 384 U.S. 213 (1966).
7. *Time, Inc.* v. *Hill*, 385 U.S. 374, 388 (1967).
8. *Thornhill* v. *Alabama*, 310 U.S. 88, 102 (1940).
9. *Winters* v. *New York*, 333 U.S. 507 (1948); *Time, Inc.* v. *Hill*, 385 U.S. 374 (1967).
10. *New York Times Co.* v. *United States*, 403 U.S. 713 (1971).
11. *Time, Inc.* v. *Hill*, 385 U.S. 374 (1967).
12. *Grosjean* v. *American Press Co.*, 297 U.S. 233, 250 (1936).
13. *Mills* v. *Alabama*, 384 U.S. 214, 219 (1966).
14. *New York Times Co.* v. *United States*, 403 U.S. 713, 717 (1971) (concurring opinion).
15. *DeGregory* v. *New Hampshire Attorney General*, 383 U.S. 825, 829 (1966); see also, *Gibson* v. *Florida Legislative Investigation Committee*, 372 U.S. 539 (1963); *Shelton* v. *Tucker*, 364 U.S. 479 (1960).
16. *Lewis* v. *Baxley*, 368 F.Supp. 768 (M.D. Ala. 1973).
17. See *Branzburg* v. *Hayes*, 408 U.S. 665 (1972) (protection of a reporter's confidential sources is not a valid basis for refusal to testify before a grand jury); but see *Bursey* v. *United States*, 466 F.2d 1059 (9th Cir. 1972) (First Amendment generally applicable to limit grand jury investigation of reporters).
18. See *Near* v. *Minnesota*, 283 U.S. 697 (1931).
19. *Bantam Books, Inc.* v. *Sullivan*, 372 U.S. 58, 70 (1963).
20. *New York Times Co.* v. *United States*, 403 U.S. 713

(1971); but see, *Marchetti* v. *United States*, 466 F.2d 1309 (4th Cir.), *cert. denied*, 409 U.S. 1063 (1972).

21. *Near* v. *Minnesota*, 283 U.S. 697 (1931).
22. See, *e.g.*, *Oliver* v. *Postel*, 30 N.Y. 2d 171 (1972); *Wood* v. *Goodson*, 485 S.W.2d 213 (Sup. Ct. Ark. 1972); *cf.*, *United States* v. *Dickenson*, 465 F.2d 496 (5th Cir. 1972), *on remand*, 349 F. Supp. 227 (E.D. La. 1972), *aff'd*, 476 F.2d 373, *cert. denied*, 414 U.S. 979 (1973).
23. See, *e.g.*, *Freedman* v. *Maryland*, 380 U.S. 51 (1965).
24. *ABC* v. *Smith Cabinet Mfg. Co.*, 43 Law Week 2009 (June 12, 1974).
25. *Roe* v. *Doe*, 42 App. Div. 2d 559, 345 N.Y.S. 2d 560 (1st Dept. 1973).
26. See, *e.g.*, *United States* v. *Schiavo*, ——F.2d——, 15 Cr. L. Rep. 2484 (3d Cir., Aug. 8, 1974, en banc).
27. *Columbia Broadcasting System* v. *Democratic National Committee*, 412 U.S. 93 (1973).
28. *Pittsburgh Press Co.* v. *Pittsburgh Commission on Human Relations*, 413 U.S. 376, 391 (1973).
29. *Id.* at 402.
30. *Miami Herald Publishing Co.* v. *Tornillo*, ——U.S.——, 42 U.S. Law Week 5098 (June 25, 1974).
31. *Near* v. *Minnesota*, 283 U.S. 697 (1931).
32. See, *e.g.*, *Pennekamp* v. *Florida*, 328 U.S. 331 (1946); *Craig* v. *Harney*, 331 U.S. 367 (1947).
33. See, *e.g.*, *Miller* v. *California*, 413 U.S. 15 (1973).
34. See, *e.g.*, *Curtis Publishing Co.* v. *Butts*, 388 U.S. 130 (1967); *Time, Inc.* v. *Hill*, 385 U.S. 374 (1967); *Gertz* v. *Robert Welch, Inc.*, ——U.S.——, 42 U.S. Law Week 5123 (June 25, 1974); *Briscoe* v. *Reader's Digest Association, Inc.*, 4 Cal. 3d 529 (1971).
35. See, *State* v. *Weston*, 255 Ark. 567, 501 S.W. 2d 622 (1973); *App. dism. for want of jurisdiction*, ——U.S.——, 42 U.S. Law Week 3710 (July 8, 1974).
36. See, *Garrison* v. *Louisiana*, 379 U.S. 67 (1974).
37. *Bigelow* v. *Virginia*, 214 Va. 341, 200 S.E. 2d 680 (1973), *prob. juris. noted*, 42 U.S. Law Week 3710 (July 8, 1974).
38. See generally, H. Edgar and B. Schmidt, *The Espionage Statutes and Publication of Defense Information*, 73 Colum. L. Rev. 929 (1973).
39. See, *e.g.*, *People* v. *Kunkin*, 9 Cal. 3d 245 (1973).
40. *Branzburg* v. *Hayes*, 408 U.S. 665, 682 (1973); see generally, Note, *The Rights of the Public and the Press to Gather Information*, 87 Harv. L. Rev. 1505 (1974).

41. See *Stanford* v. *Texas,* 379 U.S. 476, 481-82 (1965).
42. *Id*; see also, *Stanford Daily* v. *Zurcher,* 353 F.Supp. 124 (N.D. Cal. 1972).
43. *Pell* v. *Procunier,* ——U.S.——, 42 U.S. Law Week 4998 (June 24, 1974); *Saxbe* v. *Washington Post Co.,* —— U.S.——, 42 U.S. Law Week 5006 (June 24, 1974).
44. See, *United States* v. *Dickinson,* 465 F.2d 496 (5th Cir. 1972).
45. See, *e.g., Providence Journal Co.* v. *McCoy,* 94 F.Supp. 186 (D. R.I. 1950); *aff'd,* 190 F.2d 760 (1st Cir. 1951).
46. See, *e.g., Quad-City Community News Service, Inc.* v. *Jebens,* 334 F.Supp. 8 (S.D. Iowa 1971); *Kovach* v. *Maddux,* 238 F.Supp. 835 (M.D. Tenn. 1965).

II
Protecting Your Sources

Most reporters are understandably pessimistic about securing judicial protection of confidential sources and information. The prevalent attitude among journalists is accurately reflected in a Jules Feiffer cartoon which depicts a judge sitting on the bench and engaging in the following monologue:

His sources give him a story.

The story results in the exposure of corruption in high places.

A grand jury orders the reporter to reveal his sources.

The reporter refuses and is sent to jail.

The more corruption in high places the more reporters are sent to jail.

No one wishes to encourage corruption in high places.

But it's either that or a free press.[1]

Such a mood is a far cry from Thomas Jefferson's observation that, given a choice between a government without newspapers or newspapers without a government, "I should not hesitate a moment to prefer the latter."[2]

The current mood stems from the Supreme Court's decision in *Branzburg* v. *Hayes*,[3] and the jailing of several reporters in the wake of that ruling. The *Branzburg* decision involved separate appeals by reporters Earl Caldwell of *The New York Times*, Paul Branzburg of the *Louisville Courier-Journal*, and Paul Pappas of a Massachusetts television station. It was a severe setback in the campaign to secure constitutional protection for the newsgathering process in general and, in particular, for the right of reporters to safeguard their sources of information. For the first time, the Supreme Court explored the nature of the newsgathering process and the reporters' need for a constitutional right to protect confidential sources. The reporters lost.

But the defeat was not necessarily conclusive. The issue arose in the context of investigations by grand juries—government bodies whose powers of inquiry have traditionally commanded Supreme Court deference and respect. The cases were decided by a 5 to 4 margin. And the decisive vote came from Justice Lewis F. Powell, whose concurring opinion made it quite clear that he was ruling for that day only and reserving judgment on the "case-by-case" resolution of the particular competing interests that might clash in the future.[4] In fact, reporters have met with substantial success in the case-by-case process that has ensued, and where the proceeding has not involved a grand jury investigation, many judges have given a sympathetic ear to reporters' arguments.

Moreover, exactly half the states now have "shield" laws on the books, many enacted in response to the *Branzburg* decision, which afford journalists a significant amount of statutory protection for their sources of information. Although judicial interpretation of these laws has not been uniformly favorable, and occasionally has been quite hostile, they at least provide an obstacle to district attorneys or private litigants who wish to probe a reporter's sources.

In addition, nothing in *Branzburg* prevents reporters from resisting a demand for information on many grounds, First Amendment or otherwise, available to any other witness called to a deposition, brought before a court or grand jury, or subpoenaed by a legislative committee. Reporters can claim, for example, that the subpoena is an overly broad fishing expedition, that the information sought is irrelevant to the issues in the proceeding, that there has been illegal wiretapping in the case, or, perhaps, that the reporter himself might be incriminated by his own testimony. Many journalists have prevailed in court on the basis of such claims, quite independent of any constitutional right to protect sources.

Finally, the most effective weapon against press subpoenas is the determination of reporters to resist them. By quickly organizing legal assistance and mobilizing public support, as in the Agnew episode, reporters can persuade lawyers to think carefully before issuing subpoenas to the press. Partly as a consequence of such determination, very few reporters have actually gone to jail for refusing to reveal confidential sources.

One final caveat. The discussion which follows is an analysis of *legal* rights, a lawyer's attempt to predict how courts are likely to respond when the right to protect sources is claimed in any particular proceeding.

But a description of the legal picture does not tell the whole story, for the key element in any subpoena case is the reporter's willingness—and the participants' perception of that willingness—to refuse to disclose the information, no matter what. After all, with the rack a thing of the past, a reporter, although he can be ordered to testify, cannot actually be made to reveal sources or information. Like the conscientious objector whose legal claims are rejected, the reporter can, of course, be jailed. But the reporter's demonstrated willingness to go to jail if necessary to protect sources is not just mere obstinacy. Rather, it may contribute materially to the outcome of the case. For example, persisting in the refusal to testify while a civil contempt citation is being appealed may mean that by the time the subpoena is ultimately upheld, the underlying situation may have changed and you may never have to testify at all. Grand jury terms end, investigations are dropped, cases get settled—any of which may obviate the need for your evidence or the willingness of the parties to pursue the matter.

Similarly, a reporter's manifested determination to protect sources can influence the kind of sentence imposed. In 1857, a *New York Times* reporter, confined indefinitely for refusing to honor a Congressional subpoena, was released after several days when the legislators became convinced he would not identify his sources. And recently a California court ruled that the indefinite confinement of William Farr was invalid because he had made it absolutely clear that his sources would remain protected.

In short, the situation is far from bleak.

Constitutional Protection

Does the First Amendment give reporters the right to refuse to reveal confidential sources of information?

The legal answer is not clear. What is clear, however, is that the *Branzburg* decision by no means ruled out any First Amendment protection of sources in all situations.

The three cases which comprise the *Branzburg* decision involved reporters who had been subpoenaed to testify before state and federal grand juries. The reporters argued that the First Amendment afforded them a privilege to refuse to answer grand jury questions probing confidential sources of information, and, in some instances, not to appear before the grand jury at all. Without such privilege to withhold evidence, their sources would soon dry up and, ultimately, they would be less able to keep the public well informed. A majority of the Supreme Court disagreed, finding the factual assertions unpersuasive and the legal claims insufficient to override the traditional and important functions performed by grand juries.

But the Court's holding was a narrow one: "The issue in these cases is whether requiring newsmen to appear and testify before state or federal grand juries abridges the freedom of speech and press guaranteed by the First Amendment. We hold that it does not."[5] Reporters have "no First Amendment privilege to refuse to answer the relevant and material questions asked during a good faith grand jury investigation . . ." and similarly no privilege to refuse to appear at all unless the government first shows some compelling need for the testimony.[6] Thus, the force of the *Branzburg* decision is limited in many significant ways and has been so interpreted by several lower court judges since then.

Did the Supreme Court rule out the use of confidential sources by the press?

No. The Court felt that the effect of a subpoena on the relationship between a reporter and his source did not constitute a direct infringement on the use of sources. If the government tried a frontal assault on reporters' sources, that would be a different matter:

The use of confidential sources by the press is not forbidden or restricted; reporters remain free to seek news from any source by means within the law. No attempt is made to require the press to publish its sources of information or indiscriminately to disclose them upon request.[7]

Does the First Amendment protect a reporter called to testify before a grand jury?

Yes, in a general sense. The Court did not say that reporters subpoenaed by grand juries had no First Amendment rights at all, but only that the First Amendment does not confer a blanket right to refuse to appear or answer questions. Moreover, the Court pointed out that ". . . news gathering is not without its First Amendment protections, and grand jury investigations, if instituted or conducted other than in good faith, would pose wholly different issues for resolution under the First Amendment. Official harassment of the press undertaken not for purposes of law enforcement but to disrupt a reporter's relationship with his news sources would have no justification. Grand juries are subject to judicial control and motions to quash. We do not expect courts will forget that grand juries most operate within the limits of the First Amendment as well as the Fifth."[8] And Justice Lewis F. Powell, whose concurrence was necessary for the result, wrote a separate opinion just "to emphasize" that, even when called before grand juries, reporters still have rights "with respect to the gathering of news or in safeguarding their sources."[9] Grand jury harassment of reporters "will not be tolerated":

Indeed, if the newsman is called upon to give information bearing only a remote and tenuous relationship to the subject of the investigation, or if he has some other reason to believe that his testimony implicates confidential source relationships without a legitimate need of law enforcement, he will have access to the Court on a motion to quash and an appropriate protective order may be entered. The asserted claim of privilege should be judged on its facts by the striking of a proper balance between freedom of the press and the obligation of all citizens to give relevant testimony with respect to criminal conduct. . . .

In short the courts will be available to newsmen under circumstances where legitimate First Amendment interests require protection.[10]

Unhappily, these *obiter dicta* in *Branzburg* have provided small consolation to those reporters who have recently been jailed for refusing to answer a grand jury's questions. On several occasions since then, reporters argued that the particular questions were not relevant and that the court should balance the grand jury's need for the specific information against the reporter's need to protect his sources. But lower courts, relying on *Branzburg,* have rejected the claims.[11]

In a way, this is not really surprising. Reporters have traditionally not done very well trying to withhold evidence that a grand jury is seeking. In the early days they argued that they were entitled to a judge-made, common law, testimonial privilege, fashioned on the same considerations which underlay the recognition of other confidential communications, such as those between attorney and client. But those arguments were generally rejected,[12] as were claims that compelled disclosure of sources would hamper reporters' ability to earn a livelihood by discouraging sources from talking to them and thereby impairing their effectiveness as journalists.[13]

Later on, reporters did a little better. By premising their arguments on the First Amendment, reporters gained some judicial recognition that under certain circumstances they might be privileged not to answer certain grand jury questions. For example, a Wisconsin court ruled that the reporter had "a constitutional right to the privilege not to disclose his sources of information received in confidential relationships. However, when such confidence is in conflict with the public's overriding need to know, it must yield to the interest of justice."[14] In that case, since the information sought was the identity of the person who planted a bomb which killed and injured several persons, the privilege had to give way, and the reporter's six-month contempt-of-court sentence was upheld. In most of these cases, as in *Branzburg,* the reporters faced an uphill battle to overcome the historically sweeping investigative powers of the grand jury and its right to "every man's evidence." If the recent test cases had come up in some other context, perhaps the result might have been different.

In general, then, a reporter subpoenaed to testify before a grand jury has some First Amendment protection, certainly against bad-faith questions not directly relevant to the grand jury's inquiry. But, if asked specific questions about specific criminal activity that he has witnessed or has direct knowledge of, a reporter probably won't be able

successfully to claim that the need to protect sources of
information defeats the obligation to answer.

Can a grand jury subpoena all of a reporter's notes and files on a particular story or subject?

Probably not. In *Branzburg*, the three reporters were
summoned only to appear and testify (subpoena *ad testifi-
candum*). The Court thus did not have before it the situation where a grand jury witness is also instructed to bring
documents and materials with him (subpoena *duces tecum*). A demand to hand over all your files is of course
much more sweeping than a demand to appear and testify
in response to specific questions, and the harassment potential of a subpoena *duces tecum* is also more substantial.
The Supreme Court might well take a different view of
such subpoenas, which look more like the classic "fishing
expeditions" seeking to "annex the news media as an investigative arm of government" which the Court, or at
least the Justice who cast the deciding vote, purported not
to authorize.[15] One appeals court has ruled that an overly
broad subpoena *duces tecum* was invalid: "A subpoena
should be sufficiently clear to inform the witness exactly
what is being sought, and where a subpoena is overbroad
the witness is not required to cull the good from the bad."[16]
On the other hand, in one of the Watergate civil cases, a
federal judge held that subpoenas demanding various news
media to produce *all* their files for a six-month period on
Watergate political espionage were not so broad and sweeping as to be unreasonable or oppressive.[17] However, the
court went on to hold, on First Amendment grounds, that
the media did not have to produce the materials.

In general, therefore, a reporter who receives a subpoena *duces tecum* for all the files on a particular subject
has a good chance of successfully resisting the subpoena.

A subpoena for specific documents or materials presents
more difficult questions. Will Lewis, the station manager
of KPFK-FM in Los Angeles, was recently subpoenaed by
a federal grand jury to produce an original mimeographed

letter from the Weather Underground and the original tape from the Symbionese Liberation Army. Both had been anonymously left at the radio station. Copies were made available to law enforcement officials, but Lewis refused to turn over the originals, claiming an implicit confidential-source relationship between the radio station and radical groups. The federal Court of Appeals disagreed and upheld the subpoena.[18] Lewis, who spent several weeks in jail, was released by Justice William O. Douglas, pending the outcome of an appeal to the Supreme Court.

Can a reporter subpoenaed to give evidence in connection with a criminal trial resist the subpoena on First Amendment grounds?

Probably, yes.

Once a criminal case has passed beyond the grand jury stage, and specific charges have been brought against particular individuals, there may be more opportunity to resist a subpoena, either to protect sources or on other grounds. But, while you're no longer resisting the traditional prerogative of the grand jury, your arguments now face the prosecutor's interest in the administration of justice and the defendant's constitutional interest in securing exculpatory evidence. As Richard Nixon learned, those are powerful interests to contend with in claiming a legal privilege to withhold information.[19] Nevertheless, a reporter can still argue that the Supreme Court struck the balance against protection of news sources only so far as grand juries are concerned. Moreover, since the issues in the particular case being tried have now become focused, it is easier to argue that your information is of only marginal usefulness.

These principles were illustrated in the trial of the Watergate burglars. The *Los Angeles Times* had run articles based on an extensive tape-recorded interview with a key prosecution witness. Wanting the information in order to cross-examine the witness when he testified at the trial, the defendants got Judge John J. Sirica to issue a subpoena *duces tecum* to the *Los Angeles Times*'s bureau chief and reporters, directing them to produce their materials relevant to the interviews. The reporters moved to quash the subpoena on the ground that supplying the tapes would impair the paper's newsgathering ability. While Judge Sirica denied the motion, ruling that the *Branzburg* reasoning was just as applicable to a criminal defendant's request for helpful evidence as to a grand jury's investigation, he emphasized that his ruling was limited to the unique facts of the case and would have "little precedential value for defendants or prosecutors who might wish to subject newspapers to an abusive 'flood' of subpoenas. Nor is there any basis here on which parties in a criminal case might support a simply indiscriminate use of the subpoena power."[20] Not only did Judge Sirica stress the special circumstances, he also devised a series of procedures to limit the defendants' access to the tapes: (1) the tapes would be produced for the court alone for its inspection in chambers; (2) a stenographic transcript of the tape would be made in chambers, with the reporters and their attorneys present if they so chose; (3) the tapes and the transcript would be impounded and made available to the defendants, with appropriate deletions, only at the time of the trial.[21]

The reporters appealed the decision, seeking an emergency stay of Judge Sirica's order which directed the immediate confinement of the bureau chief, who spent several hours in jail for refusing to hand over the tapes. As it turned out, the appeal became moot because the source was pressed into releasing the reporters from their pledge of confidentiality, and the tapes were turned over. But the appeals court did issue a stay, and one judge wrote a useful opinion stating that the *Branzburg* decision allowed a balancing of the conflicting claims in any particular case, and that a reporter might prevail if he could show that his testimony "implicates confidential source relationships without a legitimate need of law enforcement" or has only a "remote" relationship to the subject of the investigation.[22] The appeals judge also approved and expanded the procedural protections which Judge Sirica had devised.[23]

Two recent state court decisions, applying the same First Amendment balancing test, have said that the reporters did not have to testify. In Vermont, a defendant in a drug case sought to make the reporter testify about the source of a tip that a drug bust was about to occur. The state's highest court upheld the reporter's refusal, ruling that disclosure could not be required unless (1) there is no other available source for the information, and (2) the information itself strongly bears upon guilt or innocence.[24] The Supreme Court of Virginia followed this reasoning in rejecting a murder defendant's request that a reporter identify the police source who gave her an account of the crime. The defendant argued that learning the identity of the source would enable him to cross-examine the official for inconsistencies with prior testimony. But the court ruled that a reporter could only be made to reveal evidence directly related to guilt, innocence, or punishment, and then only when such information is unavailable elsewhere.[25]

In a criminal case, can a reporter object to questions or requests for information on grounds of relevance?

Yes.

In many criminal cases reporters have succesfully refused to answer very broad questions or provide information too remote from the central issues. For example, in the Rosenberg espionage case, Ethel Rosenberg tried to prevent officials from transferring her to Sing Sing Prison, a move she contended was designed to pressure her into a confession. In connection with that proceeding she sought testimony from columnist Leonard Lyons, who had written an article suggesting that she could avoid the electric chair by confessing. The court ruled that a reporter did not have to answer questions unless they were "material and relevant to the proceedings," and that the questions put to Mr. Lyons were not.[26] In another case, a Minnesota reporter, called to testify in a post-appeal hearing in a murder case, was asked "who were your sources" for the stories about the murder. His refusal to answer was upheld by the Minnesota Supreme Court, ruling that a reporter can't be made to answer such "vague and imprecise" questions about sources, particularly in a post-conviction proceeding where the defendant must show a high degree of relevance for the information he seeks.[27]

But while reporters have had some success objecting to a question on grounds of relevance, the more valuable the information a reporter has, the more anxious the courts are to get it. The distinction between the reporter who has first-hand evidence of criminal activity and the one who has only been told second-hand that others have committed crimes was emphasized in the *Branzburg* case. Although the majority opinion quickly and harshly dispatched the argument that the First Amendment allowed a reporter to conceal the criminal conduct of a source, the Court was less adamant in rejecting the claimed need to protect the identity of sources who, although not themselves implicated in crime, have information about others who are.[30] Similarly, several state courts, in construing shield laws, have said that a person who commits a crime while the reporter is observing is not a "source" protected by the statute, while a person who tells a reporter about such activity probably is.[31] Somehow judges seem to feel that the latter situation embodies the reporter's more traditional reliance on a "tip" from a confidential informant.

This much is clear: if you witnessed criminal activity first-hand, you're more likely to have to testify about it than if you were simply told about such activity by a source who either participated in it himself or otherwise knew about it.

These same distinctions are also important when lawyers try to subpoena your files. For example, in the Watergate case Judge Sirica ordered the tapes turned over only because they would be important in helping the defendants cross-examine a key prosecution witness. However, in another recent case, a Delaware news photographer was upheld in his refusal to release photographs taken at an anti-busing demonstration. The police wanted the photographs to identify certain demonstrators and persuaded the State Attorney General to issue a subpoena to get the pictures from the paper's photo chief. The lower court approved the subpoena, but the state's highest court reversed, ruling that the photos were sought not for a valid Attorney General probe, but only in order to implement a routine police investigation.[32]

Although these cases suggest that the less important the material or information, the better a reporter's chances are to protect it, that's not very comforting because really "hot" information, the kind that fuels the best stories, is the most vulnerable. But at least in criminal cases, journalists will have some protection against fishing expeditions through their files and demands to disclose information of only minor relevance to the prosecution or the defense.

Can you be compelled to disclose confidential sources or information at the request of one of the parties to a civil lawsuit?

Probably not, unless the lawsuit is a libel action against you or your publication.

Courts in general, both before and after *Branzburg,* seem to feel that parties in civil cases have to show a very substantial need for the reporter's information in order to obtain it. Somehow society's stakes in compelling testimony are simply not as great in civil litigation as in a criminal proceeding. Of course it is difficult to determine in advance whether a particular source or item of information may someday become relevant in a civil rather than a criminal case. But to the extent that a reporter can predict that the information is more likely to interest a civil litigant than the parties in a criminal case, then you can count on protection with some assurance.

The leading post-*Branzburg* case is *Baker* v. *F & F Investment Co.*[33] The plaintiffs filed a civil-rights action in a Chicago federal court to challenge block-busting practices.

Several years earlier, a reporter had written an article on the problem based upon anonymous information provided by a real estate agent identified by the pseudonym "Mr. Vitchek." The reporter, Alfred Balk, had since moved to New York, and the civil-rights plaintiffs took his deposition there. Though wanting to cooperate, he refused to identify "Mr. Vitchek," claiming a First Amendment right to protect confidential sources. The district court agreed and refused to order the reporter to answer the questions.

On appeal, the court felt that an important consideration was the fact that the two states involved—Illinois, where the lawsuit arose, and New York, where the deposition was taken—both had enacted shield laws protecting confidential sources. And even though both laws were passed after the reporter had written his article, they were on the books at the time of the deposition, and they reflected "a paramount public interest" in maintaining a vigorous press and a recognition that disclosure of sources "unquestionably threatens" a journalist's ability to secure confidential information and inhibits investigative reporting.[34] Accordingly, the competing interests would have to be resolved in each particular case, and the presumption was in favor of the reporter:

While we recognize that there are cases—few in number to be sure—where First Amendment rights must yield, we are still mindful of the preferred position which the First Amendment occupies in the pantheon of freedoms. Accordingly, though a journalist's right to protect confidential sources may not take precedence over that rare overriding and compelling interest, we are of the view that there are circumstances, at the very least in civil cases, in which the public interest in non-disclosure of a journalist's confidential sources outweighs the public and private interest in compelled testimony. The case before us is one where the First Amendment protection does not yield.[35]

Since the reporter was not a party to the underlying lawsuit, other sources of information leading to the identity of "Mr. Vitchek" were available, and because his true identity "simply did not go to the heart of the case," the reporter could not be made to testify. So far as *Branzburg* was concerned, the court ruled that it applied only to grand jury investigations of criminal activities, not to a civil lawsuit.[36]

A similar approach was taken in one of the civil cases arising out of Watergate, *Democratic National Committee v. McCord*.[37] The defendants, various Republican Party units and officials, issued subpoenas to several news agencies seeking access to their files on Watergate. After ruling that the subpoenas were not unreasonably sweeping or oppressive, the court addressed the clash between the right of the press to gather news from confidential sources and the right of litigants to procure relevant evidence in civil cases. As in the *Baker* case, the court stressed the following factors: (1) the case was civil, not criminal, (2) the news organizations were not parties, but only potential witnesses, and (3) the parties had not demonstrated that the testimony and materials sought went to the "heart of their claim," or that alternative sources of evidence had been exhausted or even approached, or that the documents or materials were even relevant.[38] The court ruled that in most civil cases it would require parties to demonstrate that they "are unable to obtain the same information from sources other than [journalists], and that they have a compelling and overriding interest in the information thus sought."[39] In reaching these conclusions, the court emphasized its recognition of the vital role played by the press in exposing Watergate:

. . . This court cannot blind itself to the possible "chilling effect" the enforcement of these broad subpoenas would have on the flow of information to the press, and so to the public. This court stands convinced that if it allows the discouragement of investigative reporting into the highest levels of government no amount of legal theorizing could allay the public suspicion engendered by its actions and by the matters alleged in these lawsuits.[40]

Can a reporter be forced to disclose confidential sources in connection with a libel suit?

The answer is not clear.

The question of protecting sources in a libel case is particularly thorny. In the typical case a defamatory story will be partially based on confidential sources or materials. A libel suit is filed and the plaintiff wants access to the information in order to show that the news medium acted with malice because, for example, the sources were incredible or unreliable or perhaps even fabricated. (The rules on libel are discussed in Chapter VI.) The defendant refuses to reveal the sources on general First Amendment grounds. If the sources are protected, then there is the danger that journalists can avoid liability by hiding behind their sources; and there is something unseemly about allowing a reporter to libel a person and then foreclose that person from evidence which might facilitate restitution.[41] On the other hand, if the sources are not protected, then it becomes possible for someone to file a libel suit as a pretext to discover the reporter's sources and subject them to harassment.[42]

The resolution of this dilemma will depend on how important the information is to the plaintiff's case, how strong a case the plaintiff has made out, and also whether there is a state shield law involved in the situation.

In a libel case, when will a state shield law be applicable?

Libel cases are normally brought in a state court of general jurisdiction. If the state has a shield statute, its provisions will govern the question of disclosure of sources in that case. (Those provisions are discussed a little later.)

But libel suits can also be filed in a federal court if there is "diversity of citizenship," that is, if the plaintiff and defendant reside in different states. To complicate the matter, the reporter might live in yet a third state, and the plaintiff might try to take his deposition there. What happens if the reporter's state has a shield law, but the plaintiff's state, where the lawsuit will be tried, does not? In general, in a federal libel case, if *either* the state where the case is to be heard or the state where the reporter's deposition is taken has a statute which would protect sources, then the protection will probably be afforded.[43]

If no shield law is involved in a libel case, can a reporter be compelled to disclose confidential sources?

The answer is unclear. In the earlier cases, the reporter's claim was usually based on common law arguments that he was entitled to a privilege of confidential communications like a lawyer or doctor; but the argument was usually rejected. In one typical case, the plaintiff was taking the deposition of the editorial employee who wrote the supposedly defamatory editorial. The employee testified that the editorial was partly based upon a memorandum which the paper had received, but he refused to produce the memo or identify its author. The court overruled the confidential sources claim, held the information relevant and ordered the witness to produce it.[44]

The most famous example of the problem, and the first case in which a reporter invoked the First Amendment as the justification for protecting sources, involved a libel suit brought by the late Judy Garland.[45] Miss Garland had sued CBS for defamation, partly because of statements attributed to a CBS "network executive" in one of Marie Torre's *New York Herald Tribune* columns. After two CBS executives denied making the statements, Miss Torre was asked at a deposition to identify her source. She refused, the court directed her to answer, and, when she persisted, held her in contempt.

On appeal, she made the now-classic argument that compelling reporters to disclose confidential sources would burden the First Amendment by restraining the flow of news from sources to the reporters and then to the public.

The appeals court, in an opinion written by Judge Potter Stewart (now Supreme Court Justice Stewart who wrote the main dissenting opinion in the *Branzburg* case), accepted the hypothesis, but ruled that the competing claims had to be balanced to determine whether "the interest to be served by compelling the testimony of the witness in the present case justifies some impairment of this First Amendment freedom."[46] The court concluded that since there was no effort "to force a wholesale disclosure of a newspaper's confidential sources of news," and because the identity of the source, rather than being "of doubtful relevance or materiality" instead "went to the heart of the plaintiff's claim," the First Amendment afforded no right to refuse to answer.[47]

The *Garland* "heart of the claim" rule has tended to be applied in libel cases where no shield law is involved. In a Texas case, for example, suit was filed over a news story which suggested that the police had not been called into a drug case because some of the youths involved were the children of local officials.[48] When one of the reporters refused to identify his sources, the court ruled that the plaintiffs were entitled to learn those sources in order to determine whether reliance on them was reasonable.

In 1972, the *Garland* rule was strengthened in a case growing out of a *Life* magazine article that linked St. Louis Mayor Alfonso V. Cervantes with organized crime. During pre-trial discovery proceedings, the magazine turned virtually its entire files over to the Mayor for examination. But the writer refused to identify his sources within the FBI and the Department of Justice who had leaked documents and information to him. To do so, the reporter argued, would expose those officials to reprisals and physical danger and would breach necessary guarantees of anonymity. Without making the reporter disclose his sources, the trial judge granted the magazine's motion for summary judgment in its favor.[49]

The Mayor appealed, arguing that he could not possibly prove malice "if the reporter is allowed to hide behind anonymous news sources," particularly where "the information forming the core of the publication by its nature is not available to the public generally and is obtainable only from governmental employees who are under a duty not to reveal it to outsiders."[50] The appeals court thought this argument had some merit, but was more concerned with the dangers to the press of automatically allowing a libel plaintiff to learn the identity of confidential sources:

But to routinely grant motions seeking compulsory disclosure of anonymous news sources without first inquiring into the substance of a libel allegation would utterly emasculate the fundamental principles that underlay the line of cases articulating the constitutional restrictions to be engrafted upon the enforcement of state libel laws.[51]

Similarly, "to compel a newsman to breach a confidential relationship merely because a libel suit has been filed against him would seem inevitably to lead to an excessive restraint on the scope of legitimate news gathering activity."

The court then laid down the rules to resolve such conflicts. Only where there is "a concrete demonstration that the identity of defense news sources will lead to persuasive evidence on the issue of malice" should the trial court let the plaintiff discover and interrogate sources, anonymous or not. Thus, for example, if during pre-trial discovery the plaintiff finds substantial evidence that the published assertions "are so inherently improbable that there are strong reasons to doubt the veracity of the defense informant or the accuracy of his reports," or that the defendant in fact had serious doubts about the assertions, then disclosure of the sources can be compelled. But "there must be a showing of cognizable prejudice before the failure to permit examination of anonymous news sources can rise to the level of error. Mere speculation or conjecture about the fruits of such examination simply will not suffice." Applying those principles to that particular case, the court concluded that since the story had been thoroughly researched, and the mayor had been given access to hundreds of documents and deposed all relevant employees, and yet came up with only a few false items, it was proper to deny him access to the confidential sources.

The *Cervantes* case is obviously an important decision for reporters. Unfortunately, it has not been uniformly followed. A *Wall Street Journal* reporter was ordered by the Massachusetts Supreme Court to identify the local official who was her source for an allegedly defamatory article about zoning laws.[52] The *Journal* settled the libel suit and the reporter did not have to disclose her source. Similarly, Brit Hume, a former associate of Jack Anderson, was ordered by the federal appeals court in Washington, D.C., to disclose the source of a story about a union official. Although agreeing that disclosure of the reporter's sources should be a last resort, the court ruled that since the reporter had relied solely on confidential sources, not documentation, the plaintiff's need for the name of the source was strong. Nor was the plaintiff "so unlikely" to prove his case that no purpose would be served by disclosure.[53] Shortly after the decision, the source released Hume from the pledge of confidentiality.

Do the Department of Justice Guidelines on Press Subpoenas give you any enforceable right to protect sources?

The answer is unclear. The Justice Department Guidelines, set forth in the Appendix, were first promulgated in 1970 after the district court decision in the *Caldwell* case. The guidelines, applicable to all Justice Department officials, were recently supplemented and tightened to require that no reporter could be questioned or subpoenaed without the advance, express approval of the Attorney General.[54] In the *Caldwell* case, the reporter argued that the subpoena had been issued in violation of the guidelines and therefore could not be enforced. The government contended that the rules were "not intended to create any litigable rights." The Supreme Court failed to resolve the question.

It would seem, however, that the government would have to honor those guidelines before a court would enforce a Justice Department press subpoena. In various cases the courts have ruled that the federal government must follow its own procedures, whether or not such procedures themselves would be constitutionally required.[55] Indeed, this principle was recently applied by a federal judge who ruled that the firing of Watergate Special Prosecutor Archibald Cox was illegal because the summary action, even though within the President's power, did not comply with the regulations setting up the Prosecutor's office.[56] Any reporter receiving a federal subpoena should insist that any departure from the guidelines voids the subpoena. Just recently the Attorney General, in withdrawing a subpoena improperly issued to a college reporter, ruled that the college press is covered by the guidelines.

Can a legislative committee order you to disclose confidential sources?

Here too the answer depends on a number of factors.

Although most of the current controversy over disclosure of sources has focused on grand jury subpoenas, over the years legislative committees have shown a similar disregard for reporters' sources. Indeed the very first "source" battle resulted from an 1857 congressional subpoena to James Simonton, a *New York Times* reporter, who had written an exposé of corruption in the Congress. Called before a select congressional committee, Simonton refused to reveal his sources, and the House voted to hold him in contempt. He spent nineteen days in custody before being released.[57] That same pattern has persisted right up to today: a reporter exposes corruption in some public institution, a legislative committee investigates, the reporter is called to testify, asked who his sources were, and then punished for not revealing them.

But today it is questionable whether legislative demands to discover sources would automatically be upheld against the reporter's First Amendment claims. In the last decade the Supreme Court has imposed a variety of restraints on legislative investigations which infringe on First Amendment rights. And while reporters were unable to persuade the Supreme Court that those same principles afforded them a general right to resist grand jury probes, the vitality of the rules limiting legislative investigations has not been impaired. And at least one court has suggested that such investigations could be limited in ways that a grand jury inquiry could not.[58]

These issues were raised in one recent case where the publisher of a West Coast journal called *Black Politics* was subpoenaed by a Senate subcommittee looking into riots and civil disorder. The publisher was summoned to testify and bring all his files, particularly those dealing with "George Prosser," a pseudonym under which articles on revolutionary violence were written. Instead of complying, the publisher sued in federal court to enjoin enforcement of the subpoena and prevent compelled disclosure of confidential sources. The federal court of appeals indicated that the courts had the power to hear such a lawsuit, but ruled that the situation was not sufficiently grave to allow the publisher to shortcut normal legislative procedures: ". . . the possibility or even the probability that his appearance may indirectly and incidentally inhibit the flow of information from confidential sources is not a bar to congressional pursuit by the subpoena of its investigation of rioting, other disorders referred to, and their causes."[59]

In reaching this conclusion, the court emphasized that all the committee had done was issue and not withdraw the subpoena and detailed all the procedural steps which were still available: "A witness may address his claims to the subcommittee, which may sustain his objections. Were the subcommittee to insist, however, upon some response beyond the witness' concept of his obligation, and he refused to comply, no punitive action could be taken against him unless the full committee obtained from the Senate as a whole a citation of the witness for contempt, the citation had been referred to the United States Attorney, and an indictment returned or information filed. Should such prosecution occur, the witness' claims could then be raised before the trial court."[60] Thus, at the very least, these procedures afford a certain amount of time to frame your response to a congressional subpoena before there is any real jeopardy of going to jail.

It is unclear whether the same procedural steps are available in connection with state legislative committees. The Supreme Court has not yet ruled that a state legislative committee must proceed in court in order to hold a person in contempt for refusing to answer questions.[61] Thus, it is conceivable that such a committee could directly order a reporter incarcerated for refusing to disclose sources, as was the old Congressional procedure. But in the normal case, resort to the courts will occur at some point.[62]

Statutory Protection

Can the state legislatures or the Congress pass legislation allowing reporters to protect confidential sources?

Yes. The Supreme Court made it clear that both Congress and state legislatures were entirely free to enact such legislation:

At the federal level, Congress has freedom to determine whether a statutory newsman's privilege is necessary and desirable and to fashion standards and rules as narrow or as broad as deemed necessary to address the evil discerned and, equally important, to re-fashion those rules as experience from time to time may dictate. There is also merit in leaving state legislatures free, within First Amendment limits, to fashion their own standards in light of the conditions and problems with respect to the relations between law enforcement officials and press in their own areas.[63]

At the time of the *Branzburg* decision, seventeen states had such shield laws on the books. Since then, at least

eight more states have enacted such statutes. Efforts to enact federal legislation have so far been unsuccessful.

The state statutes are summarized in the Appendix.[64]

In general, what do the state shield laws provide?

More than half of these statutes provide almost absolute
protection against disclosure of news sources. The remain-
ing laws provide "qualified" protection, that is, the privilege is presumed to apply unless the person or agency
seeking the information can show some substantial reason
to get at it. Almost all of the statutes apply to proceedings
before any state body with subpoena power—judicial, legislative, or executive.

The statutes use various methods for describing who is
eligible to invoke their protection. Some statutes simply
list terms such as "publisher," "editor," or "reporter";
those of more recent vintage usually attempt to define
such terms with particularity (e.g., "reporter" means any
person regularly engaged in the business of collecting,
writing, or editing news for publication through a news
medium). Other statutes describe who is to be protected
in terms of the relationship between the person and the
news media ("employed by") or the function performed
("gathering news").[65] A few statutes, particularly older
ones, try to restrict protection to reporters for the establishment press.

The statutes also vary in terms of what kind of information is protected. Most prohibit disclosure of "the
source of any information" obtained for publication or in
the course of newsgathering. The statutes generally do not
employ the term "confidential," but courts have a tendency
to read the concept of confidentiality into the statute,
thereby limiting the scope of its protection. Some of the
statutes contain specific provisions describing under what
circumstances the statutory protection can be forfeited or
"waived." Finally, those statutes which allow the privilege
to be overcome in certain situations generally specify the
procedures to be used in making the determination.

Summaries of the specific statutory provisions are in the Appendix. You should consult the wording of the particular laws which might apply to your situation. In general, however, the courts have not been hospitable to these shield laws and have tended to interpret their protective provisions as narrowly as possible.

Have courts required that an expectation of confidentiality exist between the source and the reporter in order for the statute to apply?

So far, courts in New York have. The New York statute makes no mention of confidentiality. It simply provides that no journalist can be held in contempt for refusing to disclose "any news or the source of any such news coming into his possession" in the course of newsgathering activities.[66] Yet, in at least three cases, lower New York courts have read into this clear language the requirement that the information be communicated to the reporter in an explicitly confidential manner by a "secret" source. In one case the *Village Voice* published an article about the riots at the Tombs jail under the byline of an inmate who was subsequently indicted in connection with those disturbances. The District Attorney wanted the original manuscript to help prove his case. The *Voice* invoked the statute, but the court rejected the argument, concluding that for the law to be applied, "the information or its sources must be imparted to the reporter under a cloak of confidentiality, i.e., upon an understanding, expressed or implied, that the information or its sources will not be disclosed."[67] Since the paper had not shown that such an understanding existed, the statute was ruled inapplicable. The same reasoning was followed in another New York case where radio station WBAI read on the air a letter from the Weather Underground claiming credit for the bombing of a building. The radio station had received an anonymous phone call that the letter could be found in a phone booth. The district attorney's subpoena of the letter and envelope was upheld on the theory that the letter was not a confidential communication and that its discovery involved no "affirmative" act of newsgathering.[68] Finally, the "cloak of confidentiality" doctrine was also used to deny statutory protection to two Buffalo newsmen who refused to answer grand jury questions about events they had witnessed during the prison rebellion at Attica.[69]

While the New York courts have judicially added a confidentiality requirement to their statute, the courts in Maryland have refused to do so. In a case where a reporter obtained information from a person who did not know the reporter's identity, the court ruled that the lack of a confidential relationship was not decisive: "While the legislature may have enacted the statute with the primary purpose of protecting the identity of newsmen's confidential sources, we think the statutory privilege broad enough to encompass any source of information, without regard to whether the source gave his information in confidence or not."[70]

Can you be ordered to disclose things which you directly saw or heard while covering a story?

Apparently, yes. Where a reporter is an eyewitness to criminal activity or is told about it directly, courts have been unwilling to interpret the shield laws to allow protection. In the *Branzburg* case, for example, the reporter had witnessed people preparing illicit drugs for sale. He was asked to identify those individuals, but refused on the basis of the Kentucky statute which protects against the disclosure of "the source of any information." The court disagreed, reasoning that in such a situation the reporter himself is the "source":

Information as used in the statute refers to the things or the matters which a reporter learns and *source* refers to the methods by which or to the person from whom he learns them.
In this case the reporter learned that two men were engaged in the process of making hashish. Their identity, as well as the activity in which they were engaged, was a part of the information obtained by him, but their identity was not the source of the information.

The actual source of the information in this case was the reporter's personal observation. In addition some informant may have provided him with information that at a certain time and place he could observe the process of conversion of marijuana into hashish. If such was the case we have no doubt that the identity of the informant was protected by the Statute.[71]

Thus, the identity of criminals could be protected insofar as they were "informants," but not to the extent that they were "perpetrators." The same analysis was applied to a reporter who received "on the scene" admissions of criminal activity by a young woman shopkeeper engaged in marijuana traffic,[72] and to reporters who were admitted to Attica prison and were subsequently asked "merely . . . to testify about events which they had observed personally."[73]

The message of these cases is clear: if your information is second-hand, then you can count on statutory protection; but if your information is first-hand and direct, you probably will be ordered to disclose it, statute or not.

Does protection for the "source of any information" include more than just the identity of your informant?

The cases go both ways.

Perhaps the strongest and broadest interpretation of a state shield law protecting the "source of any information" came from the Pennsylvania Supreme Court.[74] There, newspaper officials were subpoenaed by a grand jury to produce background materials and documents from which stories about local political corruption had been written. Viewing the statute as designed to maximize the flow of information to the public, the court emphasized that it had to be "liberally and broadly construed in order to carry out the clear objective and intent of the legislature *which has placed the gathering and the protection of the source of news as of greater importance to the public interest and of more value to the public welfare* than the disclosure of the alleged crime or the alleged criminal."[75] Accordingly, the court interpreted the statute as protecting all documents and materials which the paper had gathered to do the story and all unpublished information or comments received from a news source.

On the other hand, two courts have said that where a reporter identifies a source in a story, any unpublished remarks of or information from that source are not protected, since the "source" itself has been disclosed.[76]

Can source protection under a seemingly absolute statute be overcome by overriding considerations?

Some courts have suggested that statutory protection can be withdrawn, even if the law makes no provision for doing so.

In one libel case. the question was what remarks were made by a baseball club's officials about one of their players. The ball player had questioned the officials unsuccessfully, so he attempted to get the information from the reporter. The court suggested that if it were impossible to get the information anywhere else. the reporter could be made to testify, despite the seemingly absolute California shield law.[77]

More recently, Los Angeles reporter William Farr tried to use the California shield law to avoid having to tell a judge which attorney in the Charles Manson murder trial had supplied the reporter with a secret transcript in violation of the court's orders. The court ruled that the statute could not be used to obstruct the administration of justice: "To construe the statute as granting immunity to petitioner, Farr, in the face of the facts here present would be to countenance an unconstitutional interference by the legislative branch with, an inherent and vital power of the court to control its own proceedings and officers."[78]

Finally, in the Weather Underground case, the court suggested that New York's "absolute" shield law would give way to "the furtherance of public policy requiring investigation of crime and prosecution therefor."[79]

Thus, even where a strong shield law is on the books, some courts have tried to interpret it in such a way that reporters can be ordered to reveal information which the courts feel is important.

Can shield laws protect you from revealing confidential sources of a story which has resulted in a libel suit?

The answer is unclear.

A few shield laws specifically exclude defamation actions from statutory protection—for example, the new Oregon statute.

Most statutes, however, are silent on the issue, and judicial interpretation of such laws has been mixed. In one libel case based on a magazine story about conditions in Alabama prisons, the reporter had obtained materials in confidence from various state employees whom he refused to identify. Since Alabama had a strong shield law, the court applied it and ruled that the information was protected.[80] The courts in New Jersey, however, have consistently taken the opposite view, ruling that where a newspaper defends a libel suit by claiming that the defamatory statements were based on confidential sources, there is an implied "waiver" of the statutory protection.[81] Otherwise, the court reasoned, a paper could reveal the confidential information that helped it but conceal the information that tended to prove bad faith. "This amounts to using the statute as a sword rather than as a shield as was intended when the statute was enacted."[82]

Can you inadvertently "waive" or forfeit your protection under a shield law by voluntarily revealing part of the confidential information?

Some courts have said yes, ingeniously finding a "waiver" of the statute's protection in situations where the reporter obviously had no intention of forfeiting his right to protect his sources.

In one case, Peter Bridge of the *Newark Evening News* wrote a story identifying a news source and quoting her as saying that she had been offered a bribe.[83] A grand jury asked Bridge for further details that had not been published, but he refused to comply, relying on the New Jersey shield law. But New Jersey law also provided that any evidentiary privilege could be waived if the person, "without coercion and with knowledge of his right or privilege, made disclosure of any part of the privileged matter." Seizing upon this general provision, the court ruled that because Bridge had identified the source and disclosed at least part of the information given him by the source, he waived his newspaperman's privilege and could be compelled to reveal the rest of the information.

The New York courts have been similarly adept at concluding that by supplying part of the privileged information a reporter forfeits the right to protect the rest of it. In the *Village Voice* case, the court held that by printing an article by a prisoner under his real name the paper surrendered its right to withhold the original manuscript from the district attorney: "The statute, therefore, cannot be used as a shield to protect that which has already been exposed to view."[84]

But in other states, courts have strongly taken the opposite view, ruling that a reporter who identifies his source or discloses part of his confidential information does not surrender the right to protect the rest of the material. In a Pennsylvania case the court stated: "A waiver by a newsman applies only to the statements made by the informer which are actually published or publicly disclosed and not to other statements made by the informer to the newspaper."[85]

Can your source legally prevent you from disclosing his identity or the information he gave you?

No.

The courts have consistently ruled that the statutory privilege belongs to the reporter, not the source. And if the reporter chooses to breach the confidence and reveal the information, the source cannot prevent that. In two

Indiana cases, the courts held that where a criminal defendant had made a confession to a reporter, the reporter could later decide to testify about the confession, and the defendant was powerless to stop it.[86]

Similarly, since the statutory privilege is the reporter's, he can be deemed to have waived it unintentionally, even though the source would want the information protected.[87]

Can the source by its own actions "waive" the reporter's privilege?

Apparently so.

Of course, your source can always voluntarily release you from the pledge of confidentiality, although many reporters question the ethics of revealing the identity of a source who has been pressured into releasing the reporter from the pledge of confidentiality. But some courts have also said that inadvertent actions by the source can be deemed a waiver of your rights. Thus, for example, in the *Village Voice* case it was suggested that by allowing an article to be run under his real name, a prisoner forfeited the paper's right to protect the information.[88]

If you cover a story for a news medium not specifically defined in a statute, can you still rely on its provisions?

Probably not.

In two libel cases where the state law protected "newspapers," the courts held that the law was inapplicable to magazines.[89] Many statutes remedy the problem by all-inclusive definitions of the news media to be protected.

Can a state shield law protect you against a subpoena in a federal proceeding?

The answer is not certain.

If the federal proceeding is one in which the federal

court is required to consult the applicable state law—for example, in a libel case based upon diversity-of-citizenship jurisdiction—then a state shield law may be enforceable. Similarly, in other types of civil cases, the federal courts have been inclined to honor a relevant state shield law.

But what if reporting undertaken in a state which has a strong shield law leads to a subpoena in a federal grand jury or criminal proceeding? Usually a federal court, even in a criminal proceeding, will follow state law on the question of whether a particular communication—for example, a lawyer-client discussion—can be kept confidential.[90] The courts have not yet said whether this principle encompasses a state shield law. But reporters have argued that a federal court which ignores a state shield law will be frustrating the strong public policy embodied in such a statute and, in effect, overturning that law.

If a reporter is subpoenaed, can the editor or publisher join in the legal proceeding?

Yes.

In the *Caldwell* case, *The New York Times* was granted standing to intervene as a formal party in the proceeding to quash the subpoena.[91] Similarly, in the Watergate burglary trial, subpoenas *duces tecum* were directed at the *Los Angeles Times* reporters and Washington bureau chief. The publisher was allowed to file a motion to quash the subpoena directed at the bureau chief.[92] The practical advantages of persuading the publisher to intervene are substantial. Publishers generally have more influence than reporters, and the prospect of a publisher going to jail will tend to focus the freedom-of-the-press issues more dramatically. Indeed, the strategy of having the publisher step in to face the subpoena would have been employed to resist former Vice President Agnew's efforts to interrogate the press about publicity leaks, until his resignation and plea made the issues moot.[93]

Moreover, if the material subpoenaed is in the possession of the publisher or editor, those individuals may have no choice but to be involved in the matter. In the Watergate burglary trial, the bureau chief had possession of the tapes, and he, not the reporters, wound up spending a brief stay in jail. Similarly, in a recent case under the Ohio shield law, a trial judge quashed a subpoena because, although the law protected testimony not notes, the reporter had turned her notes over to the publisher and no longer had control over them.[94]

But, as the next section indicates, such a tactic may have its disadvantages.

Who owns a reporter's notes or materials?

The answer is unclear. The problem is the other side of the coin of bringing the publisher or editor into any legal proceeding brought against a reporter. Suppose that the editor or publisher is willing to disclose confidential information or material over the objection of the reporter, can the reporter take legal steps to prevent that? None of the subpoena cases deal with this question. If there is a shield law in the picture, the reporter might contend that the statute gives him an enforceable right to protect confidential sources, even against his own publisher or editor. It has also been suggested that, at the very least, reporters and publishers have a joint property or legal interest in the notes or materials, sufficient to allow either one to prevent the other from surrendering such rights.[95]

Can the police get a search warrant to seize your confidential files, notes, and documents?

One court has said no, ruling that while law enforcement officials might be able to subpoena your materials, they can't seize them by simply getting a search warrant.[96]

The case involved a warrant authorizing police to search the offices of the Stanford University paper in order to find photographs taken during a campus disturbance. The court ruled that search warrants against newspapers whose employees are not suspected of criminal activity could not routinely be issued. Instead, the police have to proceed by way of a subpoena *duces tecum*, which does not allow the police to rummage through a newspaper office and which affords the opportunity—through a motion to quash the subpoena—to challenge the subpoena before it can be enforced. As the court put it,

A reporter or photographer responding to a subpoena will bring to the grand jury room only those materials mentioned in the subpoena; the police officers executing a warrant, however, will be in a position to see notes and photographs not even mentioned in the warrant. As is apparent from the affidavits, newspaper offices are much more disorganized than, say, the average law office; a search for particular photographs or notes will mean rummaging through virtually all the drawers and cabinets in the office. The "indiscriminate nature" of such a search renders vulnerable all confidential materials, whether or not identified in the warrant, and the concomitant threat to the gathering of news—which frequently depends on confidential relationships—is staggering.[97]

In reaching its conclusion, the court ruled that by virtue of the First Amendment, newspaper reporters have greater rights under the Fourth Amendment than the average citizen. Otherwise, the First Amendment would be relegated "to redundancy."[98]

What rights and procedures do you have available if you are subpoenaed to appear before a grand jury?

Although reporters in particular have not done very well before grand juries recently, in general the rights of witnesses before such bodies have been expanded in the last few years. The proceedings are of course still secret, and a grand jury witness still has no right to have a lawyer in the grand jury room during the questioning; but some improvements have taken place.

One of the major practical, as well as legal, problems is the suddenness with which the whole thing happens. The prosecutor can routinely obtain a grand jury subpoena, have it served on you, and make it "returnable," i.e., order you to appear before the grand jury, in just a few days. Unless you work for a major news organization with experienced counsel promptly available, it may take you three days just to find a lawyer.[99] If you are unable to arrange for counsel in the limited time available, explain this to the district attorney or grand jury official and request an adjournment. But there is no way that you can safely ignore the subpoena. You must respond to it.[100]

Once you obtain counsel, you can determine whether there are any grounds for either quashing the subpoena or refusing to provide specific materials or answer particular questions. For example, you can object if there were technical defects in the manner by which the subpoena was served upon you.[101]

There is also the possibility of pleading the Fifth Amendment, if there is any chance you were somehow involved in criminal activity, or were a witness to it. Indeed, one of the most famous Supreme Court decisions upholding the privilege against self-incrimination involved two reporters who refused to answer a grand jury's questions about the confidential sources of a story.[120] When they persisted, President Woodrow Wilson offered them a pardon for any crimes they might reveal. They declined to accept it and were upheld by the Supreme Court, which ruled that a pardon implied guilt and did not have to be accepted in exchange for testifying.

Of course, the government can choose to grant you immunity in exchange for your testimony, and at that point you may very well have to testify or face confinement. And the Supreme Court has ruled that the government need only promise that it will not prosecute you on the basis of your testimony or leads it produces ("use" immunity); the government need not offer you complete immunity from prosecution for the events that you testify about ("transactional" immunity).[103]

The Supreme Court has held that a grand jury witness who has been the subject of illegal wiretapping can refuse to answer questions based upon information so obtained.[104]

These days, that is an objection which might be available to many reporters. It should be considered where there is any reason to think there has been a wiretapping. Unfortunately, the Court recently ruled that a grand jury witness could not refuse to answer grand jury questions even though based upon evidence seized in violation of the Fourth Amendment.

Can you raise any First Amendment objections to a grand jury's inquiries? *Branzburg* of course makes it difficult to claim that the First Amendment allows you to resist grand jury questions which interfere with confidential sources of information, except to the extent that you can show harassment, bad faith, or marginal relevance. But there are some First Amendment objections still available, even against a grand jury. Thus, one federal court has suggested that while a journalist or scholar must answer factual questions, there is no obligation to answer questions asking his "opinions" about things.[105] And it has also been held that, apart from questions which inhibit newsgathering and confidential sources, journalists can still raise general First Amendment objections to grand jury questions which probe the editorial processes of a news agency.[106]

And you can try to raise the claims rejected in the *Branzburg* case, so that the issue is at least preserved for appellate review, should the judicial climate change.

What happens if you refuse to answer questions asked or provide information sought by a grand jury or a court?

Once you have appeared and refused to answer particular questions asked by a grand jury or to provide information or documents called for, then the grand jury will usually take the matter before a judge who will order you to show cause why you should not respond. One recent decision has held that you must be given a reasonable time, usually at least five days, between the refusal to answer and the contempt hearing.[107] Unfortunately, that ruling did not help KPFK manager Will Lewis, who refused to honor a grand jury subpoena and was literally in jail before sundown.

There may also be time pressures if a subpoena commands your attendance at a criminal trial itself, rather than a grand jury proceeding; but the court and the parties might be willing to resolve the issues in advance rather than risk an interruption of the trial caused by the need to litigate a reporter's testimony.[108]

In civil litigation the issues usually come up in a somewhat more leisurely manner. In the federal courts, for example, there is a great emphasis on pre-trial discovery, and there are provisions for motions to quash subpoenas and for the fashioning of protective orders for witnesses. Thus, if a reporter receives a subpoena in connection with a civil proceeding, there is usually more time to prepare a defense. And even after a refusal to answer questions during a deposition, the party seeking the information has to make a motion to the judge to compel a response. That may take additional time.

Although state procedures may vary, in the federal courts there is a codified provision generally governing "recalcitrant witnesses." It provides that:

(a) Whenever a witness in any proceeding before or ancillary to any court or grand jury of the United States refuses without just cause shown to comply with an order of the court to testify or provide other information including any book, paper, document, record, recording or other material, the court, upon such refusal, or when such refusal is duly brought to its attention, may summarily order his confinement at a suitable place until such time as the witness is willing to give such testimony or provide such information. No period of such confinement shall exceed the life of

(1) the court proceeding, or
(2) the term of the grand jury, including extensions, before which such refusal to comply with the court order occurred, but in no event shall such confinement exceed eighteen months.[109]

The statute also provides for bail pending an appeal, unless the appeal is "frivolous and taken for delay," and further provides for a prompt disposition of any such appeal.

These procedures are ones usually associated with "civil" contempt. The differences between "civil" and "criminal" contempt are frequently unclear. But in general, civil contempt is prospective, seeking to coerce the person to perform an affirmative act; criminal contempt is generally retrospective, seeking to punish a completed prior act.[110] Very often, particularly with regard to the refusal to answer questions or provide materials, the two features are combined.[111] The distinction becomes important primarily in terms of the procedures which will be afforded; the more "criminal" the proceeding looks, the more likely that normal criminal procedures will apply. Also, confinement for criminal contempt is usually for a fixed period of time, and if it's more than six months, you might be entitled to a jury trial.[112]

Footnotes to Chapter II

1. *The Village Voice*, January 18, 1973, p. 4. © 1973 Jules Feiffer 1-14.
2. *The Papers of Thomas Jefferson* (1955), Vol. XI, p. 49.
3. 408 U.S. 665 (1972).
4. *Id.* at 709-10.
5. *Id.* at 667.
6. *Id.* at 708.
7. *Id* at 681-82.
8. *Id.* at 708. See also, *Bursey* v. *United States*, 466 F.2d 1059 (1972).
9. 408 U.S. at 709-10.
10. *Id.* at 710.
11. See, *e.g.*, *Lightman* v. *State*, 15 Md. App. 713, 294 A.2d 149 (1972), *aff'd*, 266 Md. 500, 295 A.2d 212, *cert. denied*, 411 U.S. 951 (1973); *In re Bridge*, 120 N.J. Super. 460, 295 A.2d 3 (1972), *cert. denied*, 410 U.S. 991 (1973). In *Lightman*, the grand jury wanted to know the identity of a young shopkeeper who told the reporter of her involvement and police complicity in marijuana activities. In *Bridge*, the grand jury asked five questions to determine who had offered a bribe to a municipal housing official. The court held that balancing was not necessary and that the questions were relevant to the grand jury investigation.
12. See, *e.g.*, *People ex rel. Mooney* v. *Sheriff*, 269 N.Y. 291, 199 N.E. 415 (1936); *Clein* v. *State*, 52 So.2d 117 (Fla. 1950).
13. See, *e.g.*, *Plunkett* v. *Hamilton*, 136 6a. 72, 70 S.E. 781 (1911). Recently, however, a Georgia judge ruled that the state right-to-work law protected a reporter from having to reveal his sources.
14. *State* v. *Knops*, 49 Wis.2d 647, 183 N.W.2d 93, 99 (1971); see also, *Levin* v. *Marshall*, 317 F. Supp. 169 (D. Md. 1970); but see, *State* v. *Buchanan*, 250 Ore. 244 436 P.2d 729 (1968).

15. See Benno C. Schmidt, Jr., "Beyond the *Caldwell* Decision—The Decision is Tentative," Columbia Journalism Review, September/October 1972.

16. *People* v. *John Doe (In re WBAI)*, 39 App. Div.2d 869, 870, 333 N.Y.S. 2d 876 (1st Dept. 1972). In that case, the Manhattan District Attorney secured a subpoena *duces tecum,* directed to the manager of radio station WBAI, ordering him to produce:

> All Tape Recordings, Program Logs and all Material Broadcast with relation to the Riots at the Manhattan House of Detention for Men (Tombs) during the period between October 2, 1970 to October 5, 1970.

The district attorney utimately conceded, and the court agreed, that the subpoena was too broad.

17. *Democratic National Committee* v. *McCord*, 356 F. Supp. 1394 1396 (D. D.C. 1973).

18. *In re Lewis*, ——F.2d—— (9th Cir. July 19, 1974).

19. *Nixon* v. *United States*, ——U.S.——, 42 U.S. Law Week 5237 (July 24, 1974).

20. *United States* v. *Liddy*, 354 F. Supp. 208, 216 (D. D.C. 1972).

21. *Id.* at 217, note 35.

22. *United States* v. *Liddy*, 478 F.2d 586, 587-88 (D.C. Cir. 1972).

23. The additional procedures suggested were as follows: (1) the material would not be disclosed to the defendants' attorneys until the key witness had completed his direct testimony at trial; (2) the court would explore "less drastic means" of resolving the problem, for example, asking the witness to permit release of the tapes or state his reasons for not doing so; (3) the judge, after the witness has testified, will not release the material unless he determines it is needed; (4) it will first be released to counsel in chambers; and (5) will be made public at the trial only if the judge decides that is necessary. 478 F.2d at 588.

24. *State* v. *St. Peter*, 315 A.2d 254 (Vt. Sup. Ct. 1974)

25. *Brown* v. *Commonwealth*, 204 S.E.2d 429 (Sup. Ct. Va. 1974).

26. *Rosenberg* v. *Carroll (In re Lyons)*, 99 F. Supp. 629 (S.D. N.Y. 1951).

27. *Thompson* v. *State*, 284 Minn. 274, 170 N.W.2d 101 (1969).

30. 408 U.S. at 692-98.
31. See, *e.g.*, *Branzburg* v. *Pound*, 461 S.W.2d 345 (1971), *aff'd on other grounds*, 408 U.S. 665 (1972); *Lightman* v. *State*, 15 Md. App. 713, 294 A.2d 149 (1972), *aff'd*, 266 Md. 550, 295 A.2d 212, *cert. denied*, 411 U.S. 951 (1973).
32. *Petition of McGowan*, 303 A.2d 645 (Sup. Ct. Del. 1973).
33. 470 F.2d 778 (2d Cir. 1972), *cert. denied*, 411 U.S. 966 (1973).
34. *Id.* at 782.
35. *Id.* at 783.
36. *Id.* at 784-85.
37. 356 F. Supp. 1394 (D. D.C. 1973).
38. *Id.* at 1397-98.
39. *Id.* at 1398.
40. *Id.* at 1397.
41. The problem is discussed in the testimony of Professor Anthony Amsterdam in the *Hearings on Newsmen's Privilege Before the Senate Subcommittee on Constitutional Rights*, 93rd Cong., 1st Sess. at 212 (hereafter cited as *Senate Hearings*).
42. This problem is described by Brit Hume, a reporter who was sued for libel by an official of the United Mine Workers Union. See *Senate Hearings* at 116-17; *Carey* v. *Hume*, 492 F.2d 631 (D.C. Cir. 1974).
43. See generally, *Cervantes* v. *Time, Inc.*, 464 F.2d 986 (8th Cir. 1972), *cert. denied*, 409 U.S. 1125 (1973); *Application of Cepeda*, 233 F. Supp. 465 (S.D.N.Y. 1964); *Ex Parte Sparrow*, 14 F.R.D. 351 (N.D. Ala. 1953).
44. *Brewster* v. *Boston Herald-Traveler Corp.*, 20 F.R.D. 416 (D. Mass. 1957).
45. *Garland* v. *Torre*, 259 F.2d 545 (2d Cir.), *cert. denied*, 358 U.S. 910 (1958).
46. *Id.* at 548.
47. *Id.* at 549-50. The court also refused to create a privilege apart from the First Amendment. At that time, New York, where the case arose and the deposition was taken, had no statute and the court found no support for a common-law privilege in previous cases.
48. *Adams* v. *Associated Press*, 46 F.R.D. 439 (S.D. Tex. 1969).
49. Summary judgment is the procedure whereby a party seeks final judgment on the basis of the pleadings, affidavits, and other records in the case without the necessity

of a full trial of the facts. It is a procedure which is particularly important in libel actions. See Chapter VI.

50. *Cervantes* v. *Time, Inc., supra,* 464 F2d at 991.

51. *Id.* at 993.

52. *Dow Jones & Co.* v. *Superior Court,* 303 N.E. 2d 847 (Mass. Sup. Ct. 1973). See generally, Comment, *Reporters and Their Sources: The First Amendment Privilege in Constitutional Libel Actions,* 58 Iowa L. Rev. 618 (1973); cf. *Gialde* v. *Time, Inc.,* 480 F.2d 1295 (8th Cir. 1973).

53. *Carey* v. *Hume,* 492 F.2d 631 (D.C. Cir. 1974).

54. *New York Times,* Oct. 5, 1973, p. 13, col. 1; 42 Law Week 2232.

55. See, *e.g., Service* v. *Dulles,* 354 U.S. 363 (1957); See *Senate Hearings* at 680, 752 (describing *U.S.* v. *Miller,* 9th Cir. No. 71-2623).

56. *Nader* v. *Bork,* 366 F. Supp. 104 (D. D.C. 1973).

57. See Whalen, *Your Right to Know* (Vintage, 1973), pp. 18-33; *Ex parte Lawrence,* 116 Cal. 298, 48 Pac. 124 (1897).

58. *United States* v. *Doe (Appeal of Popkin),* 460 F.2d 328 (1st Cir. 1972), *cert. denied, sub. nom., Popkin* v. *United States,* 411 U.S. 909 (1973).

59. *Sanders* v. *McClellan,* 463 F.2d 894 (D.C. Cir. 1972).

60. *Id.* at 899. That cumbersome procedure helped keep Dr. Frank Stanton, the former President of CBS, from being held in contempt of Congress. CBS refused to comply with a House subpoena for outtakes of "The Selling of the Pentagon." The committee voted to issue a contempt citation, but the full House declined by a narrow margin. *Senate Hearings* at 172.

61. See, *Groppi* v. *Leslie,* 404 U.S. 496 (1972).

62. See, *e.g., Sweezy* v. *New Hampshire,* 354 U.S. 234 (1957).

63. 408 U.S. at 706. The Court also observed that state courts were free to construe their own state constitutions "so as to recognize a newsman's privilege, either qualified or absolute." *Id.* at 706. However, the efforts to persuade state courts to do that have so far been unsuccessful. See *In re Bridge,* 120 N.J. Super. 460, 295 A.2d 3, 7 (1972), *cert. denied,* 410 U.S. 991 (1972).

64. An extremely useful analysis of the statutory provisions and judicial interpretation of them was prepared by Arthur B. Hanson, General Counsel of the American News-

paper Publisher's Association. It is contained in *Senate Hearings* at 723-41.

65. See *Senate Hearings* (Hanson Memorandum) at 724-27. Some of the more recent statutes specifically provide that the protection is available even if the reporter is no longer employed by a news medium at the time the information is sought. This is a response to the case of *Farr* v. *Superior Court,* 22 Cal. App.3d 60, 99 Cal. Rptr. 342 (1971), where the court indicated that California's statute could not be utilized by a person who, although a reporter at the time he secured the confidential information, was no longer employed by a newspaper when the court ordered him to disclose his sources.
66. N.Y. Civ. Rights Law, §79-h, par.(b) (McKinney, 1970).
67. *People* v. *Wolf,* 69 Misc.2d 256, 329 N.Y.S.2d 291, 297 (Sup. Ct. N.Y. Co.), *aff'd,* 39 App. Div.2d 864, 333 N.Y.S.2d 299 (1st Dept. 1972).
68. *In re WBAI* v. *Proskin,* 42 App. Div.2d 5, 344 N.Y.S.2d 393 (3rd Dept. 1973). A strongly worded dissent criticized the majority for ignoring the plain meaning of the statute and disregarding the fact that a great many news items are supplied anonymously and gratuitously. An appeal to the highest state court has been taken.
69. *People by Fischer* v. *Dan,* 41 App. Div.2d 687, 342 N.Y.S.2d 731 (4th Dept. 1973). See also *Branzburg* v. *Pound,* 461 S.W.2d 345 (1970), *aff'd, sub nom., Branzburg* v. *Hayes,* 408 U.S. 665 (1972).
70. *Lightman* v. *State,* 15 Md. App. 713, 294 A.2d 149 (1972), *aff'd,* 266 Md. 550, 295 A.2d 212, *cert. denied,* 411 U.S. 951 (1973).
71. *Branzburg* v. *Pound,* 461 S.W.2d 345, 347 (Ky. 1970), *aff'd on other grds., sub. nom., Branzburg* v. *Hayes,* 408 U.S. 665 (1972).
72. *Lightman* v. *State, supra.*
73. *People by Fischer* v. *Dan,* 41 App. Div. 2d 687, 342 N.Y.S.2d 731 (4th Dept. 1973).
74. *In re Taylor,* 412 Pa. 32, 193 A.2d 181 (1963).
75. 193 A.2d at 186-87.
76. See *In re Bridge, supra; State* v. *Sheridan,* 248 Md. 320, 236 A.2d 18 (Ct. of App., Md. 1967). In an earlier New Jersey case it was held that the statute did not allow an editor to refuse to disclose the identity of the messenger who brought certain news releases to the paper's offices. The identity of the source might be privileged, but the

identity of the go-between was not. *State* v. *Donovan*, 219 N.J.L. 478, 30 A.2d 421 (1943).

77. *Application of Cepeda*, 233 F. Supp. 465 (S.D.N.Y. 1964).

78. *Farr* v. *Superior Court*, 22 Cal. App.3d 60, 99 Cal. Rptr. 342 (1971), *cert. denied*, 409 U.S. 1011 (1972).

79. *In re WBAI-FM*, 68 Misc.2d 355, 236 N.Y.S.2d 434, 437 (Albany Co. Ct. 1971), *aff'd, sub nom, WBAI* v. *Proskin*, 42 App. Div.2d 5, 344 N.Y.S. 2d 393 (3rd Dept. 1973).

80. *Ex Parte Sparrow*, 14 F.R.D. 351 (N.D. Ala. 1953).

81. *Brogan* v. *Passaic Daily News*, 22 N.J. 139, 123A2d 473 (1956); *Beechcroft* v. *Point Pleasant Printing and Pub. Co.*, 82 N.J. Super. 269, 197 A.2d 416 (1964).

82. *Brogan* v. *Passaic Daily News, supra*, 123 A.2d at 480. See also, *Application of Cepeda*, 233 F. Supp. 465 (S.D.N.Y. 1964).

83. *In re Bridge*, 120 N.J. Super. 460, 295 A.2d 3 (1972), *cert. denied*, 410 U.S. 991 (1972).

84. *People* v. *Wolf*, 39 App. Div.2d 864, 333 N.Y.S.2d 299 (1st Dept. 1972). See also, *People by Fischer* v. *Dan*, 41 App. Div.2d 687, 342 N.Y.S. 2d 731 (4th Dept. 1973).

85. *In re Taylor*, 412 Pa. 32, 193 A.2d 181, 186 (1963); See also *In re Howard*, 136 Cal. App.2d 816, 289 P.2d 537 (1955).

86. *Lipps* v. *State*, 254 Ind. 141, 258 N.E.2d 622 (1970); *Hestand* v. *State*, ——Ind.——, 273 N.E.2d 282 (1971); see also *Beechcroft* v. *Point Pleasant Print & Pub. Co.*, 82 N.J. Super. 269, 197 A.2d 416 (1964) (in a libel case, the privilege belongs to the paper, not the source).

87. *Lightman* v. *State*, 15 Md. App. 713, 294 A.2d 149, 156 (1972), *aff'd*, 266 Md. 550, 295 A.2d 212 (1972), *cert. denied*, 411 U.S. 951 (1973).

88. *People* v. *Wolf*, 69 Misc. 2d 256, 329 N.Y.S. 2d 291 (Sup. Ct. N.Y. Co. 1972), *aff'd*, 39 App. Div. 2d 864, 333 N.Y.S. 2d 299 (1st Dept. 1973).

89. *Application of Cepeda*, 233 F. Supp. 465 (S.D.N.Y. 1964) (*Look* Magazine); *Dultec, Inc.* v. *Dun and Bradstreet, Inc.*, 187 F. Supp. 788 (N.D. Ohio, 1960).

90. See, *e.g.*, *Love* v. *United States*, 386 F.2d 260 (8th Cir. 1967).

91. *Application of Caldwell*, 311 F. Supp. 358, 359 (N.D. Cal. 1970).

92. *United States* v. *Liddy* (*In re Times Mirror Co.*), 354 F. Supp. 208 (D.D.C. 1972).

93. See *New York Times*, Oct. 12, 1973, p. 29, col. 2.

94. See *Press Censorship Newsletter*, No. III, p. 11 (Reporters Committee for Freedom of the Press).

95. *Id.* p. 38.

96. *Stanford Daily* v. *Zurcher*, 353 F. Supp. 124 (N.D. Cal. 1972).

97. *Id.* at 134-135.

98. *Id.* at 134.

99. See *Senate Hearings* at 201-02, 287-88.

100. Grand jury problems are discussed generally in an ACLU publication entitled "Your Rights Before the Grand Jury."

101. The manner of service is usually spelled out in a statute or rule. See Rule 17, F.R. Cr.P. If that method was disregarded, you can move to quash the subpoena. In one case, a State Attorney General subpoena was invalidated because instead of summoning a photographer to appear before the Attorney General, it simply ordered him to turn his negatives over to a policeman. *Petition of McGowan*, 303 A.2d 645 (Sup. Ct. Del. 1973).

102. *Burdick* v. *United States*, 236 U.S. 79 (1915); *Curtin* v. *United States*, 236 U.S. 96 (1915).

103. *Kastigar* v. *United States*, 406 U.S. 441 (1972).

104. *Gelbard* v. *United States*, 408 U.S. 41 (1972).

105. *United States* v. *Doe* (Appeal of Popkin), 460 F.2d 328 (1st Cir. 1972), *cert. denied*, 411 U.S. 909 (1973). That case involved a grand jury probe into the transmission of the Pentagon Papers. The witness was asked his opinion about which individuals had been involved, a question which the court said he didn't have to answer. 460 F.2d at 335.

106. *Bursey* v. *United States*, 466 F.2d 1059 (9th Cir. 1972).

107. *United States* v. *Alter*, 482 F.2d 1016 (9th Cir. 1973); see generally *United States* v. *Marra*, 482 F.2d 1196 (2d Cir. 1973).

108. This was the procedure followed in *United States* v. *Liddy*, 354 F. Supp. 208 (D. D.C. 1972).

109. 28 U.S.C. Section 1826 (Supp. 1972).

110. See Hobbs, *Contempt of Court*, 56 Col. L. Rev. 183, 235 (1971); Goldfarb, *Consultant's Report on Contempt*, Working Papers of the National Commission on Reform of Federal Criminal Laws (July, 1970), Vol. I., pp. 646-47.
Even after the trial is over, a court may rule that it possesses power to compel a reporter's testimony. In the

Farr case, the judge concluded that since the main criminal case was on appeal, and the issue of who supplied the reporter with inflammatory information was still unresolved, the court retained power to determine who the sources were. Recently, an appeals court ruled that if Farr could prove that the contempt punishment would not really force him to reveal his sources, then the sentence would be punitive rather than remedial and, under California law, could not exceed 5 days. *In Re Farr,* 36 Cal. App.3d 557, 111 Cal. Rptr. 649 (2d Dist. 1974).

111. In *United States* v. *Liddy,* 354 F. Supp. 208 (D. D.C. 1972) the reporter was found in criminal contempt for refusing to obey a court order for the production of tapes, while in *Application of Caldwell,* 311 F. Supp. 358 (N.D. Cal. 1970), the reporter was held in civil contempt for refusing to appear before the grand jury.

112. *Cheff* v. *Schackenberg,* 384 U.S. 373 (1966). Refusal to obey a legislative or administrative subpoena is usually punishable by criminal contempt, following a prosecution brought by the agency. See *Goldfarb, supra* at 647-49.

III

Gathering the News

Although the problem of protecting sources has received more attention, the difficulties encountered in the general process of gathering the news probably affect more reporters. Newsgathering—gaining access to the people, places, and things which make up the news—is at the very heart of the journalistic enterprise. It is the larger issue, of which protecting confidential sources is but a part.

The courts have not addressed the newsgathering issue very often. When they have, the general conclusion has been that while the press does not necessarily have a special right of access to news, it cannot be denied the same right of access to information available to the public generally, and unreasonable discrimination among various news media will not be tolerated.[1]

Does the First Amendment protect the newsgathering process?

Yes. In *Branzburg,* the Supreme Court stated, for the first time, that the process of newsgathering has constitutional stature:

Nor is it suggested that newsgathering does not qualify for First Amendment protection; without some protection for seeking out the news, freedom of the press would be eviscerated.

. . . newsgathering is not without its First Amendment protections.[2]

The Court thus made explicit what many lower courts had recognized.[3]

But, having recognized the right to gather news, the Court went on to describe the ways in which the right has been limited:

Despite the fact that newsgathering may be hampered, the press is regularly excluded from grand jury proceedings, our own conferences, the meetings of other official bodies gathered in executive session, and the meetings of private organizations. Newsmen have no constitutional right of access to the scenes of crime or disaster when the general public is excluded, and they may be prohibited from attending or publishing information about trials if such restrictions are necessary to assure a defendant a fair trial before an impartial tribunal.[4]

This description of the law on newsgathering was dictum, i.e., the observations were not necessary to the court's disposition of the issues before it.

Unfortunately, this dictum by the Court was applied two years later in another ruling on the constitutional right of reporters to gather the news. In two cases challenging prison rules prohibiting press interviews with specific individual inmates, a 5 to 4 majority, led by Justice Potter Stewart, ruled that "the Constitution does not . . . require government to accord the press special access to information not shared by the members of the public generally."[5] Conceding the right of journalists to seek out sources of news unavailable to the general public, the Court ruled the government did not have to make such sources available. Justice Lewis F. Powell switched to the press position, noting in his dissent that the ban on prisoner-press interviews "impermissibly restrains the ability of the press to perform its constitutionally established function of informing the people on the conduct of their Government."

Can the police arbitrarily deny a press pass to a reporter?

No.

Press passes are frequently important in gaining access to locations from which the public is generally excluded. Crossing police lines is a typical example. If the police can arbitrarily control the issuance of such credentials, they can inhibit the newsgathering function. So far, the courts have not been willing to give law enforcement agencies that kind of discretion.

Not surprisingly, the "establishment" media generally have little difficulty getting official credentials for their reporters, and the few cases where the denial of credentials has been challenged have been brought by reporters for the "underground" press.

The first, and worst, case involved the *Los Angeles Free Press*, a dissident weekly newspaper whose reporters were denied police press passes.[6] The police department practice was to restrict the number of passes issued, to grant them only to individuals, not to news organizations, and generally to issue passes only to individuals working for the regular media. Passes were denied to the *Free Press* because it was "not regularly engaged in the gathering and reporting of spot, hard-core police-beat and fire news," but rather was devoted to "feature articles with some essay-type reports ... focused largely on sociological considerations."[7] A California appeals court ruled that the publisher of a weekly paper has no First Amendment right of access to the scenes of crimes and disasters superior to that of the general public, and that police department favoritism toward media which regularly cover such events was not unreasonable or arbitrary.

The next case came up in Providence, Rhode Island, where street people who put out a paper called *Extra*

were having difficulties selling the paper on the street and
getting behind police lines.[8] The police claimed that they
utilized informal guidelines which required that the applicant provide identification and be engaged in service to a
publication. The court thought that requiring press passes
was not inherently unreasonable, because the police may
regulate access to emergencies in the interest of safety.
But since such regulations did burden "the vital newsgathering function of the free press," the police must act
pursuant to "clear and narrow guidelines."[9] "If identification of members of the press is to be the sole governing
criterion and if, upon identification, passes will issue minis-
terially, then that should be clearly stated and made
known. It is not necessary that there be a written regulation, so long as there is a uniform practice under the
broad general authorization."[10] Since there was such a
regular practice, and because the reporters had not complied with the rather minimal identification requirements,
but had submitted only a very casual application, the court
upheld the denial of credentials.

Though ruling against the reporters, the Rhode Island
case made it clear that actual police discrimination in denying credentials to reporters from the underground press
would not be tolerated. And, indeed, when such harassment was attempted in Davenport, Iowa, it was vigorously
condemned. There, the police department, without any
standards or reasons, denied reporters of the Quad-City
Community News Service virtually every benefit accorded
to the establishment press. In court, the police justifica-
tions for refusing to issue credentials—that two of the ap-
plicants had prior felony convictions—were rejected as "a
classic example of post-factor rationalization of preconceived determination to deny Quad-City's application. . . ."[11] Noting that the denial of credentials is just
as potent an inhibition on the press as imposing prior
restraints on what can be published, the court ruled that
passes cannot be denied through the use of vague or un-
known criteria or by discriminating against reporters who
are not connected with an "established" newspaper:

Whatever standard [the police] employ to license journalists who are to be admitted to sites of newsworthy events must be narrowly drawn, reasonable and definite, and they must be publicly available. Furthermore, refusal to timely inform an applicant as to the reasons for denial of a pass, that is, in what respect(s) its application is found deficient according to the standards is as void of due process as is the lack of standards in the first instance.[12]

To insure that any new standards would be even-handedly applied, the court ordered that the plaintiffs were entitled to press passes until new regulations were promulgated and that the passes could not be withdrawn unless all reporters were made to apply for them under the new guidelines.[13]

Can the police interfere with a reporter engaged in newsgathering activities in public places?

No. Except for allowing reasonable restrictions on access behind police lines, courts have generally condemned police interference with reporters engaged in newsgathering activities in public places.

In Chicago, for example, a group of news photographers brought suit against the police as a result of the notorious press harassment during the 1968 Democratic Convention. The photographers claimed that the police had threatened reporters and repeatedly interfered with their efforts to gather, report, and photograph the news. The reporters also demanded that high police and city officials be held legally responsible for the situation and be compelled to improve it. A federal appeals court ruled that the reporters had asserted a valid legal complaint "that First Amendment rights have been chilled as a result of both government action and inaction" and were entitled to a trial on the merits.[14]

A few years earlier, another federal court reached a similar conclusion in a case where a reporter for a Dayton paper had been physically removed from the scene of a fire which other reporters were being allowed to cover.[15]

The newspaper brought suit, alleging that its right to send reporters out for legitimate newsgathering purposes had been infringed. The court agreed, noting that the police can only restrict access to public streets in the interest of public safety, not to interfere with a particular reporter. The court also made it clear that the news organization itself could go to court whenever its reporters are interfered with: "We do not construe the complaint as merely a suit to redress the civil rights of [the paper's] reporter, but rather as an effort to vindicate its right as a newspaper to gather news for publication without discrimination or uncalled for interference."[16]

Perhaps the most affirmative declaration of the right to gather news in public places came in a case brought by a Duluth, Minnesota, television station.[17] The station had sent a cameraman to cover a burglary in progress at a ski shop. As the suspects were led out the front door, the cameraman turned on his lights and began filming. A police sergeant ordered him to stop, seized the camera, and confiscated it when the reporter refused to promise that the police could censor the film. First, the court ruled that the seizure of the camera violated the Fourth Amendment because there was no search warrant and no reason to arrest the cameraman. Also, the confiscation of the film was an invalid prior restraint on publishing the news, of the kind condemned in the Pentagon Papers case: "If publication cannot be prevented indirectly by injunction after a hearing in a case involving the national security, *a fortiori*, the direct seizure and holding of a camera and film belonging to a newsman on any lesser ground is surely constitutionally invalid."[18] Similarly, the police could not extract a promise to allow censorship of the film as a condition of returning it. The court reaffirmed the principles that "employees of the news media have a right to be in public places and on public property to gather information, photographically or otherwise," and that the police may not inhibit that right so long as reporters "do not unreasonably obstruct or interfere with [police] investigation of physical evidence or gain access to any place from which the general public is prohibited for essential safety purpose."[19]

Likewise, the use of television lights at night can be restricted only if the police reasonably believe that the lights interfere with or endanger their work. Since the public had not been excluded from the particular area, and the lights were on for only a few seconds, the court concluded that there was no justification for the police action.

More recently, a Texas appeals court ruled that reporters for an underground paper could not be punished for photographing an undercover narcotics agent as he emerged from an open court hearing.[20]

Yet, while the courts have generally recognized a broad right to gather news in public places, a recent decision has made it clear that the right is not unlimited. The case involved Ron Gallela, a self-styled "paparazzo," who consistently hounded Jacqueline Kennedy Onassis and her children, attempting to photograph them whenever he could find them. Suits and countersuits were filed, and, after a long and acrimonious trial, the judge enjoined Gallela from photographing the family, except from a great distance.[21] The appellate court agreed that "crimes and torts committed in newsgathering are not protected" by the First Amendment, but ruled that the trial court's injunction went too far:

Relief must be tailored to protect Mrs. Onassis from the "paparazzo" attack which distinguishes Gallela's behavior from that of other photographers; it should not unnecessarily infringe on reasonable efforts to "cover" [Mrs. Onassis]. Therefore, we modify the court's order to prohibit only (1) any approach within twenty-five (25) feet of [Mrs. Onassis] or any touching of [her] person . . . ; (2) any blocking of her movement in public places and thoroughfares; (3) any act foreseeably or reasonably calculated to place the life or safety of [Mrs. Onassis] in jeopardy; and (4) any conduct which would reasonably be foreseen to harass, alarm or frighten the defendant.

Any further restriction on Gallela's taking and selling pictures of defendant for news coverage is, however, improper and unwarranted by the evidence.[22]

The appeals court also eased the restrictions placed on Gallela's coverage of the Kennedy children.

Can a reporter be denied access to open meetings of legislative or executive bodies?

Probably not. Rarely does a government body try to exclude the press from open meetings, and in one case where it was attempted, a federal court intervened.[23] The Tennessee Senate, which normally allowed reporters into committee meetings and onto the Senate floor during a session, decided to vote on a particular proposal in secret and resolved to exclude the press from that discussion. A reporter for the *Nashville Tennessean* refused to leave, protesting that the exclusion violated freedom of the press. The following day, the state senate passed a resolution denying *Tennessean* reporters access to the Senate floor until they promised to "abide by the rules of this body," and reporters from that paper were kept out of the Senate chamber, although other reporters were let in. In the court's view, the applicable principles were clear:

The freedom with which we are here concerned has been universally recognized as including the right of the press to have access to the open sessions and proceedings of legislative assemblies. Without the opportunity to gather and obtain the news, the right to publish or comment upon it would be of little value.[24]

Of course, legislative bodies can protect themselves "against contemptuous and disorderly conduct on the part of non-members," and could exclude "all reporters and newspaper representatives from the room of any committee desiring to hold a secret or executive session."[25] But the senate could not banish *Tennessean* reporters from open sessions as a form of punishment which imposed "a substantial impairment and denial of its opportunity to gather the news as it occurs during the course of the deliberations of the Senate."[26] Nor could restoring access be conditioned on a promise, couched in the vaguest of terms, to obey senate rules. Whether access to the senate floor is labeled a "right" or a "privilege," it was a vital interest which could be infringed only for valid reasons, such as limitations of space, and not in order to punish freedom of the press.

More recently, these same principles were applied to the press-credential rules of the United States Congress.[27] The suit was brought by the Consumers Union seeking access to the periodical-press galleries for correspondents of its monthly magazine. The advantages of such access were considerable, and the rules governing such credentials were vague and uncertain and were administered by the periodical-correspondents' association. The federal court declared that the denial of the Consumers Union request was unconstitutional. Although reporters may not have "an unrestricted right to go where they please in search of news," "the elimination of some reporters from an area which has been voluntarily opened to other reporters for the purpose of newsgathering presents a wholly different situation."[28] Moreover, unreasonable or arbitrary denial of access to news "constitutes a direct limitation upon the content of news." Nor is the situation remedied because the rules are actually administered by reporters themselves, under power delegated by Congress. The court made its conclusion clear: "The situation . . . flouts the First Amendment. . . . There must be an end to this self-regulation by indefinite standards and artificial distinctions developed to censor the ownership or ideas of publications. The Constitution requires that congressional press galleries remain available to all members of the working press, regardless of their affiliation. Exclusion of a publication from the galleries can only be sanctioned under carefully drawn definite rules developed by Congress and specifically required to protect its absolute right of speech and debate or other compelling legislative interest."[29]

These same principles were also tested as a result of a new Alabama "ethics" law which requires that reporters who cover the state legislature and the activities of public officials must first file a financial-disclosure statement. Under this law, in order to gain admittance to legislative chambers, press rooms, or any press conference, a reporter must obtain a special pass available only after the financial statement has been filed. Alabama reporters and publishers promptly filed suit, and a federal court ruled the statute unconstitutional.[30] Agreeing that reporters had a First Amendment right of reasonable access to the sources of news, the court held that the state's general interest in regulating lobbyists could not automatically be enforced against all reporters.

These restraints on excluding the press apply to executive officials as well as legislatures. The Mayor of Honolulu tried to banish a particular reporter from press conferences, charging that his coverage was "biased and irresponsible." A federal judge quickly overturned the exclusion: "Requiring a newspaper's reporter to pass a subjective compatibility-accuracy test as a condition precedent to the right of that reporter to gather news is no different in kind from requiring a newspaper to submit its proposed news stories for editing as a condition precedent to the right of that newspaper to have a reporter cover the news. Each is a form of censorship."[31]

Can a reporter take more than a pencil and paper into an open session of a legislative or executive body?

There is no clear answer to the question of electronic coverage of public meetings.[32]

Lawsuits seeking the right to televise public hearings have not been very successful. In one case, public television representatives wanted to cover hearings of New York's Metropolitan Transportation Authority, but the court ruled that the cameras would disturb, interfere with, and distract from the proceedings.[33]

Reporters have done a little better in their efforts to bring tape recorders into such meetings. In a California case, a reporter wanted to tape a city council meeting, despite a council rule against it. The court was persuaded that the tape recorder was no more obtrusive than a pen or pencil, and that "accuracy in reporting the transactions of a public body should never be penalized."[34] But in New York, tape recorders were successfully kept out of a city council meeting,[35] and in New Hampshire they were banned from a session of the public utilities commission.[36] And, just recently, a Maryland appellate court upheld a ban on reporters taking tape recorders in to cover sessions of the state legislature.[37] The court recognized a First Amendment right to gather news, but ruled that the ban on tape recorders did not unnecessarily impair that right and was not arbitrarily applied.

In short, a public body probably cannot be compelled to permit television cameras into its meetings, but may have a more difficult time excluding tape recorders. Obviously, as the House Judiciary Committee impeachment hearings demonstrated, a legislature can permit televising if it so chooses.

On the other hand, getting a camera into an open public meeting which does not involve a governmental body may be easier. In Texas, a judge ruled that keeping television cameras out of a university speech given by Justice William O. Douglas (ironically, at his request) was an improper discrimination against the electronic media.

Does a reporter have a right to get into a secret, executive session of a public body?

As a First Amendment matter, probably not. As the Supreme Court noted, "The press is regularly excluded from . . . the meetings of other official bodies gathered in executive session."[38] But you may be able to invoke state law in order to keep a particular governmental body from meeting in executive session.

On this issue, press efforts have been directed at the legislative rather than the judicial arena. Largely because of pressure from the news media, approximately forty states have enacted "sunshine" laws.[39] These laws generally provide that public agencies shall have open meetings and open records. As would be expected, there are frequently a host of exemptions, either based upon the agency involved (e.g., parole boards) or the kind of proceeding taking place (e.g., employee discipline).[40] Enforcement mechanisms include criminal penalties against the offending official and civil injunctive actions by members of the public.

The press has frequently resorted to these statutes, and with some success. For example, in California a court ruled that a county supervisors meeting which was continued over lunch at a private club had not become an executive session from which the press could be excluded.[41] And just recently the Florida Supreme Court held that a school board could not hold a secret meeting even when discussing "quasi-judicial" matters.[42]

Similarly, a new federal law, the 1972 Federal Advisory Committee Act, requires that meetings and records of the more than 1,500 government advisory committees must be open to the public. A federal judge recently ruled that under this law and the First Amendment, reporters for a trade journal could not be barred from a Treasury department conference on liquor labeling.[43]

Does a reporter have a right to enter prisons or other restricted places in order to cover a story?

The answer is unclear.

In the last few years, reporters have mounted a concerted effort to ease or eliminate restrictions on their access to places such as prisons. Initially the campaign was quite successful, with many lower courts ruling that prisons could not be declared completely off-limits to the press and that press access to such institutions was the only effective way for the public to be informed of conditions in prisons and of official responses to such conditions. As one judge put it, "prisons are not walled off sanctuaries like the Pentagon Map Room or the Justices' conference table at the Supreme Court"; rather they are villages in themselves where families, lawyers, clergymen, and others frequently visit.[44]

Unfortunately, the Supreme Court recently reversed

these rulings, holding that prison bans on press interviews with specifically designated prisoners did not violate the rights of the prisoners or the reporters.[45] (The prisons justified the rules on the basis of the "big wheel" theory, i.e., that rebellious inmates would be encouraged by such special press attention.) But it is important to note that in each of these cases bans on such interviews were about the only restrictions imposed on reporters. They were free to visit prisons, stop prisoners at random and interview them, and probe prisoner complaints. In short, the Court found no general attempt to hide prison conditions from reporters. The clear implication is that any blanket ban on press access to prisons will not be tolerated.

Presumably the same approach is applicable to other restricted facilities such as mental institutions,[46] military installations,[47] and migrant labor camps.[48]

If you cover a story by accompanying people engaged in criminal activity, are you subject to prosecution yourself?

The answer is uncertain, but the courts seem very reluctant to allow the First Amendment to be a defense to activity which would otherwise be criminal. Indeed, the Supreme Court called it "frivolous" to argue "that the First Amendment, in the interest of securing news or otherwise, confers a license on either the reporter or his news sources to violate valid criminal laws."[49]

Most recently the problem arose in the case of Thomas Oliphant, a *Boston Globe* reporter who covered the airlift of supplies to Wounded Knee by accompanying the pilots on their mission. Oliphant was subsequently indicted for crossing state lines to promote a riot and obstructing federal officials in the performance of their duties, the same charges which were brought against those who were involved in the siege. Oliphant resisted being extradited to South Dakota, and the criminal charges were dropped.

In response to public criticism of this and other epi-

sodes, former Attorney General Elliot Richardson promulgated guidelines requiring the personal approval of the
Attorney General before any reporter can be questioned,
arrested or indicted for an offense arising from coverage
of a news story.[50]

Assuming that a reporter does not actually and directly
engage in the criminal activity, then any legal problems
which might arise would probably involve provisions governing aiding and abetting, or misprision of felony.

For example, federal law provides that "whoever commits an offense against the United States or aids, abets,
counsels, commands, induces or procures its commission,
is punishable as a principal."[51] The statutory definition is
not very illuminating. Apparently, however, merely being
present when a crime is being committed and knowing it's
going to occur does not amount to aiding and abetting;
you must be doing something to forward the commission
of a crime. It is the difference between being a participant, and merely being "a knowing spectator."[52] The
lesson is plain: if you're along for the ride, don't drive the
car.

The more frequent problem will involve what is referred to as "misprision of felony," a modern version of
the common law duty to raise the "hue and cry," that is, to
report felonies to the authorities. Federal law provides
that "Whoever, having knowledge of the actual commission of a felony cognizable by a court of the United
States, conceals and does not as soon as possible make
known the same to some judge or other person in civil or
military authority under the United States" is guilty of
misprision of felony.[53] In *Branzburg,* the Supreme Court
pointedly discussed this provision, observing that "concealment of crime" is not "looked upon with favor."[54] But at
least the Court went on to note that the statute has been
construed to require "both knowledge of the crime and
some affirmative act of concealment or participation."[55]
So, simply failing to volunteer information to the police
will not render a reporter criminally responsible.

In a related matter, a respected federal judge recently

criticized the practice of federal prosecutors in New York who briefed reporters about an imminent major city-wide drug raid, and allowed reporters and photographers to cover the raid.[56] The judge was concerned about the effect of such coverage on the ability of the defendants to secure a fair trial.

If arrested, what should you do until the lawyer comes?

Fortunately, reporters are not often arrested in connection with covering a story. One reporter who was, Les Whitten, has offered some helpful suggestions for reporters who find themselves in that situation. Here are some of his important do's and dont's.

Do carry the phone number of at least two lawyers with you at all times (the second in case the first is not in).

Don't carry sensitive telephone numbers of sources or others on your person; the police can subject you to a thorough search upon arrest and will confiscate your possessions. Also, if possible, don't carry any personal checks or banking identification; with such information the police can proceed to investigate your checking account.

Protest the arrest at every opportunity as a violation of your First Amendment rights.

Finally, don't answer any questions or make any statements without an attorney present. As they say on television, "Anything you say may be used against you." Even the most innocent remark may prove incriminating.

If government documents are available to the public, does a reporter have a right to them?

Yes. A great number of documents in the possession of government agencies are supposed to be available freely to the general public, including reporters. Occasionally, however, public officials attempt to withhold such documents from particular news organizations or impose obstacles to the availability of such materials. On the few occasions where reporters have taken the issue to court, they have prevailed. In one case, access to public tax records was conditioned upon approval of the city council, although such records were freely available to members of the public and to reporters for certain papers. The court ruled that withholding those documents from one particular paper violated freedom of the press and denied equal protection of the laws.[57] More recently, the same result was reached in a case where police files and records, customarily available to members of the press, were withheld from reporters for an underground newspaper.[58] The court said that whether or not there is a First Amendment right to obtain confidential police reports, once the information was made available to the press, the police could not pick and choose which reporters would get it. Doing so not only violated the Constitution, but also infringed the state "public records" law:

The practice of *de facto* ruling that reports are not confidential to certain individuals but are "confidential" when sought by others is a continuation of the very abuse that so-called public information acts were designed to alleviate.[59]

Thus, public agencies must take an even-handed approach toward the availability of documents and reports.

Do reporters have a constitutional right to obtain documents and reports not publicly available?

Courts have tended to say no, even though the First Amendment has traditionally been held to encompass the right to receive information.[60] A typical case involved a reporter's efforts to gain access to Congressional payroll records.[61] The court ruled that neither the relevant statutes on Congressional documents nor the First Amendment provided a right to have the material:

... the liberty of the press ... does not comprise any alleged right of access to material not available to others, any more than it would include the privilege of attending closed meetings at which news of interest might possibly be gathered. ...

The conclusion is inevitable that the Constitutional privilege of freedom of the press does not include a right on the part of representatives of the press to inspect documents not open to members of the public generally.[62]

Just recently the Pennsylvania Supreme Court reached the same conclusion in rejecting the efforts of reporters from the *Philadelphia Inquirer* to obtain a list of welfare recipients.[63]

Do reporters have a right apart from the First Amendment to obtain public documents and records?

Yes. At both the federal and state levels there are statutory provisions which can be utilized to gain access to official information.

The majority of states have public-records laws providing for inspection and copying of public records. As with open-meetings legislation, these statutes frequently contain numerous exceptions for records which are deemed confidential (e.g., police reports, medical records, personnel files, student records). But in general these laws serve two useful functions. First they make it difficult for officials to withhold information which is not confidential, and second, they frequently allow for court action to determine whether a particular document should be confidential. Reporters have met with some success using these state laws to get information.[64]

At the federal level there is the Freedom of Information Act of 1966.[65] The Act applies only to the executive branch, not to the Congress or the federal courts. It sets forth three major categories of information which federal agencies must make available to the public: (1) information which must be published in the Federal Register (the agency's general organization and structure, and its procedural and substantive rules); (2) information which must be published or made available for inspection or sale (e.g., the decisions in administrative cases, statements and interpretations of policy); and (3) other "identifiable records," i.e., everything else. Each agency upon request must make the material "promptly available." In essence, the Act provides that all documents must be made available unless they are specifically exempted. If the agency declines to turn them over, the person seeking the information can file suit in federal court and get an expedited hearing at which the burden rests upon the government to justify its refusal.[66]

But, of course, the Act contains a series of exemptions. It does not apply to matters that are:

(1) specifically required by Executive Order to be kept secret in the interest of national defense or foreign policy;

(2) related solely to the internal personnel rules and practices of an agency;

(3) specifically exempted from disclosure by statute;

(4) trade secrets and commercial or financial information obtained from a person and privileged or confidential;

(5) inter-agency or intra-agency communications, of the kind which show how officials view various policy alternatives;

(6) personnel and medical files whose disclosure would constitute an invasion of privacy;

(7) investigatory files compiled for law enforcement purposes;

(8) reports evaluating financial institutions;

(9) geological or geophysical reports.

Judicial interpretation of these exemptions has been only partly favorable to disclosure. For example, the "national security" exception, which helps perpetuate the massive system of overclassification, was given a very broad reading by the Supreme Court. In a case brought by members of Congress seeking the release of classified reports describing the environmental impact of underground nuclear testing, the Court ruled that any classified information is exempt from disclosure and that the courts may not review the propriety of the decision to classify a particular document.[67] As a result, by stamping a document classified, federal agencies will continue to be able to suppress information even where its release could not possibly harm the national security. Courts have a similar record in interpreting the other statutory exceptions. And just recently the federal appeals court in Washington, D.C. ruled that FBI files on the investigation of President Kennedy's assassination were exempt from disclosure under the investigatory-files exception.[68]

Notwithstanding judicial reluctance to give full enforcement to the Freedom of Information Act, it remains available as a somewhat effective device to prod federal bureaucrats into disclosing information. And it is a device which reporters and news organizations are starting to use more effectively.[69]

Can a reporter be criminally prosecuted for obtaining, in an unofficial fashion, information and documents relating to the national defense?

The answer to the legal aspect of this question is extremely unclear. The matter was put into sharp focus by the Pentagon Papers litigation, the subsequent prosecution of persons alleged to have supplied those documents to various news media, and the veiled threats of prosecution against the papers and their reporters. Those events directed attention to a traditional practice with which most journalists were familiar—that reporters frequently gain access to classified documents and information made available to them by past or present government officials, activated by a variety of motives. The problem now raised is whether, in obtaining such materials, the reporter runs any risk of criminal prosecution.[70]

The fact that a document is classified does not automatically mean that acquiring or possessing it is criminal. The classification system is established by Executive Order, not Congressional legislation, and violation of its provisions is not automatically punishable.[71] In the statutes dealing with national defense information, the term "classification" appears only in connection with government employees transmitting classified information to foreign agents, or anyone publishing classified information concerning codes or communications intelligence.[72]

The only criminal statutory provisions which directly deal with the possession of national defense materials are two sections of the espionage laws governing "gathering, transmitting, or losing defense information."[73] The first three provisions of that statute deal with traditional espionage activities (e.g., gathering information about defense installations, copying or obtaining documents containing such information) done "with intent or reason to believe that the information is to be used to the injury of the United States or to the advantage of any foreign nation."[74] Although by their literal terms such provisions might encompass a reporter who receives defense or foreign policy documents, the legislative history of these sections suggests that they were not intended to cover "the activities of reporters, newspapers, and others who intend to engage in public speech about defense matters."[75] And indeed in the Pentagon Papers case, the government did not seek to rely on these provisions to justify an injunction on continued publication.

What the government ultimately did rely on was section (e) of the statute:

Whoever having unauthorized possession of, access to, or control over any document, writing [code books, etc.] or note relating to the national defense, or information relating to the national defense which information the possessor has reason to believe could be used to the injury of the United States or to the advantage of any foreign nation, wilfully communicates, delivers, transmits [or causes or attempts the same] to any person not entitled to receive it, or wilfully retains the same and fails to deliver it to the officer or employee of the United

States entitled to receive it ... shall be fined not more than $10,000 or imprisoned not more than ten years or both.[76]

The difficult question is whether a reporter can be punished under this section for obtaining secret documents, discussing them with colleagues, and failing to hand them over to the government. In one of the Pentagon Papers cases, the district judge suggested that section (e) could not be applied to prepublication preparation by newspapers and reporters.[77] In the Supreme Court, however, certain Justices took a different view and stated that it was "undeniable" that editors and reporters "are vulnerable to prosecution" if they withhold the documents covered by the statute, and even without proof of an intent to injure the United States.[78] But scholars disagree with this view and argue that if these statutes are given a literal reading and are constitutionally sound, then,

... public speech in this country since World War II has been rife with criminality. The source who leaks defense information to the press commits an offense; the reporter who holds on to defense material commits an offense; and the retired official who uses defense material in his memoirs commits an offense.[79]

Other than arguing that Congress never intended such results or that the statutes themselves are too vague, reporters have little legal assurance that the laws will not be invoked against them. But at least, despite the invitation extended by certain Supreme Court Justices, neither the newspapers nor the reporters have been prosecuted under these laws—so far.

Can a reporter be criminally prosecuted for unofficially obtaining any other kind of government documents?

Here too the answer is unclear. Although the courts have said that the First Amendment does not give reporters a "license" to violate valid criminal laws,[80] not every receipt of a "purloined" government document is illegal.[81]

At the federal level, while there is not yet a specific crime called "theft of government information," there are certain criminal laws potentially applicable to a reporter who receives or obtains government documents. One statute prohibits theft, embezzlement, or criminal conversion "of any record, voucher, money, or thing of value of the United States" or receiving the same knowing it to have been "embezzled, stolen, purloined or converted."[82] This statute is the one under which Les Whitten, Jack Anderson's associate, was arrested for possessing Bureau of Indian Affairs documents; the charges were later dropped.[83] But the language and purpose of this statute have to be stretched to cover the situation where a reporter is allowed to look at or is given xeroxed copies of government documents in the possession of an official entitled to have them.[84] Indeed, in the Pentagon Papers case, of the Justices who suggested that the newspapers and reporters might be criminally punished, none referred to this statute, and only one Justice mentioned as potentially applicable the kind of crime covered by the statute.[85] However, where it is clear that documents have been stolen from government files by outsiders, then the receiving-stolen-property statute might apply.[86]

Many of these issues were discussed in the context of a California statute dealing with receipt of stolen property. The law was used against editors of the *Los Angeles Free Press* who had obtained and published a list of undercover narcotics agents.[87] The list was received from a person who had been employed by the state attorney general's office. The lower court upheld the conviction on the ground that a xeroxed (or even hand-copied) government document is "property" which has concrete value and can be "stolen" and "received." The lower court agreed that if the information had been supplied verbally the statute would not apply, but reasoned that the existence of a document or a copy "gives the thief credibility and vouches for the accuracy of his information."[88] Concluding that reporters had no First Amendment newsgathering right to break the law and "traffic in stolen documents," the court affirmed the conviction.

The California Supreme Court reversed. Even assuming that the xeroxed list of agents was "property" and had been "received" by the editors, the state still had to prove that the employee obtained the list by theft or extortion *and* that the editors were aware of that. As to theft or extortion, the Court said that if the source received no money from the reporters and manifested an intention to return the document to its file, then his taking it would not be criminal. But since he had stopped working for the government, he was no longer conveniently able to return the document, and therefore the jury could conclude that the list had been stolen.

But did the editors know this? The prosecution pointed to seven items of circumstancial evidence which allegedly proved that they did: (1) the source referred to the list as "secret," (2) the nature of the list, (3) the physical appearance of the source, (4) his request for anonymity, (5) his hesitation to let the editors retain the list, (6) the editors' willingness to pay for it, and (7) the fact that they locked it in a safe. The California appellate court disagreed with these arguments. The source did not tell the editors he was no longer employed by the government and indicated that he was only letting the editors have a look at the document. Moreover, sources frequently request anonymity, newspapers frequently pay for information, and such documents are usually locked in a safe place. As for the sensitive nature of the material, although its publication provided "just cause for outrage at the defendants' gross and callous irresponsibility," the nature of the list of agents itself did not allow a presumption that it was stolen:

The Attorney General's list of suspicious circumstances confuses circumstances which might well serve to put a publisher on notice that official displeasure would result from publication of information released to whomever without authorization, with circumstances which should signal that the property tendered has been taken by theft or larceny.[89]

Can a reporter be subject to civil liability for receiving and utilizing documents?

So far, the answer seems to be no.

In two cases, both involving the late columnist Drew Pearson, the courts refused to impose civil liability on a reporter given documents or information which were improperly taken in the first instance by the source.

In one case, an employee of Liberty Lobby, a political-action organization, copied documents and files and made them available to Drew Pearson and his associate Jack Anderson. The organization sought an injunction against the reporters' continued use of those materials on the ground that they were "private papers illegally taken in violation of rights of privacy and property."[90] In an opinion written by then-Federal Circuit Judge Warren E. Burger, the claim was rejected.

Upon a proper showing the wide sweep of the First Amendment might conceivably yield to an invasion of privacy and deprivation of rights in private manuscripts. But that is not this case; here there is no clear showing as to ownership of the alleged private papers or of an unlawful taking and no showing that [Pearson] had any part in the removal of these papers or copies from the offices of [Liberty Lobby] or any act other than receiving them from a person with a colorable claim to possession.[91]

The second case involved a damage suit by the late Senate Thomas Dodd claiming invasion of privacy and taking of property. Two of Dodd's assistants had xeroxed materials from the Senator's files and turned them over to Pearson and Anderson. Dodd sued, and the lower court held that he had made out a claim for a wrongful taking of the documents.[92] Pearson appealed, and the decision was reversed. The court assumed that the Senator's aides had acted improperly by copying confidential files and showing them to unauthorized outsiders, and, further, that the reporters knew this had been done. Was that enough to establish liability for damages? The court said no:

If we were to hold [the reporters] liable for invasion of privacy on these facts, we would establish the proposition that one who receives information from an intruder, knowing it has been obtained by improper intrusion, is guilty of a tort. In an untried and developing area of tort law, we are not prepared to go so far. A person approached by an eavesdropper with an offer to share in the information gathered through the eavesdropping would perhaps play the nobler part should he spurn the offer and shut his ears. However, it seems to us that at this point it would place too great a strain on human weakness to hold one liable in damages who merely succumbs to temptation and listens.[93]

As to the Senator's separate claim of an improper taking of his property, the court ruled that the mere act of xeroxing the files was not enough to make out a case because the documents were not physically taken and the Senator was not substantially deprived of their use.[94] Finally, although in some situations the law protects more than the mere physical possession of documents and also safeguards the improper use of the information contained, the court concluded the nature of the materials copied did not come within that protection:

The information included the contents of letters to [the Senator] from supplicants, and office records of other kinds. . . . Insofar as we can tell, none of it amounts to literary property, to scientific invention, or to secret plans formulated by [the Senator] for the conduct of commerce. Nor does it appear to be information held in any way for sale . . . , analogous to the fresh news copy produced by a wire service.[95]

Although these decisions show that courts have afforded substantial protection to that aspect of newsgathering which involves obtaining files and documents in an unauthorized manner, they should not be read as blanket permission for reporters to actively instigate such practices.

One final word of caution. While the courts have given considerable latitude to aggressive newsgathering activities, there are occasions when the courts have condemned reporters for going too far. In one case, where reporters employed subterfuge to gain access to the private home of a "quack" and surreptitiously recorded and photographed one of his sessions, the court drew the line:

We agree that newsgathering is an integral part of news dissemination. We strongly disagree, however, that the hidden mechanical contrivances are "indispensable tools" of newsgathering. Investigative reporting is an ancient art; its successful practice long antecedes the invention of miniature cameras and electronic devices. The First Amendment has never been construed to accord newsmen immunity from torts or crimes committed during the course of newsgathering. The First Amendment is not a license to trespass, to steal or to intrude by electronic means into the precincts of another's home or office.[96]

Footnotes to Chapter III

1. See generally Comment, *Has Branzburg Buried the Underground Press?*, 8 Harv. Civ. R. Civ. L. L. Rev. 181 (1973) (hereafter referred to as "Comment, Underground Press"); Note, *The Right of the Press to Gather Information*, 71 Colum. L. Rev. 838 (1971); Note, *The Rights of the Public and the Press to Gather Information*, 87 Harv. L. Rev. 1505 (1974).

2. *Branzburg* v. *Hayes*, 408 U.S. 665, 681, 707 (1972).

3. See, *e.g.*, *Kovach* v. *Maddux*, 238 F. Supp. 835 (M.D. Tenn. 1965) ("Without the opportunity to gather and obtain the news, the right to publish or comment upon it, would be of little value." *Id.* at 839); *Burnham* v. *Oswald*, 342 F. Supp. 880 (W.D. N.Y. 1972) (The right of the public to be informed depends "to a very large degree upon the right of the press to gather information and to have access to news sources." *Id.* at 885); but see, *e.g.*, *Tribune Review Publishing Co.* v. *Thomas*, 254 F.2d 883 (3rd Cir. 1958) ("We think that this question of getting at what one wants to know, either to inform the public or to satisfy one's individual curiosity, is a far cry from the type of freedom of expression, comment, criticism, so fully protected by the first and fourteenth amendments to the Constitution." *Id.* at 885).

4. 408 U.S. at 684-85.

5. *Pell* v. *Procunier*, ——U.S.——, 42 U.S. Law Week 4998, 5003 (June 24, 1974), *Saxbe* v. *Washington Post Co.*, ——U.S.——, 42 U.S. Law Week 5006 (June 24, 1974).

6. *Los Angeles Free Press* v. *City of Los Angeles*, 9 Cal. App.3d 448, 88 Cal. Rptr. 605 (2d Dist. 1970), *cert. denied*, 401 U.S. 982 (1971). The case is discussed in Freedom of Information Center Report No. 262, *Press Passes: Patent or Privilege?* (June 1971).

7. 9 Cal. App.3d at 452-53.

8. *Strasser* v. *Doorley*, 309 F. Supp. 716 (D. R.I. 1970), *aff'd in part, modified in part*, 432 F.2d 567 (1st Cir. 1970).
9. 309 F. Supp. at 730.
10. *Id.* at 730.
11. *Quad-City Community News Service, Inc.* v. *Jebens*, 334 F. Supp. 8, 16 (S.D. Iowa 1971).
12. *Id.* at 17.
13. *Id.* at 18-19. One case recently filed involves the denial of White House press credentials to Thomas Forcade and Robert Sherill. *Forcade* v. *Rowley* (D. D.C. Civil Action No. 73-1258).
14. *Schnell* v. *City of Chicago*, 407 F.2d 1084, 1086 (7th Cir. 1969).
15. *Dayton Newspapers Inc.* v. *Starick*, 345 F.2d 677 (6th Cir. 1965).
16. *Id.* at 679.
17. *Channel 10, Inc.* v. *Gunnarson*, 337 F. Supp. 634 (D. Minn. 1972).
18. *Id.* at 637.
19. *Id.* at 638.
20. *Ex Parte Arnold*, 503 S.W.2d 529 (Tex. Ct. Crim. App. 1974).
21. *Gallela* v. *Onassis*, 353 F. Supp. 196 (S.D.N.Y. 1972), *aff'd in part, modified in part*, 487 F.2d 986 (2d Cir. 1973).
22. 487 F.2d at 998.
23. *Kovach* v. *Maddux*, 238 F. Supp. 835 (M.D. Tenn. 1965).
24. *Id.* at 839.
25. *Id.* at 840-41.
26. *Id.* at 841.
27. *Consumers Union* v. *Periodical Correspondents' Association*, 365 F. Supp. 18 (D. D.C. 1973).
28. *Id.* at 25-26.
29. *Id.* at 26.
30. *Lewis* v. *Baxley*, 368 F. Supp. 768 (M.D. Ala. 1973).
31. *Borreca* v. *Fasi*, 369 F. Supp. 906 (D. Haw. 1974).
32. In one recent instance, an official even tried to confiscate a reporter's notebook and pencil, on the ground that they were improper "recording devices"; but the local county attorney intervened. See, "Big-Time Pressures, Small Town Press," *The New York Times*, March 24, 1973, p. 33, col. 8.
33. *Educational Broadcasting Corporation* v. *Ronan*, 68

Misc.2d 776, 328 N.Y.S.2d 107 (Sup. Ct. N.Y. Co. 1972). The court relied on the Supreme Court decision in *Estes* v. *Texas,* 381 U.S. 532 (1965) which prohibited television cameras from court rooms.

In an older case, a citation for contempt of Congress was thrown out on the ground that the witness was entitled to refuse to testify with a battery of cameras, flashbulbs, and radio microphones arrayed around him. *United States,* v. *Kleinman,* 107 F. Supp. 407 (D. D.C. 1952).

34. *Nevens* v. *The City of Chino,* 44 Cal. Rptr. 50 (Dist. Ct. of App., 5th Dist. 1965).

35. *Davidson* v. *Common Council of the City of White Plains,* 244 N.Y.S. 2d 385 (Sup. Ct. Westchester Co. 1963).

36. *1590 Broadcasting Corp.* v. *Public Utilities Commission,* 306 A.2d 49 (Sup. Ct. N.H. 1973). The issues are discussed in Freedom of Information Center Report No. 279, *Electronic Coverage: Public Meetings* (March, 1972).

37. *Sigma Delta Chi* v. *Speaker of Maryland House of Delegates,* 270 Md. 1, 310 A.2d 156. (1973).

38. *Branzburg* v. *Hayes,* 408 U.S. 665, 684 (1972).

39. The history of these laws is described in Note, *Open Meeting Statutes: The Press Fights for the "Right to Know,"* 75 Harv. L. Rev. 1199 (1962).

40. The texts of the open meetings and records laws enacted through 1968 are set forth in Freedom of Information Center Report No. 202, *State Access Statutes* (June 1968). A rundown of state practices with regard to legislative committees is contained in Freedom of Information Center Report No. 240, *Access to State Committees Survey* (April 1970). In addition, state attorneys general have often given favorable interpretative rulings to these statutes. See Freedom of Information Center Report No. 307, *FOI And State Attorneys General* (July 1973).

41. *Sacramento Newspaper Guild* v. *Sacramento County Board of Supervisiors,* 263 Cal. App.2d 41, 69 Cal. Rptr. 480 (3rd Dist. 1968).

42. *Canney* v. *Bd. of Pub. Instruction of Alachua County,* ——*Fla.*——, 278 So.2d 260 (1973). The general experience with sunshine laws is described in Comment, *Government in the Sunshine: Promise or Placebo?,* 23 U. Fla. L. J. 361 (1971).

43. See *Press Censorship Newsletter* No. V, p. 63 (Reporters Committee for Freedom of the Press).

44. *Washington Post Co.* v. *Kleindienst,* 357 F. Supp. 770

(D. D.C. 1972), *on remand,* 357 F. Supp. 779 (D. D.C. 1972); *aff'd,* 494 F.2d 994 (D.C. Cir.), *rev'd, sub. nom., Saxbe* v. *Washington Post Co.,* ——U.S.——, 42 U.S. Law Week 5006 (June 24, 1974); see also *Houston Chronicle Pub. Co.* v. *Kleindienst,* 364 F. Supp. 719 (S.D. Tex. 1973); *Burnham* v. *Oswald,* 342 F. Supp. 880 (W.D.N.Y. 1972): But see, *Seattle-Tacoma Newspaper Guild* v. *Parker,* 480 F.2d 1062 (9th Cir. 1973).

45. *Pell* v. *Procunier,* ——U.S.——, 42 U.S. Law Week 4998 (June 24, 1974); *Saxbe* v. *Washington Post Co.,* —— U.S.——, 42 U.S. Law Week 5006 (June 24, 1974).

46. Access to mental institutions was one of the unresolved issues in the *Titticut Follies* case. See *Commonwealth* v. *Wiseman,* 249 N.E.2d 610 (Sup. Ct. Mass. 1969); *cert. denied,* 398 U.S. 960 (1970); *Cullen* v. *Grove Press, Inc.,* 276 F. Supp. 727 (S.D. N.Y. 1967). A film-maker had been allowed to spend several weeks at the Bridgewater State Hospital for the criminally insane. The State of Massachusetts was partly successful in restricting the audiences to whom the film could be shown.

47. Courts have consistently held that the open portions of military bases cannot be declared off-limits for First Amendment purposes. See, *e.g., Spock* v. *David,* 469 F.2d 1047 (3rd Cir. 1972).

48. *People* v. *Rewald,* 318 N.Y.S.2d 40 (Cayuga County 1971) involved trespass charges against a reporter who visited a migrant labor camp. The court refused to convict, holding that reporters "... may not be denied without good cause shown the right of reasonable visitation for purposes of gathering and disseminating news." *Id.* at 45.

49. *Branzburg* v. *Hayes,* 408 U.S. 665, 691 (1972).

50. *New York Times,* October 5, 1973, p. 13, col. 1; 42 Law Week 2252.

51. 18 U.S.C. Section 2.

52. *United States* v. *Garguilo,* 310 F.2d 249, 253 (2d Cir. 1962). A typical statement of the rule is that "in order to aid and abet another to commit a crime, it is necessary that the defendant wilfully associate himself with the venture and wilfully participate in it as something he wishes to bring about and that he wilfull seeks by some act of his to make it succeed...." *United States* v. *Tijerina,* 446 F.2d 675, 677-78, n.1 (10th Cir. 1971). Presumably, knowing of a crime in advance, but failing to

report it to the police, does not make you criminally responsible.

In *Bursey v. United States,* 466 F.2d 1059 (9th Cir. 1972) the court suggested that editorial employees of the Black Panther paper could not be responsible for "aiding and abetting" any crime which might have been committed when a speech threatening the life of the President was reported in the Panther paper.

53. 18 U.S.C. Section 4.
54. 408 U.S. at 696-97.
55. *Id.* at 696, n. 36. See, *Comment, Constitutional Protection for the Newsman's Work Product,* 6 Harv. Civ. R. Civ. L. L. Rev. 119, 136, n. 69 (1970).
56. *United States* v. *Capra,* 372 F. Supp. 609 (S.D.N.Y. 1974).
57. *Providence Journal Co.* v. *McCoy,* 94 F. Supp. 186 (D. R.I. 1950), *aff'd,* 190 F.2d 760 (1st Cir. 1951). See also, *Lee v. Hodges,* 321 F.2d 480 (4th Cir. 1963) (black publisher improperly denied access to high school personnel records for recruitment of employees).
58. *Quad-City Community News Service, Inc.* v. *Jebens,* 334 F. Supp. 8 (S.D. Iowa, 1971).
59. *Id.* at 15.
60. See, *Stanley* v. *Georgia,* 394 U.S. 557, 564 (1969).
61. *Trimble* v. *Johnston,* 173 F. Supp. 651 (D. D.C. 1959).
62. *Id.* at 656.
63. *McMullan* v. *Wohlgemuth,* 308 A.2d 888 (Pa. Sup. Ct. 1973).
64. See, *e.g., Quad-City Community News Service, Inc.* v. *Jebens,* 334 F. Supp. 8 (S.D. Iowa 1971) (police records); *Minneapolis Star & Tribune Co.* v. *State,* 163 N.W.2d 46 (Minn. 1971) (records of state board of medical examiners); but see, *e.g., Matter of New York Post Co.* v. *Moses,* 10 N.Y.2d 199 (1961), *rev'g,* 12 App. Div. 2d 243 (1st Dept. 1961) (bridge authority records); *Cervi v. Russell,* 519 P.2d 1189 (Colo. Sup. Ct. 1974) (birth and death statistics).
65. 2 Weekly Compilation of Presidential Documents 895, July 11, 1966. The Act is set forth at 5 U.S.C. Sections 551 *et seq.* The ACLU has published a useful pamphlet entitled "Your Right to Government Information: How to Use the FOIA."
66. In an important recent case the federal court of appeals in Washington, D.C. ruled that in order to justify a refusal to disclose information, the agency must make a de-

tailed demonstration of why the document should remain secret and what portions are not discloseable. The agency can no longer simply tell the court that the material falls under one of the exceptions from disclosure, *Vaughn* v. *Rosen*, 484 F.2d 820, (D.C. Cir. 1973).

67. *Environmental Protection Agency* v. *Mink*, 410 U.S. 73 (1973).

68. *Weisberg* v. *United States Department of Justice*, 489 F.2d 1195 (D.C. Cir. 1973).

69. See, *e.g.*, *Tennessean Newspapers Inc.* v. *Federal Housing Administration*, 464 F.2d 657 (6th Cir. 1972); *Stern* v. *Richardson*, 367 F. Supp. 1316 (D. D.C. 1973). The use of the Act is discussed in Theodore Jacqueney, "Nibbling at the Bureaucracy," [MORE], October 1973, p. 15.

70. See generally H. Edgar and B. Schmidt, *The Espionage Statutes and Publication of Defense Information*, 73 Colum. L. Rev. 929 (1973) (hereafter referred to as *Espionage Statutes*); *Developments in the Law—The National Security Interest and Civil Liberties*, 85 Harv. L. Rev. 1130 (1972) (hereafter referred to as *Developments—National Security*).

71. The current classification system is contained in Executive Order 11652.

72. 18 U.S.C. Sections 783(b), 798; see *Espionage Statutes, supra* at 1052; see also D. Wise, *Pressures on the Press*, pp. 17-18 (paper presented to the May 1973 Conference on Government Secrecy, sponsored by the Committee for Public Justice).

73. 18 U.S.C. §793. There are special provisions governing the protection of "restricted data" classified by the Atomic Energy Commission, 42 U.S.C. §§ 2161, *et seq.*, but the Pentagon Papers apparently contained no such material, see *New York Times Co.* v. *United States*, 403 U.S. 713, 743, n.3 (1971), and it is doubtful that reporters would have occasion to receive such documents.

74. 18 U.S.C. Section 793 (a), (b), (c).

75. *Espionage Statutes, supra* at 996-98, 1058-60.

76. 18 U.S.C. Section 793 (e).

77. *United States* v. *New York Times Co.*, 328 F. Supp. 324, 328-30 (S.D.N.Y. 1971).

78. *New York Times Co.* v. *United States*, 403 U.S. 713, 739 n.9 (1971) (concurring opinion of Justice White).

79. *Espionage Statutes, supra* at 1000.

80. *Branzburg* v. *Hayes*, 408 U.S. 665, 691 (1972); *Dietmann* v. *Time, Inc.*, 449 F.2d 245, 249 (9th Cir. 1971).

81. *Cervantes* v. *Time, Inc.*, 464 F.2d 986, 992, n. 8 (8th Cir 1972). The court seemed to reject the argument that because confidential documents were received from FBI officials in violation of federal government policy, the news medium which relied on those documents would lose its defense to a libel charge. However, New York courts hold the opposite, namely that a newspaper which improperly obtains confidential official records might be denied the defense of fair comment on public proceedings. See *Danziger* v. *Hearst Corp.*, 304 N.Y. 244 (1952); *Shiles* v. *News Syndicate, Inc.*, 27 N.Y.2d 9 (1970).

82. 18 U.S.C. Section 641. There is also a federal statute which makes it a crime to receive any stolen "goods, wares, merchandise" worth more than $5,000 and transported in interstate commerce. 18 U.S.C. Sections 2314, 2315. However, this law has been held not to apply to stolen FBI documents. *In re Vericker*, 446 F.2d 244 (2d Cir. 1971) ("We are not aware that papers showing that individuals are or may have been engaging in criminal activity or what procedures are used by the FBI in tracking them down are ordinarily bought or sold in interstate commerce . . ." *Id.* at 248.)

83. See L. Whitten, "Old Indian Refrain: Treachery on the Potomac," *New York Times*, Feb. 8, 1973, p. 43, col. 2; Wise, *Pressures on the Press, supra*, p. 28.

84. The history of the statute is traced in *Morisette* v. *United States*, 342 U.S. 246, 263-73 (1952).

85. Justice White canvassed the various espionage statutes, but made no mention of Section 641. *New York Times Co.* v. *United States, supra*, at 730-40. However, Justice Harlan's opinion noted that one of the unresolved issues was whether the newspapers "are entitled to retain and use the documents notwithstanding the seemingly uncontested facts that the documents, or the originals of which they are duplicates, were purloined from the Government's possession and that the newspapers received them with knowledge that they had been feloniously acquired." 403 U.S. at 754.

86. *In re Vericker*, 446 F.2d 244 (2d Cir. 1971).

87. *People* v. *Kunkin*, 9 Cal.3d 245, 107 Cal. Rptr. 184 (1973), *rev'g*, 24 Cal. App.3d 447, 100 Cal. Rptr. 845 (2d Dist. 1972).

88. 100 Cal. Rptr. at 853.
89. 107 Cal. Rptr. at 191.
90. *Liberty Lobby, Inc.* v. *Pearson*, 390 F.2d 489, 491 (D. D.C. Cir. 1968).
91. *Id.* at 491.
92. *Dodd* v. *Pearson*, 279 F. Supp. 101 (D. D.C. 1968).
93. *Pearson* v. *Dodd*, 410 F.2d 701, 705 (D.C. Cir. 1969).
94. *Id.* at 707.
95. *Id.* at 708.
96. *Dietmann* v. *Time, Inc.*, 449 F.2d 245, 249 (9th Cir. 1971).

IV
Publishing the News

The previous two chapters have focused upon the difficulties reporters face in attempting to gather the news. The remainder of this book is primarily concerned with problems that reporters may confront in their efforts to disseminate the news. The emphasis shifts from the law applicable to preparation of a story to the legal consequences which may result from its publication because of its content.

Can a reporter be prevented from publishing a story because it might endanger the national security?

No. The Pentagon Papers case reaffirmed the historic understanding that a primary purpose of the First Amendment was to prevent "previous restraint" upon publication. Accordingly, any system of prior restraints bears "a heavy presumption against its constitutional validity."[1] In that case, a majority of the Court concluded that the Government had failed to show that publication of the documents would so endanger the national security as to justify breaching "the concededly extraordinary protection against prior restraints enjoyed by the press under our constitutional system."[2] This "extraordinary protection" means that the publication of news can virtually never be

105

prohibited in advance. And the Pentagon Papers case is historic precisely because the Government tried—and briefly succeeded—doing just that.

But the Court did not say it could never be done. Indeed, a majority of the Justices who ruled for the newspapers indicated that they might reach a different conclusion if the government could show that the information to be published "must inevitably, directly and immediately cause the occurrence of an event kindred to imperiling the safety of a transport already at sea"[3] or "will surely result in direct, immediate, and irreparable damage to our Nation or its people."[4] But such a finding could rarely be made, and reporters can safely assume that they can publish almost anything they wish to without fear of prior restraint.

So far the same has unfortunately not been true in one case involving a prior restraint successfully imposed against Victor Marchetti, a former CIA official, on the basis of national security considerations.[5] Marchetti was enjoined from publishing accounts of his experiences in the CIA without agency approval. In reaching that result, the federal court relied on a secrecy agreement against revealing classified information which he had signed as a condition of his employment. Recently, however, Marchetti and his publisher brought their own lawsuit to seek clearance of passages in the book. A federal district judge ruled that the CIA could censor only those items of information which had actually been classified.[6]

Apart from national security, are there any other grounds for imposing a prior restraint on what reporters may publish?

With certain possible exceptions, the answer is no.

It is clear that an injunction against publication cannot be sought in order to prevent the dissemination of "malicious, scandalous, and defamatory" matter. In a classic case of prior restraint, the Supreme Court overturned a ban on publishing a newspaper which contained extreme attacks on local public officials and on certain religious groups. "The fact that the liberty of the press may be abused by miscreant purveyors of scandal does not make any the less necessary the immunity of the press from previous restraint in dealing with official misconduct. Subsequent punishment for such abuses as may exist is the appropriate remedy, consistent with constitutional privilege."[7] This rule—subsequent punishment but no prior restraints—has consistently been applied ever since.

Perhaps the major exception to the prohibition of prior restraints, and one which involves few reporters, comes in the area of pornography. Pornographic materials—movies, books, magazines—can be confiscated, and, if found to be obscene, may be suppressed.[8] But the censor must act expeditiously, bringing the materials into court for judicial consideration within a few weeks, so that there is no prior restraint in the form of administrative delay.[9] The theory behind such censorship is that obscenity is not protected by the guarantees of freedom of speech and press, and therefore its dissemination can be interdicted, a view reaffirmed in the recent Supreme Court obscenity decisions.[10] But the kind of material which can be prohibited is limited to "hard-core" pornography.[11]

Another exception to the rule against prior restraints involves copyright infringement, where the publication of a work found to be "infringing" can be enjoined.[12] The primary problem which reporters may have in this area is the reliance on books and articles in the course of researching a story. The general rule is that ideas cannot be copyrighted, although the manner in which they are expressed can be. In the Pentagon Papers case, Justice William Brennan observed: ". . . copyright cases have no pertinence here; the Government is not asserting an interest in the particular form of words chosen in the documents, but is seeking to suppress the ideas expressed therein. And the copyright laws, of course, protect only the form of expression and not the ideas expressed."[13] Moreover, the use of previous books and articles does not create a presumption of infringement.[14] The doctrine of "fair use" allows a reporter to rely on, paraphrase, and quote from a previous work, without consent, so long as the writer does not lift "material and substantial" portions of the previous work or "bodily appropriate" it.[15] Thus, only in those situations where a reporter has really plagiarized an earlier work should there be any concern about the possibility of a prior restraint on copyright grounds.

Finally, there is the question of prior restraint of anticipated invasions of privacy. The issue arose in the *Titticut Follies* cases, where efforts were made to enjoin the distribution of a documentary film depicting life in a Massachusetts mental institution.[16] In one suit, brought by the state on behalf of the patients, the court said that while distribution of the film could not be completely prohibited, its viewing could be limited to professional audiences such as legislators, doctors, and students in the field, and commercial distribution to general audiences could be prohibited. However, in the other case, filed by guards at the institution, the court ruled that general commercial distribution could not be prohibited since the film was not a deliberately or recklessly false portrayal of conditions at the hospital. Thus, while neither case allowed a complete ban on showing the film, each court indicated that there were certain circumstances where some restrictions on distribution might be tolerated in the interests of protecting the privacy of the subjects of the story.

In a similar case, which at this writing is pending in the Supreme Court, the New York courts upheld an injunction against distribution of a book of anonymous psychiatric case histories.[17] The former patient complained that she could still be identified and that the book thus violated her right of privacy and the doctor-patient relationship.

Can a reporter be prosecuted for publishing national-security secrets and information?

The answer is unclear. Although the Supreme Court ruled against prior restraint of the Pentagon Papers, certain Justices indicated that subsequent punishment of the newspaper officials for violation of the World War I espionage laws would be in order. Interestingly, one of the original prosecutions under those laws resulted from the publication of newspaper articles condemning the war effort and urging resistance to military service.[18]

As was true with regard to acquiring secret information, the mere publication of classified information is not *per se* criminal, although the fact of classification may be relevant to proving criminal intent.[19] (Under current proposals to change the law, the unauthorized disclosure of classified information would automatically be criminal.) On the other hand, it is similarly clear that the publication of specific kinds of information, such as photographs or depictions of vital military installations, could be criminal.[20]

Beyond that, clarity soon disappears. For example, one section of the espionage laws prohibits publication of classified information concerning cryptographic systems or communication-intelligence activities or any information obtained from communication-intelligence operations.[21] In the Pentagon Papers case, neither the government nor the district court thought the provision applicable, while one Justice thought it was and would "have no difficulty in sustaining convictions" of the newspapers under it.[22]

In the two general sections of the espionage laws, the word "publishes" appears only once, in connection with disseminating information about troop movements; the other provisions make it a crime to "communicate" various kinds of information.[23] There is disagreement over whether this distinction in language means that "communicates" refers only to clandestine activity and excludes the open publication of information through a news medium.[24]

Finally, there is the problem of the kind of intent or purpose with which the information is communicated and the character of the recipient to whom it is made available. The provision of the espionage laws with the most direct bearing on news media speaks of communication with "intent or reason to believe that the information is to be used to the injury of the United States, or to the advantage of any foreign nation."[25] There is serious dispute over whether these statutes can or should be applied to the publication of information directed to the public and designed to advance public debate about foreign policy or defense matters.[26] Moreover, in enacting portions of the law, Congress included the proviso that "nothing contained in this Act shall be construed to authorize, require or establish military or civilian censorship or in any way to limit or infringe upon freedom of the press or of speech. . . ."[27] Although one Justice relied on this proviso to conclude that the newspapers could not be punished for publishing the Pentagon Papers, scholars have suggested that it was nothing more than a placebo.[28] To compound the uncertainty, the espionage laws have only infrequently been applied and construed by the courts. Fortunately they have not, as yet, been directly applied to the press, although there have been threats and attempts to do so.[29]

In short, it is nearly impossible to determine in advance what rights reporters have or what consequences they may face with regard to publishing national-security information. But although there can be no assurances, there can be some reliance on the government's apparent disinclination to prosecute reporters for informing the public, and some comfort in the understanding that to the extent that the Congress had a fixed purpose in mind in enacting the espionage laws, it was not to punish journalists.[30]

Can reporters be punished for taking a stand in print on public issues?

No. Other than the potential sanctions for libel, invasion of privacy, or interference with the judicial process (which are discussed in the next two chapters), reporters can take any stand they wish on public issues. The point was made clear in a case where the editor of a paper was convicted for violating a law against electioneering by writing an editorial on election day urging citizens to vote a certain way on the issues. The Supreme Court unanimously threw out the conviction:

Suppression of the right of the press to praise or criticize governmental agents and to clamour and contend for or against change, which is all that this editorial did, muzzles one of the very agencies which the Framers of our Constitution thoughtfully and deliberately selected to improve our society and keep it free. The [law] by providing criminal penalties for publishing editorials such as the one here silences the press at a time when it can be most effective. It is difficult to conceive of a more obvious and flagrant abridgment of the constitutionally guaranteed freedom of the press.[31]

Not only can there be no punishment for a story urging citizens to vote a particular way, but reporters, like citizens generally, can publish any views and advocate any positions, even including violation of the law. The Supreme Court has ruled that "the constitutional guarantees of free speech and free press do not permit a state to forbid or proscribe advocacy of the use of force or of law violation except where such advocacy is directed to inciting or producing imminent lawless action and is likely to produce such action."[32] Thus, although fifty years ago a man was convicted for publishing an anti-draft, anti-war article,[33] it is extremely unlikely that the expression of any idea by a reporter, particularly in writing, would be found to constitute an incitement to imminent lawless action.

Can a reporter be punished for using profanity in a story?

No. The absence of four- (or even twelve-) letter words from most reporting is dictated by editorial taste, not constitutional law. The courts have made it clear that the public use of profanity, written or spoken, is not punishable. Indeed, the Supreme Court reversed the conviction of a young man for wearing a sign on his jacket which said "Fuck the Draft"[34] and invalidated the expulsion of a young woman who distributed a newspaper on campus with the headline "Motherfucker Acquitted."[35] In the latter case, the Court specifically ruled that the headline could in no way be considered "obscene." The same result has been reached by lower courts in cases where teachers have been disciplined for using profanity as a teaching device or assigning reading material which contained profanity.[36] The use of profanity is constitutionally protected.

Only hard-core pornography can be banned, and laws which refer to material which is "lewd," "lascivious," "filthy," "indecent," or "immoral" will be treated as though they prohibited only hard-core obscenity.[37] Similarly, a publication cannot be punished because it contains ideas which are "sacrilegious."[38]

Notwithstanding these clear rules, the government has recently tried to crack down on certain radio shows, pursuant to a federal statute which makes it a crime to utter "any obscene, indecent or profane" language by means of radio communication.[39] In one case, the government indicted a disc jockey for playing an album by Country Joe and the Fish, where the audience spells out F-U-C-K; but the Justice Department soon dropped the charges.[40] More recently, the FCC fined an Illinois radio station $2,000 for broadcasting "topless radio" where listeners phone in and discuss sexual matters.[41] The ruling is being appealed to the courts. Presumably the courts will hold, in conformity with the recent Supreme Court obscenity decisions, that only communications "which, taken as a whole, appeal to the prurient interest in sex, which portray sexual conduct in a patently offensive way [i.e., 'representations or description of ultimate sexual acts, normal or perverted, actual or simulated, ... masturbation, excretory functions, and lewd exhibition of the genitals'], and which, taken as a whole, do not have serious literary, artistic, political, or scientific value" may be prohibited.[42]

Footnotes to Chapter IV

1. *New York Times Co.* v. *United States*, 403 U.S. 713, 714 (1971) (quoting from *Bantam Books, Inc.* v. *Sullivan*, 372 U.S. 58, 70 (1963)).
2. *Id.* at 730-31 (opinion of Justice White).
3. *Id.* at 726-27 (opinion of Justice Brennan), referring to *Near* v. *Minnesota*, 283 U.S. 697 (1931).
4. *Id.* at 730 (opinion of Justice Stewart).
5. *United States* v. *Marchetti*, 466 F.2d 1309 (4th Cir.) *cert. denied*, 409 U.S. 1063 (1972).
6. *Knopf* v. *Colby*, —— F. Supp. —— (E.D.Va. 1974).
7. *Near* v. *Minnesota*, 283 U.S. 697, 720 (1931). This principle was recently ignored when a local judge enjoined ABC from running a report on inflammable baby cribs, on the ground that it defamed the manufacturer. The injunction was later overturned. *ABC* v. *Smith Cabinet Mfg. Co.*, 43 Law Week 2009 (Ind. App. Ct. 1974).
8. See generally *Heller* v. *New York*, 413 U.S. 483 (1973).
9. See generally *Freedman* v. *Maryland*, 380 U.S. 51 (1965); *United States* v. *Thirty-Seven Photographs*, 402 U.S. 363 (1971).
10. *Miller* v. *California*, 413 U.S. 15 (1973); *Paris Adult Theatre I* v. *Slaton*, 413 U.S. 49 (1973).
11. *Miller* v. *California, supra*.
12. See generally, Nimmer on Copyright (1973), § 157.
13. 403 U.S. at 726.
14. *Rosemont Enterprises, Inc.* v. *Random House, Inc.*, 366 F.2d 303 (2d Cir. 1966), *cert. denied*, 385 U.S. 1009 (1967). In that case Howard Hughes had apparently bought up the copyright on a 1954 *Look* magazine series written about him. Relying on copyright law, he then tried to enjoin a 1966 Random House biography, the research for which had included the *Look* articles.
15. *Id.* at 306-07. In *Liberty Lobby, Inc.* v. *Pearson*, 390 F.2d 489 (D.C. Cir. 1968), the court suggested that First

Amendment rights to publish the news "might conceivably yield to . . . deprivations of rights of property in private manuscripts." *Id.* at 491.

16. *Commonwealth* v. *Wiseman,* 249 N.E. 2d 610, *cert. denied,* 398 U.S. 960 (1970); *Cullen* v. *Grove Press, Inc.,* 276 F. Supp. 727 (S.D. N.Y. 1967).

17. *Roe* v. *Doe,* 42 App. Div. 2d 559, 345 N.Y.S.2d 560 (1st. Dept. 1973).

18. *Frohwerk* v. *United States,* 249 U.S. 204 (1919).

19. See *Developments in the Law—the National Security Interest and Civil Liberties,* 85 Harv. L. Rev. 1130, 1232-33 (1973) (hereafter referred to as *Developments-National Security*); *Gorin* v. *United States,* 312 U.S. 19 (1941); *United States* v. *Drummond,* 354 F.2d. 132 2d Cir. (1965).

20. Sections 795, 796 and 797 of Title 18, U.S.C. prohibit unauthorized photographing or sketching of vital military installations, and publication of such information. Although one Justice thought one of these sections potentially applicable, see 403 U.S. at 735, the Government did not invoke them in the Pentagon Papers litigation, and apparently no prosecution has ever been based upon them. See, H. Edgar and B. Schmidt, *The Espionage Statutes and Publication of Defense Information.* 73 Colum. L. Rev. 929, 1069-1073 (1973) (hereafter referred to as *Espionage Statutes*).

21. 18 U.S.C. Section 798.

22. 328 F. Supp. at 329; 403 U.S. at 737.

23. 18 U.S.C. Sections 793, 794.

24. Compare 328 F. Supp. at 328-39 and 403 U.S. at 720-24 (opinion of Justice Douglas) with 403 U.S. at 738-39: see generally, *Espionage Statutes, supra* at 1032-1038.

25. 18 U.S.C. Section 793.

26. See, *Developments—National Security, supra* at 1232-43; *Espionage Statutes, supra* at 996-98, 1030-58.

27. See 403 U.S. at 722.

28. *Espionage Statutes, supra* at 1026-28.

29. See D. Wise, "Pressures on the Press." (Paper prepared for the Government Secrecy Conference of the Committee for Public Justice, May 1973), pp. 18-20.

30. See 403 U.S. at 745-46 (opinion of Justice Marshall).

31. *Mills* v. *Alabama,* 384 U.S. 214, 219 (1966).

32. *Brandenburg* v. *Ohio,* 395 U.S. 444, 447 (1969).

33. *Frohwerk* v. *United States,* 249 U.S. 204 (1919).

34. *Cohen* v. *California,* 403 U.S. 15 (1971).

35. *Papish* v. *Board of Curators of the University of Missouri*, 410 U.S. 667 (1973).
36. See, *e.g.*, *Keefe* v. *Geanakos*, 418 F.2d 359 (1st Cir. 1969); *Parducci* v. *Rutland*, 316 F. Supp. 352 (M.D. Ala. 1970).
37. *United States* v. *12 200 Foot Reels*, 413 U.S. 123, 130, n. 7 (1973).
38. *Burstyn* v. *Wilson*, 343 U.S. 495 (1952).
39. 18 U.S.C. Section 1464.
40. *United States v. Nesci* (E.D. Va. No. CR-181-72-N).
41. *In re Sonderling Broadcasting Corp.*, FCC 73-713, No. 97882.
42. *Miller* v. *California*, 413 U.S. 15, 24-26 (1973).

V

Covering the Courts

In 1830, federal Judge James H. Peck imprisoned a man named Lawless for having published a criticism of one of Judge Peck's opinions in a case which was then pending on appeal. For this action, Judge Peck was impeached by the House of Representatives. Although he was subsequently acquitted, Congress acted immediately to limit the power of federal courts to hold persons in summary contempt for publishing critical comments about judges and courts.[1] "The years that followed were marked by a feeling of jealous solicitude for freedom of the press in areas touching upon the administration of justice."[2] With one exception, short-lived and aberrational,[3] the Supreme Court consistently threw out contempt convictions imposed on newspapers for criticizing, cajoling, or commenting upon the actions of the courts.[4] And even when thoroughly castigating the press for the massive and prejudicial pretrial publicity which surrounded the trial of Dr. Sam Sheppard, the Court prefaced its lecture with the following praise:

A responsible press has always been regarded as the handmaiden of effective judicial administration, especially in the criminal field. Its function in this regard is documented by an impressive record of service over several centuries. The press does not simply publish information about trials but guards against the miscarriage of justice by subjecting the police,

117

prosecutors, and judicial processes to extensive public scrutiny and criticism.[5]

But the Court did say a *"responsible"* press, and there has always been controversy over the precise boundaries of press responsibility in covering judicial proceedings, and over the power of the courts to enforce those limits. While American legal history is "studded with notorious examples of the impact of widespread and uncontrolled inflammatory publicity upon the administration of criminal justice,"[6] the running controversy took on an additional, complicating dimension in 1959, when, for the first time, the Supreme Court invalidated a federal criminal conviction because some jurors had read news articles stating that the defendant had two previous felony convictions.[7] Two years later, again for the first time, the Court overturned a state court conviction because of persistent and pervasive prejudicial publicity about the defendant.[8] In 1963 the Court threw out a Louisiana conviction because the defendant's confession to the police had been televised repeatedly to an estimated 100,000 viewers in the community, rendering it impossible for the jury to be impartial.[9] The conviction of financier Billy Sol Estes, whose trial had been televised, was reversed in 1965 on the ground that the presence of cameras in the courtroom was prejudicial to the defendant.[10]

Finally, in 1966, the Supreme Court decided the famous *Sheppard* case and in the process added more fuel to the "free press–fair trial" debate.[11] There were so many excesses in that trial, by both media and law enforcement, that it is difficult to tell whether any single factor by itself would have caused the Court to conclude that Sheppard had been denied a fair trial. Among the practices which the Court pointed to were the following: (1) In the days and weeks after the murder of Sheppard's wife there was increasing editorial clamor for Sheppard's arrest and indictment, criticism of his refusal to submit to a lie-detector test and his insistence on not being questioned without counsel, and extensive coverage of Sheppard's compelled reenactment of the events surrounding the murder and of his testimony at a public coroner's inquest; (2) news stories, based on law enforcement sources, described in great detail damaging "evidence" which was never introduced at trial; (3) the names, addresses, and photographs of all potential jurors were published, and each one of them was contacted about the case; (4) once the proceedings commenced, media representatives "took over practically the entire courtroom" and were given "absolute free rein" to install and use facilities throughout the courthouse, to interview and photograph all participants, particularly jurors as they came and went, and to make it extremely difficult for counsel and witness to be heard; and (5) the transcript of each day's testimony and photographs of evidence were published daily, even though the jury was not sequestered.

The harm done to the defendant by these press practices was magnified by the judge's refusal to grant a postponement or change of venue, to sequester the jury, to instruct them forcefully not to expose themselves to news accounts of the proceedings, and to prevent law enforcement release of prejudicial information. The combination of all these various factors deprived Sheppard of a fair trial.

The Court concluded its historic opinion by observing that "unfair and prejudicial news comment on pending trials has become increasingly prevalent" and that given "the pervasiveness of modern communications and the difficulty of effacing prejudicial publicity from the minds of the jurors, the trial courts must take strong measures to ensure that the balance is never weighed against the accused.... The courts must take such steps by rule and regulation that will protect their processes from prejudicial outside interferences."[12]

Before the *Sheppard* decision and with greater intensity since then, courts have done just that, attempting in various ways to insulate their processes from undue outside influences. Such measures have included holding closed hearings or trials, prohibiting the use of electronic or photographic equipment in or near the courthouse, restricting the mobility of reporters in the courtroom itself, sealing court pleadings or documents, prohibiting the press from publishing certain kinds of information about cases and punishing reporters and editors for doing so, and frequently imposing contempt citations on the press for criticizing the courts.

Indeed, the problem of covering the courts is a microcosm of the difficulties which reporters face generally: restrictions on access to the news, prior restraints on reporting the news, and subsequent punishments for publishing the news.

Access and Newsgathering

Can a judge close a trial to the public in order to punish reporters?

No. In 1971 a judge in New York City, angered by news stories mentioning the prior record of a criminal defendant and by the reporters' refusal to heed the court's warnings, granted the defendant's motion to exclude the public and press from the trial. The judge did not attempt to hold the reporters in contempt; he simply closed his courtroom. Even though the trial had ended, the reporters sued the judge to get a definitive decision on the issue. The highest court in New York ruled that although a judge could close a courtroom in exceptional circumstances, he could not do so in order to punish reporters for writing stories about the case.

In short, then, it is our conclusion that the [judge's] order was an unwarranted effort to punish and censor the press, and the fact that it constituted a novel form of censorship can not insulate or shield it from constitutional attack.[18]

A trial judge in Washington tried to take similar measures when reporters failed to heed his prohibition on publishing certain information about a pending case. Not only did he hold them in contempt; he also barred them from the courtroom. The appellate court immediately overturned that ruling.[14]

Can a judge close a trial or a hearing for any other reasons?

Yes, in certain exceptional circumstances a judge can conduct all or portions of a particular proceeding in secret. But he must have some other purpose in mind than simply a desire to exclude the public or the press.[15]

Often the issue is raised by a criminal defendant who objects to a closed proceeding on the ground that it deprives him of a public trial. In a skyjacking case, a federal appeals court ruled that the confidentiality of the antiskyjacking procedures justified a secret hearing on the issue of whether those procedures had been followed in the arrest of the defendant.[16] But in a later skyjacking case, the same court ruled it was improper to hold the *entire* hearing on the motion to suppress evidence *in camera* when only a small portion of the testimony related to the secret procedures:

Moreover, because of the importance of providing an opportunity for the public to observe judicial proceedings at which the conduct of enforcement officials is questioned, the right to a public trial should extend to suppression hearings rather than permit such crucial steps in the criminal process to become associated with secrecy.[17]

Thus, courts have closed off proceedings in order to protect air travel, to guard against harassment of witnesses, to preserve order and deal with an obstreperous audience, or to protect the defendant. Courts have also excluded the public in order to protect the identity of an undercover agent,[18] or where sordid and obscene evidence was to be presented,[19] or to protect the sensibilities of youthful spectators.[20]

But the extent of the exclusion must be narrowly tailored to the reason which justifies it, and courts have said that even if in some cases the public can be excluded from the courtroom, the press can still be allowed to remain. Thus, if the purpose of a secret proceeding is to protect the identity of a government agent, then it is sensible to exclude everyone. However, if the court is trying to protect a prosecution witness against intimidating gestures from spectators, there is obviously no need to exclude the press or other members of the public.[21] Similarly, if the concern is with youthful spectators watching a prostitution case, there is no need to exclude adults generally or the press in particular.[22]

Indeed, many courts have suggested that where there are valid reasons for excluding the general public, it becomes more important that the press be allowed in so that, in effect, it can represent and report to the public. For example, in one case involving a trial for contributing to the delinquency of minors, the judge allowed the public in but tried to keep out reporters unless they promised not to print the names of youthful witnesses.[23] The appellate court ruled this improper:

In our opinion, there is nothing that better protects the rights of the public than their presence in proceedings where these rights are on trial. The news media should be accorded some priority in this respect for they have the facilities to disseminate the information of what transpires to a much broader audience than those who can gather in a crowded courtroom.[24]

May a criminal defendant automatically bar the press from the courtroom?

The answer depends on a number of factors. If the presence of reporters becomes a disruptive influence affecting the proceedings, the judge has an obligation to protect the defendant's right to a fair hearing and the power to control reporters in the courtroom.[25] Whether the defendant can keep the press out completely is another matter. In general the courts have not allowed that, even if the defendant wants a secret trial:

The fact that the defendant has waived his right to a public trial is insufficient to deprive the public and the press of their rights, for the right to a public trial is not only to protect the accused but to protect as much the public's right to know what goes on when men's lives and liberty are at stake.[26]

The same rule has been applied when defendants try to exclude the public or the press from pre-trial hearings on motions to suppress evidence.[27] However, some states have laws which allow a defendant to exclude the public from a preliminary examination where the issue is whether there is enough evidence to warrant holding the defendant for trial, and the courts have generally upheld such laws against the efforts of reporters to cover those proceedings.[28] But in one recent case the Arizona Supreme Court held that reporters could not be kept out of preliminary examination unless a public proceeding would pose a clear and present danger to the defendant's right to a fair trial.[29]

If the court tries to keep the press out, do reporters have legal standing to challenge the exclusion?

Yes. On several occasions the courts have allowed reporters or their news organizations to file suit to challenge such bans.[30] And while the lawsuit may not be resolved quickly enough to open up the particular trial in question, the case will not be moot and the courts will usually reach a final decision on the issues.

Once the trial is open, can the court restrict the reporter's mobility in the courtroom?

Yes. In the *Sheppard* case, the Supreme Court expressed dismay at the way that the judge allowed press representatives virtually to take over the courtroom:

The fact is that bedlam reigned at the courthouse during the trial and newsmen took over practically the entire courtroom, hounding most of the participants in the trial, especially Sheppard. At a temporary table within a few feet of the jury box and counsel table sat some 20 reporters staring at Sheppard and taking notes. The erection of a press table for reporters inside the bar is unprecedented.... Having assigned almost all of the available seats in the courtroom to the news-media the judge lost his ability to supervise that environment. The movement of the reporters in and out of the courtroom caused frequent confusion and disruption of the trial. And the record reveals constant commotion within the bar. Moreover, the judge gave the throng of newsmen gathered in the corridors of the courthouse absolute free rein. Participants in the trial, including the jury, were forced to run a gantlet of reporters and photographers each time they entered or left the courtroom.[81]

Accordingly, the Court gave trial judges extremely broad power to control the conduct of reporters, as well as any other spectator, within the courtroom.[32]

Indeed, of all the diverse elements of the *Sheppard* ruling, the Court was most emphatic in telling judges to take strong action within the courtroom. And courts have followed this lead. For example the Judicial Conference of the federal courts has authorized the adoption of local court rules governing press access to "widely publicized and sensational cases."[33] Such rules contain provisions for the seating of news media representatives including:

(a) An order that no member of the public or news media representative be at anytime permitted within the bar railing;
(b) The allocation of seats to news media representatives in cases where there are an excess of requests, taking into ac-

count any pooling arrangement that may have been agreed to among the newsmen.[84]

Notwithstanding such rigid rules, which reporters have generally gone along with, if a reporter winds up sitting in a restricted area of the courtroom without objection from the parties and without causing any commotion, the court will probably not do anything.[85]

Is radio or television broadcasting of court proceedings allowed?

Usually not. The judicial attitude to the presence of electronic media in courtrooms has been extremely wary.

In the Billie Sol Estes case, the Supreme Court ruled that televising and broadcasting the trial over his objections deprived him of the "judicial serenity and calm" to which he was entitled, and thus denied him a fair trial.[36] The cameras were enclosed in a specially constructed booth at the back of the courtroom, and live telecasting of the testimony was prohibited. Nevertheless, the majority of the Court ruled that televising the trial was inherently prejudicial to the defendant.

In reaching this result, the Court reasoned that televising a trial had a pervasive and distorting effect on all the participants, especially the jurors, but also the judge, the attorneys, the witnesses, and the defendant himself.[87] The jurors will think they are involved in a "cause célèbre"; they will be distracted not just "by the physical presence of the camera and its telltale red lights" but by the awareness that the proceeding is being televised; if not sequestered, they will come home each night to replays of portions of the trial. Witnesses and attorneys will play to the cameras. Judges will be reluctant to deny media requests to televise a particular trial. Finally, the defendant himself will suffer the psychological torment of the ever-present camera focused on him. For these reasons, the majority concluded that "trial by television is . . . foreign to our system." "The television camera is a powerful weapon. Intentionally or inadvertently it can destroy an accused and his case in the eyes of the public."[38]

This has by and large been the rule. Even before the *Estes* decision, only a very few states allowed televising of trials. Those that did reasoned that television was not *necessarily* prejudicial to the defendant, that television was entitled to the same rights as other media, and that the issue should be resolved on a case-by-case basis.[39] Now, televising trials is all but completely prohibited by bar-association or court rules.

However, since the purpose of the prohibition is to protect judicial proceedings and the participants, there would be little reason to prevent a reporter from filming the courtroom when no proceedings were taking place, to use the film, for example, as background for a report on a forthcoming trial.

Does this mean that trials can never be televised or broadcast?

Not necessarily. The result in the *Estes* case was reached by a narrow margin.[40] The dissenters were troubled at the suggestion "that there are limits upon the public's right to know what goes on in the courts. . . . The idea of imposing upon any medium of communication the burden of justifying its presence is contrary to . . . the presumption . . . in the area of First Amendment freedoms."[41] Indeed even the majority, in rejecting the argument that television was being discriminated against, did not propose to ban television from the courtroom for all time:

Nor can the courts be said to discriminate where they permit the newspaper reporter access to the courtroom. The television and radio reporter has the same privilege. All are entitled to the same rights as the general public. The news reporter is not permitted to bring his typewriter or printing press. When the advances in these arts permit reporting by printing press or by television without their present hazards to a fair trial we will have another case.[42]

As one of the dissenters observed, given the closeness of the vote and the reasoning involved, "today's decision is *not* a blanket prohibition against the televising of state criminal trials."[43]

In fact, certain trials have been televised, with the defendant's consent, for educational purposes. Colorado has been experimenting with televising trials. And some courts are using videotaped testimony, where a witness is examined in advance of trial with no judge or jury present, and the testimony is edited to eliminate inadmissible statements.[44] With improved technology, particularly more compact and mobile equipment, and with a willingness to minimize the prejudicial aspects of television coverage, it is possible that cameras may one day be permitted back into the courtroom.

Can photographs be taken inside a courtroom?

During a proceeding, probably not. The courts have generally not allowed photographs to be taken inside a courtroom, and have promulgated rules to that effect. Reporters have lost the occasional challenges to such rules.

In Pennsylvania, for example, photographers and publishers brought suit against a state court rule which said that "No pictures or photographs shall be taken, immediately preceding or during sessions of this court or recesses between sessions, in any of the court rooms or at any place in the courthouse within forty feet of the entrance to any courtroom." The rule was upheld as a reasonable exercise of the court's power to maintain order and decorum.[45]

In the federal courts, the situation is somewhat unclear. The rule applicable in all federal proceedings only covers criminal cases: "The taking of photographs in the courtroom during the progress of judicial proceedings or radio broadcasting of judicial proceedings from the court room shall not be permitted by the court."[46] Under this wording, reporters theoretically could take photographs of any civil proceeding and during breaks in criminal cases. However, the United States Judicial Conference has urged each local district to prohibit taking photographs "in the courtroom or its environs in connection with any judicial proceeding." And many districts have done so.[47]

Of course, if the local court does not have a flat ban on photographing in the courtroom, then reporters can be prevented from using cameras only if they become disruptive. In one case a defendant was not denied a fair trial simply because photographers were in the courtroom and were occasionally allowed to take pictures without flashbulbs. The court reasoned that the controlled use of still cameras posed none of the inherent dangers of television.[48]

Can a reporter take photographs in the immediate vicinity of the courtroom?

Probably not. News photographers, generally respecting the ban on photos in the courtroom itself, have strenuously challenged prohibitions on taking photographs anywhere else in the courthouse, but without much success.

The judicial attitude toward the taking of photographs near the courtroom was reflected in the *Sheppard* case, where the Court critically noted that "participants in the trial, including the jury, were forced to run a gantlet of reporters and photographers each time they entered or left the courtroom."[49] And in *Estes*, one Justice observed that "the line is drawn at the courthouse door and within, a reporter's constitutional rights are no greater than those of any other member of the public."[50]

The issue became a journalistic cause célèbre in Pennsylvania, where the courts banned the taking of photographs within forty feet of a courtroom entrance, or of any party, juror, or witness inside the courthouse except with consent, or of any prisoner or inmate on his way to or from court.[51] Wanting to photograph a prisoner about to be sentenced for murder, some news photographers created a distraction, pretending to photograph the prisoner, while another photographer surreptitiously took pictures from the opposite direction. The photographs were published the next day, and a contempt-of-court proceeding was brought against the newsman for violating the court rule. The Pennsylvania Supreme Court criticized the reporters for taking sensational photographs designed to pander to the public: "Courtrooms and courthouses are not places of entertainment, and trials are not had for the purpose of satisfying any sadistic instinct of the public seeking sensationalism."[52] The fact that the photographs were not taken in court but in the "precincts" of the court was irrelevant, as was the fact that the photographers caused no disturbance. The rule was a reasonable effort to protect the dignity of the court and the privacy of prisoners. There was a lengthy dissent emphasizing the importance of newsgathering and extolling the virtues of action photos, but it failed to carry the day.[53]

At about the same time, the Florida courts upheld a contempt citation against photographers for violating a similar rule banning photographs of prisoners on the way to court.[54] The reasoning was that since the courts have power to control access to or information about judicial proceedings—for example, closing trials to prevent disturbance, shielding the identity of rape victims, keeping juvenile records confidential, protecting prisoners from news interviews—they can exercise such powers by general injunctions against photographing participants.

The situation in the federal courts is about the same. Although the only nationwide rule bans taking photographs in court during proceedings in a criminal case, local federal courts have gone beyond that to prohibit taking photographs "in the courtroom or its environs" in connection with any case. "Environs" has been defined to include everything from just the floors which have courtrooms to the entire federal building and the surrounding areas.

The validity of such local rules came up in a Texas case where a television news photographer photographed a defendant and his lawyer standing in the hallway outside a courtroom after an arraignment.[55] The photographer was held in contempt and fined $25.00. On appeal, the conviction was affirmed. The court held that the rule against taking photographs on the same floor as any courtroom was clear, that the pictures were taken "in connection with" the arraignment, and that violation of the rule was properly punishable as contempt. Finally, the court said that the interests in judicial decorum were more important than the First Amendment ability of the press to gather news in that manner.[56]

A similar New Mexico federal court rule was also upheld in a case where the reporter took a photograph of the state attorney general filing a lawsuit in the clerk's office, which was located on the same floor as a courtroom.[57] However, since the attorney general had invited the photographer to take the picture, and since the newsman did not know about the rule in advance, the court ruled that the government failed to prove criminal intent beyond a reasonable doubt.[58]

Are there any limits to the ban on taking photographs near the court?

Yes. A number of newsmen in Chicago filed a class action against the local rule of the federal court which defined "environs" to include twelve floors of the federal building (which housed numerous federal agencies in addition to the courts) and "the plaza and sidewalks surrounding" the building. Because of this rule, photographers were unable to take pictures of a number of events inside or outside the building, completely unrelated to any judicial proceedings. The reporters conceded that courts can protect the integrity of their own proceedings, but argued that such rules must be narrowly drawn to achieve only that goal. The appeals court agreed. Although it was proper to prohibit photographing and broadcasting "in the areas adjacent to the courtrooms," as well as on any floor which housed a courtroom or the offices of federal prosecutors, magistrates, and marshals, and the area surrounding the first-floor elevators, the rest of the prohibition went too far:

... the extension of Rule 34 to the floors of the federal building where there are no courtrooms, to the large center lobby
on the first floor, and to the plaza and outside areas surrounding the building is broader than is necessary to accomplish
the stated purpose. The courtrooms in the federal building are
windowless chambers whose walls do not border the outside
walls of the building. The lowest floor housing a courtroom
presently in use is nineteen floors above the ground.... No
foreseeable noise or commotion occurring on the first floor or
outside the building would disturb the proceedings in a courtroom.[59]

"The protection of the integrity of the courtroom offers no
justification for such a broad scope of exclusion. Any prior
restraint on the press must be confined to those activities
which offer immediate threat to the judicial proceedings
and not to those which are merely potentially threatening."[60] Judges can prevent the press from blocking traffic in
the building or harassing participants in judicial proceedings, but not by use of an overly broad rule.

Similarly, in a recent Texas case, the court ruled that
two reporters from an underground newspaper could not
be held in contempt for taking the photograph of an undercover narcotics agent as he was leaving a hearing open
to the public.[61] Although there was no rule against taking
photographs, the prosecutor argued that the reporters
were guilty of "constructive" contempt. The court rejected
the contention, holding that taking the photographs did
not undermine the administration of justice.

Can a court prohibit the making of sketches of judicial proceedings?

In general, no. Some federal courts say that no photograph or sketch can be made of any juror within the environs of the court.[62] But recently a federal judge went beyond this limited prohibition. In a criminal trial of eight
antiwar activists, the court told a CBS sketch artist not to

make any sketches at all in the courtroom and not even to draw any sketches later from memory. The court then held CBS in contempt for broadcasting the sketches and fined the network five hundred dollars. But the court of appeals reversed the conviction.[63] The court agreed with CBS that sketching involves none of the potential distractions of electronic coverage and is essentially no different a process than taking notes. Thus, the ban on making sketches was not a valid exercise of the court's power to control the courtroom. Similarly, the ban on televising sketches drawn from memory was unconstitutional because the government could not show that there was an immediate peril to the judicial process. Finally, in terms of procedure, the court disapproved the use of oral orders and held that the trial judge should have referred the contempt hearing to another judge.

In another recent development, the New Jersey Supreme Court repealed its court rule against sketching.

During a criminal trial, can the court protect witnesses or jurors from press access?

Although the matter has not been tested, the Supreme Court suggested in the *Sheppard* case that both witnesses and jurors could be insulated to some degree from the press:

Moreover, the jurors were thrust into the role of celebrities by the judge's failure to insulate them from reporters and photographers. . . . The numerous pictures of the jurors, with their addresses, which appeared in the newspapers before and during the trial itself exposed them to expressions of opinion from both cranks and friends. . . .

Secondly, the court should have insulated the witnesses. All of the newspapers and radio stations interviewed prospective witnesses as well, and in many instances disclosed their testimony.[64]

In light of this criticism, many federal courts have adopted local rules against the taking of any photographs or making any sketch of a juror "within the environs of the court," and for insulating witnesses "from news interviews during the trial period."[65] Also, jurors can be instructed not to discuss the case with anyone, presumably including reporters. Apparently, such rules have not been tested. It should be remembered that such rules are intended to apply only in criminal cases, although their texts often fail to make an explicit distinction between criminal and civil cases.[66] Moreover, as to witnesses, any ban on press access to them or photographs of them prior to the actual trial would probably be unconstitutional.[67] Finally, once the trial has concluded, these various restrictions are presumably no longer in effect.

Can a reporter be punished for obtaining information about secret grand jury proceedings?

The answer probably depends on how affirmative a role the reporter plays in getting the information.

In most state and federal courts the proceedings of the grand jury are required to be secret, at least until an indictment has been returned or the session of the grand jury has ended. But the secrecy requirement tends to be imposed only on participants in the proceedings. Thus, for example, in the federal courts, "a juror, attorney, interpreter, stenographer, operator of a recording device or any typist" may not disclose matters occurring before the grand jury, except with court permission.[68] However, "No obligation of secrecy may be imposed upon any person except in accordance" with that rule. This would appear to mean that if a grand juror or prosecution attorney revealed grand jury information to a reporter, the source might be subject to a contempt-of-court charge, but the reporter would not. Theoretically, the reporter might be accused of aiding and abetting the source's act of contempt, but in the federal courts prosecutions for aiding a contempt of court are extremely rare.

The matter came up recently as a result of news reports that New York Congressman Mario Biaggi had pleaded the Fifth Amendment before a federal grand jury.[69] Biaggi made an unprecedented request for the court to read the secret transcript of his testimony and announce whether the stories were true. Instead, the court ordered disclosure of portions of the testimony. In the course of its decision, the court directed the prosecutor's office to investigate the leaks of grand jury information to the press. The prosecutor's response noted that there are no direct sanctions applicable against disclosure by persons not connected with the grand jury proceedings. However, the report went on to state that a reporter who persisted in trying to persuade a government attorney to divulge such information would be engaged in potentially illegal conduct.

However, there is no prohibition on talking to grand jury witnesses and finding out what testimony they gave, if they are willing to tell you.

Does a reporter have the right to examine a trial transcript?

Yes, if the trial itself is a public proceeding. In one case, a well-publicized New York murder trial resulted in an acquittal of the defendant. Accordingly, there was no appeal and thus no transcript of the trial. However, the *New York Post* wanted a copy of the judge's charge to the jury. When the judge instructed the court stenographer not to make the transcript available, the *Post* sued and won. The court ruled that judicial proceedings in a publicly held trial must be open to the fullest scrutiny by the press and the public. Without access to the official records "the press might well be hampered in reporting opinions or decisions for fear of transgressing the limitations imposed by the law of libel, that the report be a 'fair and true' one."[70] Moreover, under the New York public records law, the paper had a right to compel the stenographer to provide a copy of the transcript.

What about pleadings, documents and other court papers?

So long as they are not secret or sealed, as juvenile or matrimonial proceedings frequently are, such documents usually come within the state open-records laws which can be used as a basis for a legal attack on any refusal to make them available.[71]

Reporting About Judicial Proceedings

So far the discussion in this chapter has centered on the difficulties a reporter may face in gaining access to and gathering news about judicial proceedings. But reporters also face problems in reporting the news that they have been able to gather. Traditionally, reporters have had to worry about punishment, by way of contempt of court proceedings, for criticizing courts and judges. More recently, the problems have shifted to the "free press–fair trial" arena, where obstacles to reporting the news have been placed in the reporter's path in order to protect the rights of the criminal defendant.[72]

Can reporters freely criticize the decisions or actions of judges?

Yes. The press is entitled to criticize the courts freely, robustly, even maliciously. Punishment can be imposed, if ever, only when "there is no doubt that the utterances in question are a serious and imminent threat to the administration of justice." And "the danger must not be remote or even probable; it must immediately peril."[73] Thus any critical reporting about judges or courts cannot be punished unless the most rigorous kind of "clear and present danger" test would be met:

> Conceivably, a plan of reporting on a case could be so designed and executed as to poison the public mind, to cause a march on the courthouse, or otherwise so disturb the delicate balance in a highly wrought situation as to imperil the fair and orderly functioning of the judicial process.[74]

In the past thirty years the Supreme Court has never found that news reporting posed such an extreme danger as to warrant punishing the press.[75]

That has not always been the situation. For a time, the British common law doctrine of "contempt by publication" gained a foothold in the United States. In 1917, the Supreme Court upheld a federal contempt citation against a Toledo newspaper which had criticized the filing of certain lawsuits against the city.[76] The federal contempt statute allowed a federal court to punish "misbehavior of any person in its presence or so near thereto" as to obstruct the administration of justice.[77] Instead of reading the phrase "so near thereto" in a spatial sense, the Court read it in a causal sense and concluded that the publications reflected adversely on the court's integrity and tended to provoke a public attitude of resistance to the court's orders.[78] This sweeping view of the federal courts' contempt powers over critical publications prevailed for almost twenty-five years until the Supreme Court overruled its earlier decision and held that "so near thereto" meant physical proximity and precluded punishment in the form of summary contempt for publishing critical remarks about the courts.[79] Thus, federal judges have no general power to punish reporters for what they write about the courts.[80] However, a federal court does have power to hold anyone in contempt for "disobedience or resistance to its lawful writ, process, order, rule, decree, or command."[81] As we shall see later, it is through this provision that the federal courts have attempted to enforce their "free press–fair trial" guidelines.[82]

Do you have to wait until the case is over before you can criticize the court's action?

No, not anymore. The rule used to be that trial or appellate courts were supposed to be free from "any outside influence, whether of private talk or public print" until the case was finished.[83] In one case, a publisher was held in contempt for printing a cartoon which questioned the motives of the judges on the Colorado Supreme Court in deciding a case. Although the opinion had been handed down, the time for a rehearing petition had not yet expired when the cartoon was printed. Thus, the case was still "pending," and the contempt citation was upheld.

But that is no longer the law. In 1941 the Supreme Court, noting that cases can "pend" for years, ruled that criticism about the handling of a case cannot automatically be punished simply on the ground that the case is still pending.[84] However, there is greater freedom to comment about cases once they are over.[85]

Can the press urge a court to decide a case one way or the other?

Yes. Reasoning that judges are a heartier lot than most people, the Supreme Court has thrown out contempt citations against publications which put editorial or news pressure on a particular judge.

The most famous case involved separate attempts to punish the *Los Angeles Times* and labor leader Harry Bridges for publicly commenting on pending judicial matters. As one might have expected in 1940, the actual opinions voiced were diametrically opposed. In an editorial entitled "Probation for Gorillas?" the *Times* urged a trial judge to impose severe sentences on two union members convicted of assaulting non-union truck drivers. After ruling that the "clear and present danger" test had to be met in order to convict for contempt by publication, the Supreme Court held that the editorial threatened nothing more than future adverse criticism of the judge in the event of a lenient disposition of the case: "To regard it, therefore, as in itself of substantial influence upon the course of justice would be to impute to judges a lack of firmness, wisdom, or honor—which we cannot accept as a major premise."[86] Bridges had published a telegram sent to the Secretary of Labor warning that a judge's "outrageous" decision in a labor case would lead to a strike. He was held in contempt on the theory that the publication of the telegram was an effort to intimidate the judge. The Supreme Court disagreed, concluding that the tense labor situation resulted from the facts not from the telegram.

How restrained does a reporter have to be in criticizing a judge's actions?

Not very restrained at all. In a Florida case, contempt convictions were imposed upon the *Miami Herald,* which ran editorials and cartoons condemning the general structure and conduct of the local judiciary and the handling of specific cases. The reporting was less than objective. In fact, it was distorted and inaccurate, and the Supreme Court accepted the findings that the truth "was wilfully or wantonly or recklessly withheld from the public" and that the editorial motive was "to abase and destroy the efficiency of the courts."[87] Nevertheless, the Court concluded that the publications did not pose an immediate danger to the administration of justice sufficient "to close the door of permissible public comment."[88] However, the Court emphasized that the cases which drew editorial fire were non-jury proceedings and the articles did not contain "comments on evidence or rulings during a jury trial."[89]

One year later, the Court again dealt with contempt charges arising out of newspaper reporting and criticism of a court's actions. The underlying case was a private civil suit in Texas involving a veteran recently home from the war. The jury had returned a verdict for the veteran, but the judge overruled that finding. The veteran sought a new trial, and the newspaper urged the judge to grant the motion, describing his earlier action as "arbitrary" and a "travesty" and "gross miscarriage of justice," which had properly brought down "the wrath of public opinion upon his head." The journalists were held in contempt.

The Supreme Court reversed. In response to the argument that the reporting was inaccurate and unfair, the Court responded: ". . . inaccuracies in reporting are commonplace. . . . Certainly a reporter could not be laid by the heels for contempt because he missed the essential point in a trial or failed to summarize the issues to accord with the views of the judge who sat on the case."[90] As to the editorial, with its "vehement" and "intemperate" language, the Court ruled that the nature of the language used "is not alone the measure of the power to punish for contempt. The fires which it kindles must constitute an imminent, not merely a likely, threat to the administration of justice."[91] In the absence of any threatening demands that the judge reverse his position—"or else"—there could be no contempt. Finally, the fact that the underlying case was only a private lawsuit, rather than a criminal case or one involving public questions, did not diminish the right of the press to report about it (although the nature of the case might affect a determination of whether press comments posed a clear and present danger).[92] But there were dissents, including a powerful one by Justice Frankfurter who observed that "these newspapers asked of the judge, and instigated powerful sections of the community to ask of the judge, that which no one has any business to ask of a judge, except the parties and their counsel in open court, namely, that he should decide one way rather than another."[93]

There the matter rested until 1962, when the Court once again dealt with the question of contempt by publication. The case involved the published remarks not of a journalist but of a sheriff, criticizing instructions given by local judges to a Georgia grand jury to investigate "bloc voting" by blacks, the buying of votes, and other "corrupt" election practices. The sheriff condemned these instructions as racially biased effort to intimidate black voters in an upcoming election. The sheriff's charges were published and were seen by members of the grand jury which was in session. Although the remarks were aimed at influencing grand jurors, rather than judges, the Court found no evidence that any of the jurors were actually affected or that the criticism constituted "a substantative evil actually designed to impede the course of justice."[94] Moreover, the issues being aired were particularly appropriate concerns of public discussion and could properly be considered by a body with the functions of a grand jury.

But in reaching that conclusion, the Court was careful to leave open the question of published remarks which might affect the deliberations of a *trial* jury attempting to determine guilt or innocence or liability:

Moreover, we need not pause here to consider the variant factors that would be present in a case involving a petit [trial] jury. . . . "trials are not like elections, to be won through the use of the meeting-hall, the radio, and the newspaper". . . . and of course the limitations on free speech assume a different proportion when expression is directed toward a trial as compared to a grand jury investigation.[95]

Thus, although the Supreme Court has not upheld a contempt citation for published criticism of courts and judges since 1941 (nor apparently has any state court in recent years), and "seems clearly determined to extend a high degree of protection to discussion of the administration of justice,"[96] the Court has nevertheless carefully left open the question of editorial or news reporting which is aimed at affecting the deliberations of a jury trying a case.

Can reporters criticize attorneys, parties, or witnesses in a case?

You probably have a greater right to criticize attorneys and litigants than to comment about witnesses, especially ones not personally interested in the outcome of the litigation.

The issue arose in an unusual case several years ago. A Chicago television talk-show personality named Tom Duggan was named as a co-respondent in a state court divorce and child-custody action. During several of his shows, he made sarcastic and severe denunciations of all the participants—except the judge. Nevertheless, after the custody proceedings were over, the judge cited him for contempt. The citation was appealed through the state courts which ruled that the remarks on television interfered with the judicial proceedings.

Duggan then took the case to the federal court for a declaration that the contempt conviction violated the First Amendment. The District Court agreed, noting that whatever power the state courts had to punish contemptuous publications "bears, not the approval, but the mere tolerance of the Supreme Court."[97] Nevertheless, there might be grounds for contempt depending on who the targets of the attack were. Thus, while attacks on interested participants could be allowed, intimidation of jurors or neutral witnesses could not be:

... our system of justice depends upon full protection of the jurors from intimidation and coercion. They are lay people of no special training in law. Their relationship to the system is short lived, and their concern for personal matters extending beyond their court experience make them easy victims of pressure.

Generally, witnesses are in no better position than jurors, as long as they are disinterested witnesses. Attacks on them through the press can discourage their willingness to make full disclosure. But litigants in civil cases, their attorneys, and their interested and trial participating witnesses stand on a different footing. Their strength is derived from their predisposed interest in the outcome of their litigation. They have a right to a fair and impartial trial. They cannot complain as long as no outside influences unduly impinge upon their Judge, their jury and their disinterested witnesses. Our judicial system can offer them no more.[98]

Finding that the criticism on television would have angered but not intimidated the persons at whom it was directed, the court concluded that there had been no real danger that justice would be obstructed, and thus no basis for the contempt conviction.

Can a reporter be punished for publishing information which jeopardizes the right to a fair trial?

So far, probably not, but there is much uncertainty. The question implicates the entire controversy referred to as "free press–fair trial." Over the years it has engaged the attention of courts, scholars, bar association groups, and press representatives.[99] Although in practice there are few cases where news reporting actually poses a substantial danger to a fair trial, these cases tend to be the spectacular ones which arouse great public interest.[100]

In the *Sheppard* case, the Supreme Court warned trial judges, law enforcement officials, attorneys, and members of the press to put their respective houses in order. In response, three forms of control have been suggested or implemented to deal with the problem of prejudicial publicity.[101]

First, there have been efforts to interdict prejudicial publicity at the source by prohibiting participants from releasing certain items of information. These are the so-called gag orders. Thus, for example, in many federal courts, lawyers and court personnel are prohibited from divulging the defendant's prior criminal records, the existence of or refusal to make a confession, the performance of any examination, the identity or testimony of any prospective witness other than the victim, the possibility of a guilty plea, any opinion about guilt or innocence, the merits of the case, or evidence to be presented.[102] In widely publicized cases, some federal courts prohibit "extra-judicial statements by participants ... including lawyers, parties, witnesses, jurors and court officials, which might divulge prejudicial matter not of public record in the case."[103] In addition, the Department of Justice has its own guidelines, promulgated in 1965, prohibiting its officials and employees from disclosing various kinds of prejudicial information.[104] One of the claims raised by former Vice President Agnew in an effort to head off an indictment was that Justice Department officials had leaked such prejudicial information in violation of those Department regulations. Where the ban on release of information is contained in a court rule, it is enforceable by the contempt power, and also, in the case of attorneys, by disciplinary action.[105] The federal court in Chicago recently upheld a restriction on lawyers making statements which have a "reasonable likelihood" of prejudicing a fair trial or proceeding.[106]

Second, there are a number of corrective devices over the judicial proceedings which courts can employ. They can grant a change of venue or allow a continuance so that the publicity can dissipate. They can carefully poll the prospective jurors to determine how many have a preconceived notion about the case by virtue of the publicity. It is important to remember that a juror who has some knowledge about the case is not automatically deemed to be prejudiced, although a juror's proclaimed ability to render a fair verdict is not conclusive. The ultimate question is the nature and quantity of the publicity and its probable effect on the juror.[107] Thus, in one case the Court reversed a narcotics conviction where several jurors had read an article describing the defendant's previous arrests and conviction for other drug offenses.[108] During the trial itself, the court can strongly warn the jurors not to expose themselves to news reports about the trial, and, if necessary, the court may sequester the jury. Finally, if these measures prove inadequate, mistrials can be granted or convictions reversed on appeal.

The third device to protect the defendant is to impose direct sanctions against the press for publishing prohibited kinds of information or opinion. In the *Sheppard* case, the Supreme Court said that since other corrective devices would have insured a fair trial, there was no need to consider "what sanctions might be available against a recalcitrant press."[109]

The prevailing judicial view—both before and after *Sheppard*—is that direct sanctions against the press for reporting certain information about cases would run into strong, indeed insurmountable, First Amendment objections. Almost every post-*Sheppard* proposal for alleviating the "free press–fair trial" tension has rejected the imposition of direct control on the press in favor of proceeding against the sources of prejudicial information or affording the defendant a variety of procedural protections. But rules controlling what news the press can gather and report have been and continue to be promulgated by judges and courts. And attempts to punish the press for violating those rules have been made.

Can a reporter be punished for or prohibited from reporting extra-judicial information about a pending case?

Probably not. The reporting of information which does not come out in open court poses a serious problem. Prior arrests or convictions, confessions, facts about the crime, results of lie-detector tests, inflammatory inadmissible evidence, law enforcement opinions about the case ("We've got the evidence, we've got it cold")—these are the stuff of prejudicial publicity, the kind of information which tends to convict the defendant in the press before the trial has ever begun. Of course, such information is regularly and routinely reported in the press, without any effort to impose any sanctions.

The few times that courts have tried to punish journalists for reporting such items, the reporters have prevailed. Attempted punishment can be premised on two bases: (1) violation of an explicit provision of a "protective" order which, by its terms, includes news media, or (2) a retrospective determination that the conduct of the press jeopardized the possibility of a fair trial.

One of the few attempts to punish the press for prejudicial publicity involved a celebrated murder case in the Baltimore area in 1948. A few hours after the killing of an eleven-year-old girl, a black man was arrested and soon confessed. Certain Baltimore radio stations gave detailed and frequent coverage to the crime, the police investigation, the confession which "broke" the case wide open, and the criminal record of the accused.[110] (The publicity was so intense that the defendant later waived a jury trial and the case was heard by a judge alone.)

Shortly after the arrest, contempt charges were brought against the radio station and one of its announcers for violating a long-standing local court rule against the release of such information. The trial court found the broadcasters guilty, but the appellate court reversed the contempt convictions.[111] The court reasoned that the radio station was simply reporting facts verified by public officials and possibly admissible at trial and had not posed a "clear and present danger" to the defendant's right to a fair trial because various corrective devices, such as interrogating the jurors, could have been employed. Finding that the reporting had not been inflammatory, false, or designed to intimidate the participants, the court saw no need to punish the media. A strong dissent noted that the Supreme Court had left open the question of potential news impact on jurors and had warned that "a plan of reporting on a case could be so designed and executed as to poison the public mind [and] so disturb the delicate balance in a highly wrought situation as to imperil the fair and orderly functioning of the judicial process."[112]

The decision in the Baltimore case has largely set the pattern of judicial response to the question of punishing the press for reporting prejudicial out-of-court information about a criminal case. The occasional attempts to prohibit or punish such reporting have been unsuccessful.[113] In Massachusetts, for example, a trial judge instructed reporters, although informally, not to mention the prior criminal record of the defendants. The *Boston Traveler* dutifully reported the content of the judge's warning. On appeal, the defendants' conviction was reversed, and the reporters were lectured on their responsibilities.[114] Four years later, the warning was replaced by a contempt citation against the *Worcester Gazette* for reporting that a criminal defendant was currently serving a prison sentence. After a mistrial was granted, contempt charges were brought against the newspaper and its reporter. On appeal, the charges were dismissed because there had been "no wilful attempt to affect the trial" and because the reporting inadvertently violated a written editorial policy not to publish criminal records unless the information is brought out in court proceedings.[115]

In a widely publicized New York trial, the judge informally warned reporters that if they continued to publish the defendant's long criminal record, "you'll be in the can."[116] The New York Court of Appeals ruled that the judge could not have held the reporters in contempt for publishing such information:

... the law is settled that the contempt power may not be utilized to impose punishment for the publication of out-of-court statements relating to a pending court proceeding, except where such statements are shown to present "a clear and present danger" or "a serious and imminent threat to the administration of justice."[117]

Even where such reporting affected a jury trial, punishment of the press "would still require a substantial showing of justification in order to avoid the condemnation of the First Amendment."

Just recently, the federal appeals court in Philadelphia handed down an important decision in a similar case involving the *Philadelphia Inquirer*. The trial judge had verbally ordered the press not to report any information about a criminal trial except matters that came out in open court. He was particularly concerned that reporters not reveal that the defendant, being tried for perjury, had also been indicted for conspiracy to commit murder in the same episode. The press obeyed the ban, appealed the order, and won. The appeals court ruled that such protective orders had to be in writing and could not be issued until after the judge had held a hearing at which the reporters could challenge the order.[118]

Despite such rulings, trial courts still try to enforce protective orders against reporters. In a Los Angeles trial, the judge entered a comprehensive order prohibiting attorneys "and all agencies of the public media" from discussing anything about the case except what occurred in open court. The news media and the district attorney challenged the order. The appellate court drew a sharp distinction between restraints on participants and controls on the press. The latter could be sustained, if ever, only upon the strongest showing of justification, which had not been demonstrated since there was not that much press interest in the particular trial.[119] The court concluded that while limitations can be imposed on what the participants say about a case if there is a "reasonable likelihood" that a defendant will be prejudiced, no such limitations can be imposed on the press at all. Thus, the court ordered that the news media be stricken from the protective order.

But, although reporters have successfully resisted direct judicial restraints on reporting out-of-court information about criminal cases, the door has never been closed to the possibility of post-trial punishment of the press for engaging in a pattern of reporting which results in provable harm to a criminal defendant.[120] Some judges have suggested that the right of the press to report about a case "rises no higher than the criminal defendant's right to a fair trial."[121] Under this theory, if prejudicial publicity resulted in a mistrial or the reversal of a conviction, the way might be open for punishing the reporters who were responsible. So far this view has not prevailed, and such punishment has not been meted out.

One final problem should be noted. Even though most courts and experts have said that the best, and the constitutionally sound, method of protecting a defendant is to restrain and punish the sources of prejudicial publicity, a reporter may still face substantial difficulties over reporting such information. For the reporter may be caught in a cross-fire between the court and the source of the information, when the court tries to find out which of the participants in the case violated the gag order by leaking the prohibited information to the press. This is exactly what happened in the Charles Manson case, where a reporter published a highly damaging deposition, apparently provided by one of the lawyers in the case. For refusing to identify the lawyer, the reporter was held in contempt and jailed.[122]

This dilemma can indirectly bring about a result which courts have said cannot be achieved directly, namely, punishing the press in an effort to protect the defendant.

Can a reporter be prohibited from reporting what transpires in open court?

No.

The one aspect of the entire area which has some clarity is the coverage of events which take place in open court. Twenty-five years ago the Supreme Court stated:

A trial is a public event. What transpires in the courtroom is public property. . . . Those who see and hear what transpired can report it with impunity. There is no special prerequisite of the judiciary which enables it, as distinguished from other institutions of democratic government, to suppress, edit, or censor events which transpire in proceedings before it.[123]

This basic rule seems clear enough. But it has not prevented lower courts from trying in various ways to keep reporters from reporting what occurs in open court. Fortunately such actions have consistently been invalidated.

Does a reporter have a right to report any testimony given in open court?

Generally, yes. The issue came up in a recent federal case which, for reasons which will be discussed a little later, has caused great concern among reporters. A civil-rights worker in Louisiana, charged with conspiracy to commit murder, obtained a federal court hearing to determine whether state officials were acting in good faith in pressing the prosecution. At the start of the hearing, the federal judge read an order prohibiting reporters from reporting any evidence given at the hearing:

It is ordered that no, no report of the testimony taken in this case today shall be made in any newspaper or by radio or television, or by any other news media. This case will, in all probability, be the subject of further prosecution; at least there is the possibility that it may. In order to avoid undue publicity which could in any way interfere with the rights of the litigants in connection with any further proceedings that might be had in this or other courts, there shall be no reporting of the details of any evidence taken during the course of this hearing today.[124]

Two reporters present at the hearings wrote stories summarizing the day's testimony in detail. The judge asked the reporters to show cause why they should not be held in contempt, found them in contempt, and fined them $300 each.

On appeal, the invalidity of the order presented little difficulty: ". . . a blanket ban on publication of Court proceedings so far transgresses First Amendment freedoms that any such absolute proscription 'cannot withstand the mildest breeze emanating from the Constitution.' "[125] The appeals court noted several reasons why the reporting in no way posed a danger to the administration of justice: (1) any jury trial would not be held until well in the future when any prejudicial effect of the reporting would probably be dissipated; (2) the hearing itself was the opposite of a "Roman Holiday" and had generated the interest of few reporters or readers; (3) it was particularly important that the public be aware of and informed about allegations of prosecutorial bias; (4) the order sought to control the conduct of two reporters who were not parties to the proceeding, and the hearing itself was of marginal importance to the issues which might arise at the conspiracy trial; and (5) the state courts could employ alternative cures to deal with any prejudice that might linger as a result of the reporting.

Even when protective orders are directed at an imminent trial, rather than an ancillary proceeding, courts have used this same reasoning to find such orders unconstitutional. In one California case the court ruled that prior restraints on reporting what occurs in open court "should rarely be employed against the communications media."[126] In an Arizona case, the court ruled that a reporter could not be prevented from publishing testimony given at a habeas corpus hearing, even though the trial was about to begin:

> Courts are public institutions. The manner in which justice is administered does not have any private aspects. To permit a hearing held in open court to be kept secret, the order of secrecy being based entirely on the defendant's request, would take from the public its right to be informed of a proceeding to which it is an interested party.[127]

Supreme Court Justice Lewis F. Powell applied this reasoning in voiding a Louisiana judge's order against reporting about a trial soon to be held.[128] Since there was no showing that the reporting posed an "imminent threat" to a fair trial, the stories could not be restrained. The practical effect of the Justice's order was that both the trial and the reporting were allowed.

However, where a statute specifically provided for non-public preliminary hearings in order to protect the defendant if the charges are dismissed, a Nevada court upheld an order that reporters could observe but not report the proceedings.[129] The court implied that the reporters could obtain a copy of the transcript (and presumably write about it) at a later date.

If evidence is given in open court, but ruled inadmissible, can a reporter publish it anyway?

Yes, but the issue is a troublesome one. Although the Supreme Court has invalidated convictions because of news reports containing evidence which would be inadmissible or which was not produced at trial,[130] protective orders which prohibited the reporting of evidence presented in open court but ruled inadmissible have been invalidated.

The leading case arose in Washington, where judges, lawyers, and reporters had discussed the "free press–fair trial" issue for some time, and voluntary press guidelines had been adopted. Prior to a widely publicized murder trial, the judge entered an order saying that only proceedings in open court could be reported, and even then "no report shall be made by such news media ... of matters or testimony ruled inadmissible or stricken by the trial judge at the time of the offer of matter or testimony."[131] The editors of the *Seattle Times* decided to challenge the order. They had their opportunity on the third day of trial. The defense objected to certain prejudicial testimony about the facts surrounding the arrest of the defendants in California and their implication in another murder. The testimony was being given in the jury's absence, but to a courtroom full of spectators. The trial judge ruled some of the evidence inadmissible. The reporters described it in their stories the next day and were immediately cited for contempt. On appeal, the Washington Supreme Court reversed the ruling and held that reporters could not be told in advance to refrain from reporting "those events which occur during an open and public court proceeding."[132] The court noted that although the trial judge had not sequestered the jury, he had warned them not to read any newspapers and could have declared a mistrial if any had. Moreover, the mere possibility that prejudicial matter will reach the jury outside of the courtroom does not justify a ban on reporting what occurs inside.

Most courts have generally, though sometimes reluctantly, adhered to this rule about reporting unsuccessful efforts to introduce evidence.[133]

Can a reporter be prevented from publishing the names or identities of witnesses who testify in open court?

No. If the testimony is given in open court, there can be no bar on reporting the identity of the witness.

The point was made in a recent California case. An inmate was murdered at the Chino prison, and the trial of the alleged killers was about to start. The prosecutor claimed that if his witnesses were identified or photographed they would not testify because of fear of retribution from other inmates, or they would suffer physical violence when they returned to prison. The trial judge agreed, and ordered the reporters not to print the names or pictures of the witnesses. The press appealed on grounds that the order constituted an invalid prior restraint on news reporting, with no reasonable justification. The appellate court concurred and invalidated the order.[134] The court concluded that sanctions or restraints against reporters were rarely, if ever, to be allowed. Since the prosecutor claimed only that the witnesses "might" be deterred, there was no showing of the kind of imminent danger to the administration of justice that would theoretically allow a prior restraint on reporting.

Similarly, in a Kentucky prosecution for contributing to the delinquency of a minor, where the trial was open to the public, the court ruled that reporters could not be barred from publishing the names of the juveniles involved in the proceeding.[135] The state statute which allowed the public to be excluded from juvenile cases was held to be inapplicable. But, in general, juvenile proceedings can be closed to the public and to the press, and reporters seem inclined to go along with this exclusion. However, there are some states and judges that permit reporters at such proceedings on the condition that they not publish names or identifying details.[136]

Can the court prevent reporters from identifying juveniles under the court's jurisdiction or victims in rape cases?

Courts have tended to say yes.

In one case, a Virgin Islands statute made juvenile court records confidential and provided that "the name or picture of any child under the jurisdiction of the court shall not be made public by any newspaper, radio, or television station except as authorized by order of the court."[137] The publisher of a daily newspaper in St. Croix reported the names of such juveniles and was fined $100. He argued that the statute violated the First Amendment and that anonymity in juvenile proceedings was not desirable. The

court disagreed, held that the goals secured by confidentiality were valid, and concluded that the restraint on publishing such information was justified:

... the Municipal Court carefully considered the advantages accruing to juveniles by shielding them from publicity and those to be gained by permitting the unrestricted publication of their names, and concluded that the limitation on the press was valid as in the interest of rehabilitating youthful offenders. We are wholly in accord. . . .[138]

But the Supreme Court, while allowing states to continue to maintain the confidentiality of juvenile records, has noted that confidentiality is usually honored in the breach and that the claim of secrecy is "more rhetoric than reality."[139] Such "confidential information" is routinely revealed to law enforcement officials, military agencies, and private employers. Given such informal disclosure, a reporter could well argue that he was equally entitled to reveal juvenile information, at least in a controlled manner.

Similarly, several states absolutely prohibit reporting the identity of female victims of sex offenses.[140] The validity of such a ban is pending before the Supreme Court at this writing. The case is a civil invasion-of-privacy action brought against a Georgia television station by the family of a young woman who was raped and murdered. The station identified her while reporting the subsequent trial. The Georgia courts upheld the invasion-of-privacy claim.[141]

Can a court order reporters not to print the names of jurors until the trial is over?

So far, the answer seems to be yes.

One of the major irritants in the *Sheppard* case was the release of jurors' names, addresses, and photographs prior to the trial, which thrust them "into the role of celebrities" and exposed them to out-of-court communications and pressures.[142] Accordingly, many federal courts have provided that the names and addresses of jurors and prospective jurors shall not be publicly released except as required by statute.

The issue came up recently in Nevada where, prior to the re-trial in a widely publicized murder case, a state judge ordered that the names of jurors and alternates not be published. The press complied, but took the issue into federal court. The court concluded that the order was a valid attempt to maintain the integrity of an impartial jury. The court reasoned that the purposes of the First Amendment—to insure free discussion on public issues—were not involved in the case: ". . . the public's right to know is wholly irrelevant to this situation. No public purpose is furthered by publication of the jurors' names on the first day of the trial rather than the last. The only imaginable use any member of the public might make of such information is an improper one—jury tampering."[143]

Can a reporter be prohibited from publishing a jury verdict because it might affect another jury's deliberations?

No.

In Arkansas, two separate juries were simultaneously deliberating verdicts in related criminal cases. The first jury returned its verdict late in the day. The trial judge, fearing that news reports about that verdict would reach the second set of jurors, phoned the publisher of the *Texarkana Gazette* and ordered him not to print the story. The publisher refused to comply and ran a prominently displayed article. The trial judge held him in contempt, but the Supreme Court of Arkansas reversed the conviction:

Every court that has had an occasion to rule upon the freedom of the press to publish court proceedings, has held that whatever transpires in the courtroom is public property and those who see and hear it may report it without judicial censorship.[144]

Since the members of the second jury had been warned not to expose themselves to media reports, there was no need for the ban on publication.

Can a reporter be punished for writing a false account of an imminent court decision?

The answer is unclear.

In 1934, the *San Francisco Chronicle* published a story saying that the California Supreme Court had entered a decision throwing out a murder conviction. The story was untrue, and the court held the newspaper in contempt. The court concluded that the story tended to create public distrust of the court by making it appear that a judge or official had leaked the news and also tended to interfere with the administration of justice by appearing to influence the court's decision.[145] In light of the later rulings invalidating contempts by publication, it is doubtful that this decision represents the law today.

Can a reporter be punished for violating a ban on publishing even though the rule itself is later found to be invalid?

The answer is unclear, and the question has caused a great deal of concern among reporters. In many situations, reporters have been content to obey a prohibition on reporting certain kinds of information about judicial proceedings—even a patently valid one—while they pursued a court challenge to the rule. But what if the order is imposed on the spur of the moment, and, because of deadline pressures, obeying it will mean sacrificing the story?

That was precisely the situation in the *Dickinson* case in New Orleans.[146] The morning of the hearing, the judge instructed the reporters not to write about the testimony. They did so and were fined for contempt, over their objection that the order itself was an unconstitutional prior restraint. On appeal, the Fifth Circuit agreed that the ban was unconstitutional. But, in the court's view, that did not end the matter, for there was still the question of whether reporters could be punished for violating the order. Or, as the court put it: ". . . whether a person may with impunity knowingly violate an order which turns out to be invalid." Relying on a Supreme Court decision in a civil-rights-demonstration case, the court ruled that judicial orders, unlike any other governmental decree or rule and no matter how invalid, must first be obeyed. (Ironically, as support for this conclusion the court pointed to the fact that the news media obeyed temporary restraining orders in the Pentagon Papers cases.) The only exceptions to this rule are (1) where the court issuing the order had no jurisdiction to do so, (2) if there is no effective way to seek judicial review of the challenged order, or (3) if the order requires "an irretrievable surrender of constitutional guarantees."[147] The reporters argued that there were no speedy avenues of review, and meantime the news would grow stale while they appealed. But the court disagreed: ". . . newsmen are citizens, too. . . . They too may sometimes have to wait. They are not yet wrapped in an immunity to decide with impunity whether a Judge's order is to be obeyed or whether an appellate court is acting promptly enough."[148] Finding that speedy appellate review of the order would have been possible, the court concluded that the reporters could properly be punished for violating the order before challenging it. The result seems particularly unusual since the federal contempt statute, by its terms, allows punishment only for disobeying "lawful" court orders; if the order was invalid, how can the refusal to obey be punishable under the statute?

In any event, other courts have disagreed with the conclusion that invalid judicial rules must nevertheless be obeyed. Indeed, another federal court of appeals overturned a contempt citation of a lawyer who discussed a pending case with the press in violation of a pre-trial publicity order.[149] And at least three state courts have ruled that reporters do not have to obey an invalid publicity order before contesting it in court. In the Seattle case, the newspaper officials published inadmissible testimony in disregard of the judge's prohibition. The Washington Supreme Court held that the reporters could violate the order and still challenge it: "the violation of an order patently in excess of the jurisdiction of the issuing court cannot produce a valid judgement of contempt."[150] The same result was reached when the *Texarkana Gazette* printed the verdict in a jury case in violation of the court's instructions. The contempt citation was summarily overturned, even though the publisher had not waited to challenge the order before he violated it.

In the recent *Philadelphia Inquirer* case, the federal appeals court noted the dilemma a reporter faces.[151] If the order is obeyed, the news is suppressed until after it is stale. If the reporter violates the order, he may be denied the right to defend the contempt charge by arguing the order was unconstitutional. Requiring the judge to give reporters a hearing before the order is formulated can help to deal with the problem.

However, until the Supreme Court resolves these issues, the uncertainty will remain.

If a reporter publishes a story in violation of a court rule, what consequences will follow?

In all probability, the court whose rule was violated will issue an order for the reporter to "show cause" why he should not be held in contempt of court.

As indicated in the chapter on protecting sources, concepts and doctrines in the contempt area are extremely fuzzy. In the context of violating a publicity order, the contempt proceeding would probably be labeled "criminal" rather than "civil," because its purpose would be to punish the reporter for a completed act, not to compel the reporter to perform some affirmative act, such as revealing sources.

The power of a court to hold a person in *summary* contempt, i.e., without a hearing, is severely limited, usually to those situations where the contemptuous act occurs in the court's presence. For example, a television news photographer who walked into a criminal trial and started filming might be punished summarily.

In the more typical situation, the actual violation of the

order will occur out of court, in the form of a reported story containing information whose dissemination has been prohibited. A federal court has the power to punish by fine or imprisonment "such contempt of its authority as ... disobedience or resistance to its lawful writ, process, order, rule, decree, or command."[152] If charged under that provision, a reporter is entitled to notice of the charges, reasonable time to prepare a defense, and a hearing on the merits.[153] Defenses might include the claim that you were not aware of the order or that it violates the First Amendment.[154] If the judge anticipates imposing a sentence of at least six months' confinement, you may be entitled to a jury trial. As with any other criminal conviction, there is a right to appeal and to be free on bail in the meantime. But the normal sentence in these cases tends to be payment of a fine with no incarceration.

Finally, judges occasionally like to give reporters an informal "warning" not to publish certain information or engage in certain conduct. The warning is disregarded and the judge then attempts to hold the reporter in contempt. In such situations the reporter can properly argue that the warning did not constitute a judicial order or rule which must be obeyed. In the CBS sketching case, the appeals court ruled that because the trial judge's order was given only verbally, he should not have presided over the contempt hearing where one of the issues was the question of precisely what prohibitions his order contained.[155] And in the *Philadelphia Inquirer* case, the federal court of appeals held that such orders could not be given orally at all.

Footnotes to Chapter V

1. The episode is described in *Nye* v. *United States*, 313 U.S. 33, 45-46 (1941).
2. *United States* v. *Dickinson*, 465 F.2d 496, 502-03 (5th Cir. 1972), *on remand*, 349 F. Supp. 227 (D. La. 1972), *aff'd*, 476 F.2d 373 (5th Cir.), *cert. denied*, 414 U.S. 979 (1973).
3. *Toledo Newspaper Co.* v. *United States*, 247 U.S. 402 (1917), *overruled in Nye* v. *United States, supra.*
4. See, *e.g., Pennekamp* v. *Florida*, 328 U.S. 331 (1946); *Craig* v. *Harney*, 331 U.S. 367 (1947).
5. *Sheppard* v. *Maxwell*, 384 U.S. 333, 350 (1966).
6. *Report of the Committee on the Operation of the Jury System on the "Free Press–Fair Trial" Issue*, 45 F.R.D. 391, 394-95 (1968); see generally Lofton, *Justice and the Press*, (1966); Friendly and Goldfarb, *Crime and Publicity* (1967).
7. *Marshall* v. *United States*, 360 U.S. 310 (1959).
8. *Irvin* v. *Doud*, 366 U.S. 717 (1961).
9. *Rideau* v. *Louisiana*, 373 U.S. 723 (1963).
10. *Estes* v. *Texas*, 381 U.S. 532 (1965).
11. *Sheppard* v. *Maxwell*, 384 U.S. 333 (1966).
12. 384 U.S. at 362-63.
13. *Oliver* v. *Postel*, 30 N.Y. 2d 171, 183 (1972).
14. *State ex rel. Superior Court of Snohomish County* v. *Sperry*, 483 P.2d 608 (Wash. Sup. Ct. 1971).
15. *Oxnard Publishing Co.* v. *Superior Court of Ventura County*, 261 Cal. App. 2d 505, 68 Cal. Rptr. 83 (1968).
16. *United States* v. *Bell*, 464 F.2d 667 (2d Cir.) *cert. denied*, 409 U.S. 991 (1972).
17. *United States* v. *Clark*, 475 F.2d 240, 246-47 (2d. Cir. 1973).
18. *People* v. *Hinton*, 31 N.Y.2d 71 (1972).
19. *Matter of United Press Association* v. *Valente*, 308 N.Y. 71 (1954); see also, *People* v. *Jelke*, 308 N.Y. 56 (1954)

(involving the same trial). See generally, Annotation, *Validity and Construction of Constitution or Statute Authorizing Exclusion of Public in Sex Offense Cases*, 39 A.L.R. 3d 852.

20. *United States* v. *Kobi*, 172 F.2d 919 (3rd Cir. 1949).

21. See, *United States ex rel. Orlando* v. *Fay*, 350 F.2d 967 (2d Cir. 1965), *cert. denied*, 384 U.S. 1008 (1966); *United States ex rel. Bruno* v. *Herold*, 408 F.2d 125 (2 Cir. 1969), *cert. denied*, 397 U.S. 957 (1970).

22. *United States* v. *Kobi*, 172 F.2d 919 (3rd Cir. 1949); see also, *Lewis* v. *Peyton*, 352 F.2d 791 (4th Cir. 1965) (defendant's right to a public trial violated by exclusion of public from testimony given by rape victim in her home); *Kirstowsky* v. *Superior Court of Sonoma County*, 143 Cal App. 2d 245, 300 P.2d 163 (1956).

23. *Johnson* v. *Simpson*, 433 S.W. 2d 644 (Ky. 1968).

24. *Id.* at 646; see also, *Scripps* v. *Fulton*, 100 Ohio App. 157, 125 N.E.2d 896 (1958); *Lancaster* v. *United States*, 293 F.2d 519 (D.C. Cir. 1961).

25. *Estes* v. *Texas* 381 U.S. 532 (1965); *Sheppard* v. *Maxwell*, 384 U.S. 333 (1966).

26. *People* v. *Holder*, 70 MISC.2d 31, 332 N.Y.S.2d 933 (*Sup Ct.*, Queens Co., 1972).

27. See, *e.g.*, *United States* v. *American Radiator and Standard San. Corp.*, 274 F. Supp 790 (W.D.Pa. 1967); *United States* v. *General Motors Corp.*, 352 F. Supp 107 (E.D. Mich. 1973); but see, *People* v. *Pratt*, 27 App. Div. 2d. 199, 278 N.Y.S.2d 89 (3d. Dept. 1967).

28. See, *Abzill* v. *Fisher*, 84 Nev. 414, 442 P.2d 916 (1968); *State* v. *Meek*, 9 Ariz. App. 149 450 P.2d 115 (Ct. of Appeals, 1969); *cert. denied* 396 U.S. 847 (1969) (reporter could be held in contempt for refusing to leave a preliminary hearing); *People* v. *Elliot*, 6 Cal. Rptr. 753 (1960) (reversible error for court to allow reporter to remain at preliminary hearing over the defendant's objection). See generally, Annotation, *Right of Person Accused of Crime to Exclude Public From Preliminary Hearing or Examination*, 31 A.L.R. 3d 816.

29. *Phoenix Newspapers Inc.* v. *Jennings*, 107 Ariz. 557, 490 P.2d 563 (1971), see generally, Annotation, *Right of Accused to Have Press or Other Media Representatives Excluded from Criminal Trial*, 49 A.L.R. 3d 1007.

30. See, *e.g.*, *Oliver* v. *Postel*, 30 N.Y.2d 171 (1972); *Oxnard Publishing Co.* v. *Superior Court of Ventura County*, 261 Cal. App.2d 505, 68 Cal. Rptr. 83 (1968).

31. 384 U.S. at 355.

32. 384 U.S. at 358.

33. See, *United States* v. *Dickinson, supra,* 465 F.2d at 505-06.

34. *Report of the Committee on the Operation of the Jury System on the "Free Press–Fair Trial" Issue,* 45 F.R.D. 391, 409-13 (1968).

35. See, *United States ex rel. Dessus* v. *Commonwealth of Pennsylvania,* 316 F. Supp. 411, 420 (E.D. Pa. 1970), *aff'd,* 452 F.2d 557 (3rd Cir. 1971), *cert. denied,* 409 U.S. 853 (1972).

36. *Estes* v. *Texas,* 381 U.S. 532, 546 (1965).

37. 381 U.S. at 544-50. Two years earlier the Court had ruled, tersely and almost unanimously, that the televising of a defendant's confession to the police was automatically prejudicial. *Rideau* v. *Louisiana,* 373 U.S. 723, 727 (1963).

38. 381 U.S. at 549. In one pre-*Estes* case, a Georgia court ruled that the presence of a recording microphone in the courtroom, a few feet from the defense table, deprived the defendant of a fair trial. *Hudson* v. *States,* 108 Ga. App. 192, 132 S.E. 2d 508 (1963).

39. See, *Lyles* v. *States,* 330 P.2d 734 (Sup. Ct. Okla. 1958); *In re Hearings Concerning Canon 35 of the Canon of Judicial Ethics,* 132 Colo. 581, 296 P.2d 465 (1956).

40. In fact, only four Justices thought that televising trials should always be prohibited. Five thought that the issue depended on the facts of each case. But since one of those Justices thought there was prejudice in the *Estes* case, he voted with the majority to reverse the conviction.

41. 381 U.S. at 614-15.

42. 381 U.S. at 540.

43. 381 U.S. at 617. In one case since *Estes,* the court ruled that the presence of a television camera in court when the verdict was rendered in a murder case did not deprive the defendant of a fair trial because the trial was almost over and the dignity of the court was not disturbed. *Bell* v. *Patterson,* 279 F. Supp. 760 (D. Colo. 1968) *aff'd.* 402 F.2d 394 (10th Cir. 1968); see also *Bradley* v. *State of Texas,* 470 F.2d 785 (5th Cir. 1972).

44. *New York Times,* Sept. 23, 1973, p. 28, col. 1.

45. *Tribune Review Publishing Co.* v. *Thomas,* 254 F.2d 883 (3rd Cir. 1958). See also, *Ohio* v. *Clifford,* 162 Ohio St. 370, 123 N.E. 2d 8 (1954) (upholding the contempt con-

    viction of a photographer who took pictures during an arraignment in violation of the judge's order).

46. Rule 53, Federal Rules of Criminal Procedure.

47. See Wright, Federal Practice and Procedure: Criminal, §861; see, *e.g.*, *Seymour* v. *United States,* 373 F.2d 629 (5th Cir. 1967).

48. *Bell* v. *Patterson,* 279 F. Supp. 760 (D. Colo. 1968), *aff'd,* 402 F.2d 394 (10th Cir. 1968).

49. *Sheppard* v. *Maxwell,* 384 U.S. 333, 355 (1966).

50. *Estes* v. *Texas,* 381 U.S. 532, 589 (1965).

51. *In re Mack,* 126 A.2d 679 (Pa. 1956).

52. 126 A.2d at 682.

53. After losing in the state courts, the reporters took the issue to the federal courts, but were unsuccessful there. The rules were upheld as a reasonable regulation of conduct in the courthouse. *Tribune Review Publishing Co.* v. *Thomas,* 254 F.2d 883 (3rd Cir. 1958).

54. *Brumfield* v. *State,* 108 So.2d 33 (Fla. 1959).

55. *Seymour* v. *United States,* 373 F.2d, 629 (5th Cir. 1967).

56. *Id.* at 631-32.

57. *In re Acuff,* 331 F. Supp. 819 (D.N.M. 1971).

58. *Id.* at 822.

59. *Dorfman* v. *Meizner,* 430 F.2d 558, 562 (7th Cir. 1970).

60. *Id.* at 563.

61. *Ex Parte Arnold,* 503 S.W.2d 529 (Tex. Ct. Crim. App. 1974).

62. See, *United States* v. *Dickinson,* 465 F.2d. 496 (5th Cir. 1972).

63. *United States* v. *Columbia Broadcasting System,* 497 F.2d 102 (5th cir. 1974).

64. *Sheppard* v. *Maxwell,* 384 U.S. 333, 353, 359 (1966).

65. See 45 F.R.D. 410-11.

66. Compare the Judicial Conference Proposals, 45 F.R.D. 391 with the local Rule for "widely publicized or sensational" cases involved in *United States* v. *Dickinson,* 465 F.2d 496, 506 N. 11 (5th Cir. 1972).

67. *United States* v. *Zeiler,* 470 F.2d 717, 719-20 (3rd Cir. 1972).

68. Federal Rules of Criminal Procedure, Rule 6(e).

69. *In re Biaggi,* 478 F.2d 483 (2d Cir. 1973); *cf. Craemer* v. *Superior Court of County of Marion,* 265 Cal. App.2d 216, 71 Cal. Rptr. 193 (2d Dist. 1968).

70. *Matter of New York Post Corp.* v. *Leibowitz,* 2 N.Y. 2d 677, 684 (1957). Libel law recognizes a defense of fair and true reporting of official proceedings.

71. See, *e.g.*, *Matter of New York Post Corp.* v. *Liebowitz, supra*; See, Freedom of Information Center Report No. 307, *FOI and State Attorneys General* (July 1973).

72. The issues are discussed generally in Emerson, *The System of Freedom of Expression* (1970) at 449-65, and Friendly and Goldfarb, *Crime and Publicity* (1967) at 113-20.

73. *Craig* v. *Harney,* 331 U.S. 367, 373, 376 (1947).

74. *Id.* at 375.

75. See, *Bridges* v. *California,* 314 U.S. 252 (1941); *Pennekamp* v. *Florida,* 328 U.S. (1946); *Craig* v. *Harney* 331 U.S. 367 (1947); *Wood* v. *Georgia,* 370 U.S. 375 (1962).

76. *Toledo Newspaper Co.* v. *United States,* 247 U.S. 402 (1917).

77. The successor statute is 18 U.S.C. §401 which reads as follows:

> A court of the United States shall have power to punish by fine or imprisonment, at its discretion, such contempt of its authority, and none other, as—
>
> (1) Misbehavior of any person in its presence or so near thereto as to obstruct the administration of justice;
>
> (2) Misbehavior of any of its officers in their official transactions;
>
> (3) Disobedience or resistance to its lawful writ, process, order, rule, decree, or command.

78. See Friendly and Goldfarb, *supra* at 115-16.

79. *Nye.* v. *United States,* 313 U.S. 33 (1941).

80. Unlike the federal courts, state courts do theoretically have the power to punish critical publications, but only if they fall within the strict "clear and present danger" test.

81. 18 U.S.C. §401(3).

82. See, *e.g.*, *United States* v. *Dickinson,* 465 F.2d 496 (5th Cir. 1972); see also *United States* v. *Seymour,* 373 F.2d (5th Cir. 1967).

83. *Patterson* v. *Colorado,* 205 U.S. 454, 462-63 (1907).

84. *Bridges* v. *California,* 314 U.S. 252, 268-69 (1941).

85. See *Pennekamp* v. *Florida,* 328 U.S. 331 (1946).

86. *Bridges* v. *California,* 314 U.S. 252, 273 (1941).

87. *Pennekamp* v. *Florida,* 328 U.S. 331, 345 (1946).

88. *Id.* at 354.

89. *Id.* at 348.

90. *Craig* v. *Harney,* 331 U.S. 367, 374-75 (1947).

91. *Id.* at 376.

92. *Id.* at 377.

93. *Id.* at 390.

94. *Wood* v. *Georgia,* 370 U.S. 375, 389 (1962).

95. *Id.* at 389-90.

96. *Emerson, supra,* at 456.

97. *Goss* v. *State of Illinois,* 204 F. Supp. 268, 274 (N.D. Ill. 1962); *rev'd on other grounds,* 312 F.2d 257 (7th Cir. 1963).

98. *Id.* at 275.

99. See generally Friendly and Goldfarb, *Crime and Publicity* (1967); Emerson, *The System of Freedom of Expression,* 459-65 (1970); *Report of the Committee on the Operation of the Jury System on the "Free Press–Fair Trial" Issue,* 45 F.R.D. 391; American Bar Association Project on Minimum Standards for Criminal Justice, *Standards Relating to Fair Trial and Free Press, Tentative Draft* (1966).

100. Since the *Sheppard* decision only a handful of convictions have been invalidated because of the effect of prejudicial publicity. This may be the result of several factors including: (1) the atypical number of aggravating factors present in *Sheppard,* making it easy for courts to "distinguish" that decision and find it inapplicable to the case before them; (2) greater self-restraint by the press in reporting about sensational cases; (3) the adoption of court rules limiting the kinds of information which participants in the proceedings are allowed to reveal; (4) strictly enforced rules to insure that the courtroom itself will be relatively calm and free from turbulence; and (5) the general reluctance of courts to invalidate convictions. The following are examples of cases which upheld convictions despite the existence of a substantial amount of pretrial publicity: *Hitchcock* v. *Arizona,* 446 F.2d 46 (9th Cir.), *cert. denied,* 404 U.S. 946 (1971); *Margoles* v. *United States,* 407 F.2d 727 (7th Cir.), *cert. denied,* 396 U.S. 833 (1969); *Corbett* v. *Patterson,* 272 F. Supp. 602 (D. Colo. 1967).

101. See Emerson, *supra,* at 459-60; see generally Robert S. Warren and Jeffrey M. Abell, *Free Press–Fair Trial: The "Gag Order," a California Aberration,* 45 So. Cal. L. Rev. 51 (1972).

102. See Rules of the United States District Court for the Southern District of New York, Criminal Rule 8.

103. See *United States* v. *Dickinson,* 465 F.2d 496, 506, n. 11 (5th Cir. 1972); *United States* v. *Anderson,* 356 F. Supp.

1311 (D.N.J. 1973) (text of a "Gag Order"); see also, 45 F.R.D. 394, 409.

104. 28 C.F.R. 50.2 (Release of Information by Personnel of the Department of Justice Relating to Criminal and Civil Proceedings) (1972); See *United States* v. *Abbott Labs.,* 369 F. Supp. 1396 (E.D.N.C. 1973), *rev'd,*——F.2d—— (4th Cir. 1974).

105. But the comments must be found to present an imminent danger, or a reasonable likelihood of such danger, to the administration of justice. See generally *United States* v. *Tijerina,* 412 F.2d 661 (10th Cir. 1969) (speech by criminal defendant about the case); *Chase* v. *Robson,* 435 F.2d 1059 (7th Cir. 1970); *In re Oliver,* 452 F.2d 111 (7th Cir. 1971); *Younger* v. *Smith,* 30 Cal. App. 2d 143, 106 Cal. Rptr. 225 (2d Dist. 1973).

106. *Chicago Council of Lawyers* v. *Bauer,* 371 F. Supp. 689 (N.D. Ill. 1974).

107. See *Sheppard* v. *Maxwell,* 384 U.S. 333, 350-52 (1966); see also, *Estes* v. *Texas,* 381 U.S. 532 (1965); *Turner* v. *Louisiana,* 379 U.S. 466 (1965); *Irvin* v. *Dowd,* 366 U.S. 717 (1961).

108. *Marshall* v. *United States,* 360 U.S. 310 (1959). Recently a federal appeals court threw out a conviction because news reports of the defendant's guilty plea, later withdrawn, reached the jury. *United States ex re Doggett* v. *Yeager,* 472 F.2d 229 (3rd Cir. 1973).

109. *Sheppard* v. *Maxwell,* 384 U.S. 333, 358 (1966).

110. See Friendly and Goldfarb, *Crime and Publicity,* at 292-98 (1967).

111. *Baltimore Radio Show* v. *State,* 67 A.2d 497 (Court of Appeals, Md., 1949), *cert. denied,* 338 U.S. 912 (1950).

112. Quoting from *Craig* v. *Harney,* 331 U.S. 367, 375 (1947).

113. See, *e.g., Atlanta Newspapers Inc.* v. *State,* 216 Ga. App. 399, 116 S.E.2d 580 (Sup. Ct. 1960).

114. *Crehan* v. *Massachusetts,* 345 Mass. 609, 188 N.E.2d 923 (1963).

115. *Worcester Telegram & Gazette Co.* v. *Commonwealth,* 238 N.E. 2d 861, 864 (1968).

116. Freedom of Information Center Report No. 277, *Sequester the Country* (Feb. 1972), pp. 10-11.

117. *Oliver* v. *Postel,* 30 N.Y.2d 171, 180 (1972).

118. *United States* v. *Schiavo,*——F.2d——(3rd. Cir. 1974) (en banc).

119. *Younger* v. *Smith*, 30 Cal. App.2d 143, 106 Cal. Rptr. 225 (2d Dist. 1973); see also, *Florida ex rel. Miami Herald Publishing Co.* v. *Rose*, 271 So.2d 483 (Ct. of App. 1972).

120. See, *e.g.*, *State ex rel. Superior Court of Snohomish County:* v. *Sperry*, 483 P.2d 608, 627 (Wash. Sup. Ct. 1971) (concurring opinion); *Phoenix Newspapers Inc.* v. *Superior Ct.*, 101 Ariz. 257, 418 P.2d 594 (1966).

121. *United States* v. *Kahaner*, 317 F.2d 459, 470 (2d Cir.), *cert. denied*, 375 U.S. 836 (1963).

122. *Farr* v. *Superior Court*, 22 Cal. App.3d 60, 99 Cal. Rptr. 342 (2d Dist. 1971), *cert. denied*, 409 U.S. 101 (1972). Two recent cases discussing the problem of identifying the source of leaks are *United States* v. *Isaacs*, 351 F. Supp. 1323 (N.D. Ill. 1972), which involved the trial of judge Otto Kerner, and *United States* v. *Archer*, 355 F. Supp. 981 (S.D. N.Y. 1972).

123. *Craig* v. *Harney*, 331 U.S. 367, 374 (1947); see also, *Sheppard* v. *Maxwell*, 384 U.S. 333, 350 (1966); *Estes* v. *Texas*, 381 U.S. 532 541-42 (1965).

124. *United States* v. *Dickinson*, 465 F.2d 496, 500 (5th Cir. 1972); *on remand*, 349 F. Supp. 227 (E.D. La. 1972), *aff'd*, 476 F.2d 373, *cert. denied*, 414 U.S. 979 (1973).

125. *Id.*, 465 F.2d at 500.

126. *Sun Company of San Bernardino* v. *Superior Court*, 29 Cal. App. 2d 815, 830; 105 Cal. Rptr. 873, 884 (4th Dist. 1973); see also, *Younger* v. *Smith*, 30 Cal. App.3d 143, 106 Cal. Rptr. 225 (2d Dist. 1973).

127. *Phoenix Newspapers Inc.* v. *Superior Court*, 101 Ariz. 257, 418 P.2d 594, 596 (1966).

128. *Times-Picayune Pub. Co.* v. *Schulingkamp*,——U.S.——, 43 Law Week 2046 (July 29, 1974).

129. *Azbill* v. *Fisher*, 442 P.2d 916 (Nev. Sup. Ct. 1968).

130. See, *e.g.*, *Marshall* v. *United States*, 360 U.S. 310 (1959); *Sheppard* v. *Maxwell*, 384 U.S. 333 (1966.)

131. *State ex rel. Superior Court of Snohomish County* v. *Sperry*, 79 Wash.2d 69, 483 P.2d 608 (1971); see also, *Freedom of Information Center Report No. 277, Sequester the Country* (Feb. 1972), pp. 7-9.

132. 483 P.2d at 612.

133. See, *e.g.*, *People* v. *Lambright*, 61 Cal.2d 482, 393 P.2d 409 (1964).

134. *Sun Company of San Bernadino* v. *Superior Court*, 29 Cal. App.3d 815, 105 Cal. Rptr. 873 (4th Dist. 1973).

135. *Johnson* v. *Simpson*, 433 S.W.2d 644 (Ky. 1968); see also, *State* v. *Morrow*, 57 Ohio App. 30, 11 N.E.2d 273 (Court of Appeals, 1937).
136. See generally, Note, *Juvenile Delinquents: The Police, State Courts, and Individualized Justice*, 79 Harv. L. Rev. 775, 794 (1966).
137. *Government of the Virgin Islands* v. *Brodhurst*, 285 F. Supp. 831, 833 (D.V.I. 1968).
138. *Id.* at 838.
139. *In re Gault*, 387 U.S. 1, 24-25 (1967).
140. See M. A. Franklin, *A Constitutional Problem in Privacy Protection: Legal Inhibitions on Reporting of Fact*, 16 Stan. L. Rev. 107, 121 (1963).
141. *Cox Broadcasting Co.* v. *Cohn*, 231 Ga. 60. 200 S.E.2d 127 (1973).
142. *Sheppard* v. *Maxwell*, 384 U.S. 333, 353 (1966).
143. *Schuster* v. *Bowen*, 347 F. Supp. 319, 322 (D. Nev. 1972).
144. *Wood* v. *Goodson*, 485 S.W. 2d 213, 216 (Sup. Ct. Ark. 1972).
145. *In re San Francisco Chronicle*, 1 Cal.2d 630, 36 P.2d 369 (1934).
146. *United States* v. *Dickinson* 465 F.2d 496 (5th Cir. 1972).
147. 465 F.2d at 511.
148. *Id.* at 512.
149. *In re Oliver*, 452 F.2d 111 (7th Cir. 1971).
150. *State ex rel. Superior Court of Snohomish County* v. *Sperry*, 483 P.2d 608, 611 (Wash. Sup. Ct. 1971).
151. *United States* v. *Schiavo*, ——F.2d—— (3rd Cir. 1974) (en banc).
152. 18 U.S.C. Section 401, see *Seymour* v. *United States*, 373 F.2d 629 (5th Cir. 1967).
153. Rule 42 (b), Federal Rules of Criminal Procedure.
154. See, *e.g., In re Acuff*, 331 F. Supp. 819 (D.N.M. 1971).
155. *United States* v. *CBS*, 497 F.2d 102 (5th Cir. 1974).

VI

Libel and Invasion of Privacy

Of all the areas of the law which may touch upon a reporter's activities, none is so deeply rooted in legal history and so thoroughly regulated by the courts as the law of defamation, encompassing both libel and slander. Nor does any legal subject have so pervasive an impact on a reporter's daily work. Hardly a news story is written which does not potentially implicate the elaborate system of legal rules governing defamation.

An exhaustive survey of those rules—which are created by state law to protect individuals against damage to reputation by reporters or anyone else—is beyond the purpose of this chapter. Rather, the general contours affecting reporters will be described, as the background against which to explain how the First Amendment has come to limit the application of those rules.[1]

In 1964, the Supreme Court virtually revolutionized the law of defamation. Prior to then, it had been held that defamatory statements were beyond the protection of the First Amendment, and the states generally fashioned their defamation rules however they chose. And while reporters were given some protections—for example, the right fairly and accurately to report defamatory statements made during the course of a public proceeding—such defenses were not available as a matter of constitutional law. A defamatory statement was legally presumed to be false. And although truth was a defense to a defamation charge, the

169

burden of proof was on the defendant, and in some states even truthful statements had to be made with pure motives.

New York Times Co. v. *Sullivan*[2] changed all that. For the first time, the Supreme Court ruled that defamatory statements were not automatically denied the protection of the First Amendment. Nor did the availability of the defense of truth provide sufficient protection for the press. Even false statements of a defamatory nature had to receive some protection so that people would not have to speak or write at the risk of being unable to prove the truth of their remarks in court. So long as the defamatory statements were made about a public official and related to his official conduct, then the official could not recover a damage judgment unless he could prove that the statement was made with "actual malice"—that is, with knowledge that it was false or with reckless disregard of whether it was false or not.[3] It must be remembered that "actual malice" is a term of art which has absolutely nothing to do with bad motives, spite, ill-will, or any other attribute of malice in the popular sense of that term. Rather, it means actually knowing a statement is false or having a total disregard of whether or not it is false.

Subsequently, the protection was expanded, with the application of the "actual malice" rule to defamation suits brought not just by public officials, but also by "public figures" as well. And for a brief time, from 1971 to 1974, the "actual malice" rule was further extended to include suits by private persons who happened to be caught up momentarily in an event "of public or general interest."

But in 1974, a decade after the *Times* decision, the Supreme Court once again fundamentally altered the law of defamation in a decision which withdrew press protection in some ways, while extending it in others. In *Gertz* v. *Robert Welch, Inc.*[4] the Court retreated from its 1971 ruling, which had applied the "actual malice" doctrine to reporting about matters of public or general interest. While the *Times* "actual malice" requirement is still applicable in suits by "public persons"—i.e., public officials and public figures—it no longer protects a reporter from liability in a suit by an ordinary private citizen.

At the same time, however, the Court strengthened press protection in several ways. First, when the press is sued by anyone who is not a "public person," the plaintiff can no longer win the suit merely by showing he was defamed. Now he must also show that the press acted negligently, i.e., carelessly, in publishing the defamatory statement. And where the defamatory nature of the statement is not apparent from its content, the plaintiff may even have to prove more than just negligence. Second, where the defamation is only the result of negligence, and not a product of "actual malice," a private individual must prove he suffered actual injury in order to recover any damages; state laws can no longer allow the existence of injury and damages to be presumed. Similarly, unless the private individual can prove he was defamed with "actual malice," there can no longer be any recovery of punitive, damages, i.e., damages designed to punish the press.

Thus, in the absence of "actual malice," the press still cannot be successfully sued by public persons at all, and are liable to private individuals only to the extent that such persons can prove that the press acted negligently and that the person actually suffered damages as a result of the defamation.

A reporter should therefore be concerned with (1) whether the statement is obviously defamatory, (2) whether the subject of the statement is a "public person," and (3) whether the potential plaintiff can prove that the statement was false and made with "actual malice," in the case of "public persons," or carelessly, in the case of private individuals.

Finally, another problem to be concerned with is invasion of privacy. While the traditional law of defamation has been increasingly restricted by the First Amendment, the more recently developed right of privacy has been expanding.[5] And in some recent lower court cases, it has been found to override a claim of press freedom, a defense of truth, and a lack of "actual malice."

As a procedural matter, libel or invasion-of-privacy

suits can be filed in either the state or the federal court. In either situation, the relevant state law will govern, except insofar as First Amendment limitations are applied.

What is a defamatory statement?

Traditionally, a defamatory statement has been defined as one which tends to hold the plaintiff up to hatred, contempt, or ridicule or to cause him to be shunned or avoided. Dean William L. Prosser believes that this traditional definition does not accurately reflect the wide variety of statements which have been held to be defamatory:

Defamation is rather that which tends to injure "reputation" in the popular sense; to diminish the esteem, respect, goodwill or confidence in which the plaintiff is held, or to excite adverse, derogatory or unpleasant feelings or opinions against him. It necessarily, however, involves the idea of disgrace. . . .[6]

The precise definition of defamation can vary from state to state, but will generally follow these guidelines.

In addition to this general description of defamation, the law has developed certain categories of statements which were deemed to be automatically ("per se") defamatory. Under the traditional common law, (1) calling a woman (more recently men were included) "unchaste" or (2) stating that a person had a "loathesome" disease came under this category. Of more relevance to most reporters are the other two categories of automatic defamation: (3) accusing a person of criminal conduct punishable by imprisonment (unless the conduct is trivial) and (4) charging a person with conduct, characteristics, or qualities incompatible with the proper conduct of his business, profession, or public office.[7]

The latter category is the most open-ended. In general it encompasses any charge that an individual is dishonest, incompetent, or mentally ill, since such attributes are always relevant to a person's capacity to perform his responsibilities. Senator Barry Goldwater successfully sued publisher Ralph Ginzburg because under New York law "a false accusation of insanity, mental imbalance, or mental disease, is libelous per se. . . ."[8] Beyond that, specific examples of defamation affecting a person's professional responsibilities have included the following:

. . . to say of a physician that he is a butcher . . . of an attorney that he is a shyster, of a school teacher that he has been guilty of improper conduct as to his pupils, of a clergyman that he is the subject of scandalous rumors, of a chauffeur that he is habitually drinking, of a merchant that his credit is bad or that he sells adulterated goods, of a public officer that he has accepted a bribe or has used his office for corrupt purposes, or that he is a Communist, or of any of these that he is dishonest, incompetent or insane—since these things obviously discredit him in his chosen calling.[9]

It is important to remember that in order for such charges to be per se defamatory, they must be relevant to the person's job responsibilities. However, even a charge without such relevance can nevertheless be defamatory, just not automatically so. The distinction can be explained as follows: calling a public official a Communist is defamatory per se, because it presumably reflects poorly on his ability to discharge his responsibilities; calling an engineer a Communist might be defamatory, but not automatically.[10] Similarly, epithets such as "bigot" are not automatically defamatory; however, saying that about a white merchant in a black neighborhood would present a different situation.[11] Also, characterizing a businessman's proposal as "blackmail" or a non-union member as a "traitor" is deemed non-defamatory rhetorical hyperbole.[12]

What is the difference between a statement that is defamatory per se and one which is not?

Prior to the *Gertz* decision, the difference between statements which were automatically defamatory and those which were not was crucial. In the former situation, damage to reputation ("general damages") was presumed to exist and the plaintiff did not have to allege or prove that pecuniary damages were actually suffered; in the latter case, the plaintiff could not win without proving actual harm. Now, unless the defamatory statement was made with "actual malice," the plaintiff must prove that he suffered "actual damages," regardless of whether the statement was automatically defamatory. Actual damages can no longer be presumed. Examples of actual damages can include, in addition to out-of-pocket losses (loss of salary, etc.), "impairment of reputation and standing in the community, personal humiliation, and mental anguish and suffering."[13]

In addition to requiring plaintiffs to prove some injury in order to receive compensatory or actual damages, the Supreme Court also limited the power of juries to impose "punitive" damages, i.e., damages designed to punish the defendant as an example to others. Now, such damages cannot be awarded at all, unless the defamatory statement was knowingly false or written with reckless disregard for the truth.

What is the difference between libel and slander?

Libel is any defamatory statement which is in written or other permanent form, while slander is any defamatory remark which is spoken. Libel rules are much more favorable to the plaintiff than slander rules. This seems to reflect the notion that something committed to writing evidences a greater intent to make the remarks and also has a more lasting impact. Spoken words tend to be both more spontaneous and evanescent.[14]

With regard to radio and television, these distinctions have resulted in the prevailing rule that defamatory remarks based upon a prepared script are treated as libel, while defamatory words uttered extemporaneously are treated as slander.[15] Thus, most reporters will be concerned with statements in the libel category.

Under the traditional common law, the major practical difference between libel and slander was that the slander plaintiff had to prove actual damages in situations where the libel plaintiff did not. But the *Gertz* decision, requiring proof of actual damages in most cases, minimizes many of these distinctions.

Does the defamatory meaning have to be apparent from the content of the statement?

No. Defamatory meaning can be shown by extrinsic facts which transform a seemingly innocuous statement into a libelous one. One of the more famous examples was an advertisement identifying the plaintiff as a butcher who sold a particular brand of bacon. Of course, it turned out that he was a Kosher butcher, and the courts upheld his libel claim.[16] But in such situations, courts occasionally required proof of actual damages as a prerequisite to recovery. Also, the *Gertz* decision seems to indicate that where the defamation is not apparent on the face of the statement, the plaintiff may be required to show more than just negligence on the part of the reporter.

Who can be defamed?

Any living person, but not one who has died. However, statements about a dead person which defame a living person are actionable (e.g., "John Smith, who died yesterday, had a long-standing relationship with his sister"). Corporations and other organized groups can sue for defamation.[17] Whether unincorporated associations can sue is unsettled.

In a related area, there probably can be no punishment, civil or criminal, for libeling the government or any of its agencies.[18] Similarly many states prohibit "group" libel, that is, derogatory remarks about any ethnic group. Although such a law was upheld by the Supreme Court in 1952, it is extremely doubtful that the application of such laws would be allowed today.[19]

How precisely does the defamatory statement have to refer to the plaintiff?

In traditional libel law, the plaintiff had to show that the statement was made and understood as "of and concerning" him. If the plaintiff is identified by name then there is no difficulty. But what if he is not? In the *Times* case, the challenged statement simply referred to actions taken by the "police" in Birmingham, Alabama, and made no explicit reference to the plaintiff, who was in charge of the police department. The official and his witnesses contended that because of his position, the criticism of police action was understood to have been directed at him. The Supreme Court rejected this theory:

We hold that such a proposition may not constitutionally be utilized to establish that an otherwise impersonal attack on governmental operations was a libel of an official responsible for those operations.[20]

Two years later, this principle was applied in a lawsuit brought by the former head of a public recreation agency. The article in question made no mention of the previous regime, but simply asked "What happened to all the money last year?"[21] The Court ruled that the jury could not find a reference to the official "merely on the basis of his relationship to the governmental agency, the operations of which were the subject of discussion."[22]

However, it is possible to make a defamatory statement about a group of people in such a manner that any member of that group could bring suit. The matter tends to depend on the size of the group and the quantitative nature of the reference. To say that "some" members of a nine-man city council are on the take would probably allow all to sue; if the council had twenty-five members, probably no one could sue.[23] "Most lawyers are shysters" does not defame any particular lawyer.

The rule turns on whether it is reasonable to interpret

the statement as specifically referring to the plaintiff. And if the status of the plaintiff brings the case within the *Times* rule, greater proof of reference will be required.

Who is legally responsible for defamatory statements?

Technically, everyone who participates in the particular enterprise—from the reporter, up through the editorial staff, to the publisher—is legally responsible for any defamatory statement which results. As a practical matter, however, suits are usually brought against the corporate entity, although sometimes the individuals are also named as defendants.[24]

Can the publication of a defamatory statement be enjoined in advance?

No. One of the most important Supreme Court cases on prior restraint involved an effort to enjoin publication of a "malicious, scandalous and defamatory" newspaper. The Court invalidated the injunction, holding that prior restraints contained the very essence of forbidden censorship.[25] The appropriate remedy is a post-publication suit for damages.

Can a reporter be held liable for simply repeating or quoting a defamatory statement made by someone else?

Yes. The traditional rule is that the repetition of a defamatory statement can itself be defamatory. A newspaper "may not defend a libel suit on the ground that the defamatory statements are not its own."[26] Thus, liability cannot be automatically avoided simply by quoting someone else:

The mere fact that a particular defamatory statement made by the media did not originate with them but was picked up from a usually reliable source, such as police comments, hospital records, or a wire service, does not in itself preclude liability. One who repeats defamatory material is just as liable as the originator.[27]

As one court has put it: "Repetition of another's words does not release one of responsibility if the repeater knows that the words are false or inherently improbable, or there are obvious reasons to doubt the veracity of the person quoted or the accuracy of his reports."[28]

However, this principle is qualified in two important respects. First, if the original statement itself was "privileged," for example, made during testimony given in a court proceeding, then the press has a right to report the statement. Second, reliance on a reputable source such as a news service will usually preclude a finding that the reporter acted with "actual malice" in repeating the statement.

In general, what are the different kinds of defenses available in a defamation suit?

Defenses to a defamation suit fall into two categories: absolute and partial. Absolute defenses completely preclude liability. Truth is an absolute defense. Partial defenses do not go to the issue of liability, but rather seek to mitigate the amount of damage which the defendant must pay.

"Privilege" (i.e., the claim that the person had a right or obligation to make the defamatory statement) is also a complete defense. It too falls into two categories: "absolute" or "qualified." An absolute privilege usually cannot be defeated. For example, any defamatory statement made in the course of judicial proceedings and relating to the subject of those proceedings is absolutely privileged, as are any such statements made by a high government official acting "within the outer perimeter" of his duties.[29] "Qualified" privileges can be lost if the person making the statement exceeds the purposes for which the privilege is afforded, or if the statements are published with improper motives. For example, there is a qualified privilege to make defamatory statements in connection with employee-evaluation reports, but the privilege would be lost if a derogatory evaluation were circulated throughout the office.[80] Similarly, there is a qualified privilege for defamatory statements made between an employee and his superior and relating to their common enterprise. That is why a defamatory statement contained in the draft of a story but eliminated by the editor does not give rise to a lawsuit even though there has been a "publication" of the defamation from the writer to the editor. Most of the expansion of the rights of the press has come in this area, with a strengthening of these "qualified" privileges.

Is truth always a defense to a defamation suit?

Yes. The truth of the statement is an absolute defense in almost all cases.[31] While a few states still require that a truthful statement of a defamatory nature must be published with good motives or for justifiable ends,[32] as a practical matter truth remains a complete defense. The traditional common law rule was that any defamatory statement was presumed to be false, with a burden of proof on the reporter to show that it was true. But the *New York Times* case turned that rule around, and now, if a defamatory statement comes within the *Times* rule, the plaintiff has the burden of proving that the statement was false. It is uncertain whether the plaintiff must prove the statement false by a preponderance of the evidence ("more probable than not") or by the more rigorous standard of "clear and convincing."[33] But the statement need not be absolutely true; if it is "substantially" true, that is sufficient.[34]

Can you report defamatory statements made during or in connection with judicial, legislative, or executive proceedings?

Yes. Almost all states recognize a conditional privilege for news media to report false and defamatory statements originally published in judicial, administrative, or legislative proceedings and records, if the account is fair and accurate and not published solely to harm the person defamed.[35] In such situations, the original speaker had an absolute privilege to make the defamatory statements, and the reporter has a qualified privilege to report those statements. The theory is that the reporter is a surrogate of the public at large, exercising its right to attend and observe such proceedings or obtain such reports. Most crime reporting is made possible by virtue of this privilege.[36] However, the report must be fair and accurate as to what was said in the proceeding or contained in the document, and you must clearly indicate that the source of the statement was an official proceeding or report.[37] Although the privilege has usually been limited to *official* proceedings, recently some courts have ruled that it also covers statements made during any *public* meeting, official or not.[38]

While the right to report about legislative and administrative proceedings is clear, there is some uncertainty about the precise time when the privilege to report judicial proceedings or documents comes into play. In most states, some judicial action must be taken with regard to the matter before the privilege can be invoked; it is not sufficient that a complaint containing defamatory statements has simply been filed in a clerk's office. However, some states do allow reporting of public court documents and pleadings as soon as the case has been filed.[39] But the privilege to report judicial records and proceedings is limited to matters which are public. Thus, where a reporter repeats statements contained in sealed documents or made during closed judicial sessions, the privilege defense might be defeated.[40] Theoretically, this rule might also be applied to the reporting of defamatory statements made in non-judicial secret documents or proceedings.

Does a reporter have the right to state defamatory opinions on matters of public interest?

Yes. The common law developed the doctrine of "fair comment" on matters of public interest. The rule turned on the distinction between statements of the fact and expressions of opinion or criticism. And although the line between fact and opinion was frequently hard to define, there was nevertheless a qualified privilege to express defamatory opinions.

As initially developed, the doctrine had two components: literary or artistic criticism, and comments about public officials and affairs. Now, the "fair comment" privilege has a broader scope:

Traditionally, privileged comment has concerned persons, institutions, or groups who have voluntarily injected themselves into the public scene or affect the community's welfare, such as public officials, political candidates, community leaders from the private sector or private enterprises which affect public welfare, persons taking a public position on a matter of public concern, and those who offer their creations for public approval such as artists, performers, and athletes.[41]

The literary-criticism privilege allows the reporter to make the most excessive and hostile kinds of comments about a book, painting, or performance. But the critic cannot misstate facts about the nature or content of the work, and while the credentials of the author or performer can be challenged, the individual cannot be attacked personally.[42]

The rule allowing fair comment about the conduct of public officials had a more complicated genesis. The traditional rule, followed in most states, allowed defamatory opinion about the conduct of public officials or the qualifications of candidates for public office, but required that the facts upon which the opinion was based had to be true or else the privilege would be lost.[43] But there was a minority rule which took a different approach. Criticism about public affairs was deemed so important that it could not be made to depend on the truth of the facts expressed or relied upon as the basis for the criticism. Instead, even factually untrue criticism had to be protected, so long as the writer honestly believed that statement was true.[44]

What the Supreme Court did in 1964 was to adopt the minority rule, elevate it to constitutional stature, and expand the "fair comment" doctrine to encompass defamatory statements of fact as well as defamatory expressions of opinion. The traditional common-law privilege of fair comment on matters of public interest has thus provided the vehicle for today's rule which allows false and defamatory reporting about any public person—so long as the reporter honestly believes the defamatory statement is true.

Can a reporter successfully be sued for making or reporting false and defamatory statements about a public official's conduct of his responsibilities?

No, unless the official can prove with "convincing clarity" that "the statement was made with 'actual malice'—that is, with knowledge that it was false or with reckless disregard of whether it was false or not."[45] That is the doctrine of *New York Times* v. *Sullivan* which dramatically changed the law of defamation as it affects reporters. Ironically, this landmark decision did not even involve reporters. Instead, it arose out of an advertisement placed in the *New York Times* by a group of well-known civil-rights supporters. The ad, headlined "Heed Their Rising Voices," was a description of the civil-rights struggle in various parts of the South and an appeal for funds. It did not even mention Mr. Sullivan, who was chief of police in Birmingham, Alabama, but simply charged that the police there "ringed" the campus of a black college, and padlocked the dining hall in order to starve the protesting students. The statements were not accurate, and Sullivan sued four sponsors who organized the ad and the *Times* for publishing it. In the state courts the case was decided on traditional defamation rules, including the doctrine that defamatory "fair comment" on the conduct of public officials had to be based on true facts. A jury award of $500,000 damages was upheld.

The Supreme Court reversed. The reasoning was as follows: (1) the mere fact that a statement is libelous does not make constitutional protections irrelevant; (2) uninhibited debate on public issues and the conduct of public affairs is at the core of First Amendment values; (3) erroneous statements are an inevitable element of such discussion; (4) punishing unintentionally false statements about public officials through defamation judgments will deter all communications except those which can be proven true in court; and (5) being subject to harsh criticism comes with the territory of public office.[46] Accordingly, neither factual error nor defamatory content, nor the combination of the two, justifies removing the constitutional shield from criticism of official conduct.

Thus, the theory is that false statements must be protected not so much because they have value in themselves, but in order to give some breathing space to true statements. The availability of truth as a defense was held to provide inadequate protection; instead a defense "for erroneous statements honestly made" was essential. And the same conditional privilege was to be applied not just to "honest misstatements of fact" but also to "honest expression of opinion" based upon them.[47] Only where the factual statements were made with "actual malice" could there be liability. Nor could the existence of "actual malice" be presumed by virtue of the defamatory nature of the statement. Instead, the plaintiff had the burden of proving that the statement was made "with knowledge that it was false or with reckless disregard of whether it was false or not." As will be shown later, this is a burden which few plaintiffs have met. Whether plaintiffs who are private individuals will more easily prove negligence under the new *Gertz* standard remains to be seen.

Finally, "misleading euphemisms" aside, what the *Times* rule "ultimately protects is defamatory falsehood."[48] The leeway is necessary to safeguard First Amendment interests. But reporters must remember that the consequences of this privilege will often include uncompensated damage to someone's reputation and must insure that such consequences are occasioned only by the broader purposes underlying the rule.

Can a reporter be criminally punished for making false, defamatory statements about public officials' conduct of office?

No, the *New York Times* doctrine limits criminal responsibility in the same way that it limits civil liability.

The point was made in a decision involving the criminal libel conviction of former New Orleans district attorney Jim Garrison, who publicly accused various local judges of being lazy, inefficient, and subject to racketeer influences. The Supreme Court ruled that a prosecution for criminal libel of public officials could not be treated any differently than a civil lawsuit by those same officials. Accordingly, the state could not decree that the defense of truth required "good motives" and could be defeated if the truthful statements were made with "malice in the sense of ill-will."[49] So long as there was no "actual malice," then an intent to inflict harm by making the statement was irrelevant.

Who is a "public official" for purposes of the rule?

Since the purpose of the "public official" privilege is to encourage debate and reporting about public issues and the conduct of government, the Court has described public officials as "those persons who are in a position significantly to influence the resolution of those issues. . . . Those responsible for government operations . . . those among the hierarchy of government employees who have, or appear to the public to have, substantial responsibility for or control over the conduct of governmental affairs."[50] Based

upon these standards, the Court has treated the following
as public officials: a mayor, a trial judge, a commissioner
of public affairs, a county attorney, a police chief, a dep-
uty sheriff, an elected court clerk, and all candidates for
elective public office.[51]

Whether the "public official" rule applies to every public
employee is less clear. In 1966, the Court suggested that
some lines must be drawn, depending on whether the position is of such apparent importance that ". . . the public
has an independent interest in the qualifications and performance of the person who holds it, beyond the general
public interest in the qualifications and performance of all
government employees. . . ."[52] Thus, presumably a clerk-
typist could not be gratuitously singled out for defamatory
attention unless the employee were involved in some
newsworthy event. However, in the *Gertz* case, the court
suggested that one factor in determining who is a public
official is whether the person holds "a remunerative governmental position."

One final observation: lawyers are not automatically
"public officials" just because they are characterized as
"officers of the court."[53] Indeed, the plaintiff in *Gertz* was
a lawyer, and the Supreme Court specifically rejected the
argument that his appearance at an administrative proceeding or his status as an officer of the court rendered
him a public official for this purpose.

Does it matter whether the public official is still in office when the story is published?

No, the *Times* doctrine is applicable to stories about individuals no longer in office, if the subject matter of the
story is "still a matter of lively public interest"; however,
". . . there may be cases where a person is so far removed
from a former position of authority that comment on the
manner in which he performed his responsibilities no longer has the interest necessary to justify the *New York
Times* rule."[54] In that case, suit was brought by the former
head of a public recreation area because of a story which

praised the new administration and by implication criticized the former officials. Since the running of the agency was still a matter of some public concern, comments about the former official were held to be protected.

What kinds of matters relate to the "official conduct" of a public official?

The general rule is that ". . . anything which might touch on an official's fitness for office" is relevant to his official conduct and brings the statement within the *Times* rule.[55] Charges of dishonesty, malfeasance, or improper motivation in the conduct of public business are always matters of public concern, and charges of criminal conduct are always relevant to fitness for office. In a case where a candidate for nomination as a United States Senator was described in a syndicated column as a "former small-time bootlegger," the Court stated:

We therefore hold as a matter of constitutional law that a charge of criminal conduct, no matter how remote in time or place, can never be irrelevant to an official's or a candidate's fitness for office for purposes of the application of the "knowing falsehood or reckless disregard" rule of New York Times Co. v. Sullivan.[56]

Also, the fact that the subject matter of a story is "only of local interest" does not matter, so long as the publication is "addressed primarily to the interested community."[57]

Nor is it a prerequisite that the story charging criminal conduct identify the person as a public official. In one case, a newspaper ran a story stating that a particular person had been charged with perjury in a federal court. The man was a mayor and a candidate in an election, which he subsequently lost. The story was false; it was the man's brother who had been charged. Nevertheless the Court ruled that the case came within the *Times* rule and suggested that the story's failure to identify the public office held was irrelevant.[58]

Finally, the Court has rejected the argument that criticism of public officials which reflects on their personal integrity can be considered as "purely private defamation": "Of course, any criticism of the manner in which a public official performs his duties will tend to affect his private, as well as his public, reputation. The New York Times rule is not rendered inapplicable merely because an official's private reputation, as well as his public reputation is harmed."[59]

But this does not necessarily mean that *any* statement about a public official automatically relates to his official conduct, responsibilities, or fitness for office. The Court has expressly left open the questions of "purely private libels, totally unrelated to public affairs" and of whether "there remains some exiguous area of defamation against which a candidate may have full recourse."[60] And while indicating that a candidate for office places "every conceivable aspect of his public and private life" before the voters,[61] the court has also declared that "some aspects of the lives of even the most public men fall outside the area of matters of public or general concern," implying that defamatory reporting about intimate marital or sexual matters might not come within the protection of the *Times* rule.[62]

Is the New York Times rule limited to statements about public officials?

No. The doctrine applies as well to stories about "public figures." The question was decided, although not conclusively, as a result of separate libel actions brought by two well-known individuals.[63] Wally Butts, a respected football coach and the Athletic Director at the University of Georgia (a position not publicly funded) sued the *Saturday Evening Post* over an article charging that he conspired to fix a game against the University of Alabama. General Edwin Walker, a conservative political figure, sued the Associated Press for a news dispatch which suggested that he was encouraging the violent resistance to integration of the University of Mississippi. In four separate opinions, and by a narrow vote of 5 to 4, the Supreme Court ruled that defamation actions brought by such public figures were governed by the same "actual malice" requirement as suits by public officials. The minority took the position that reporters had to be more careful when writing about public figures. In their view, public figures could recover damages "for a defamatory falsehood whose substance makes substantial danger to reputation apparent, on a showing of highly unreasonable conduct constituting an extreme departure from the standards of investigation and reporting ordinarily adhered to by responsible publishers" —a less rigorous test than "actual malice."[64] Based on the particular standard they thought applicable, five Justices felt that Wally Butts had proven his case, while all Justices ruled that General Walker had not. The judgment in favor of Butts is the only libel award which the Supreme Court has approved up to now.

Who comes within the description of a "public figure"?

The Supreme Court described coach Butts and General Walker as persons who "commanded a substantial amount of independent public interest" at the time the articles were written.[65] Dean Prosser has defined a "public figure" as "a person who, by his accomplishments, fame, or mode of living, or by adopting a profession or calling which gives the public a legitimate interest in his doings, his affairs, and his character, has become a 'public personage' . . . "a celebrity.' "[66] Traditionally, there was usually the implication of some affirmative action by the individual which focused public attention upon him or which projected him into the arena of public controversy.[67] And in general the "public figure" had to have occupied that status prior to and independent of the story in question before the public-figure privilege came into play.[68] In short, a public figure is "anyone who is famous or infamous because of who he is or what he has done."[69]

In applying these principles, courts have treated the following individuals as public figures: a prominent local real estate developer,[70] a famous, colorful attorney,[71] a Nobel Prize-winning scientist who actively campaigned against nuclear testing,[72] the author of a best-selling book,[73] an antiwar activist and writer,[74] a retired basketball player,[75] a former college basketball coach,[76] and a newspaper publisher who attempted to arouse public interest in a local issue.[77]

In *Gertz*, the court considered these issues at length and indicated that the person's voluntary quest for public notoriety was an important factor: "Hypothetically, it may be possible for someone to become a public figure through no purposeful action of his own, but the instances of truly involuntary public figures must be exceedingly rare."[78] Normally, two types of situations will exist. "In some instances an individual may achieve such pervasive fame or notoriety that he becomes a public figure for all purposes and in all contexts. More commonly, an individual voluntarily injects himself or is drawn into a particular public controversy and thereby becomes a public figure for a limited range of issues. In either case, such persons assume special prominence in the resolution of public questions."[79] Applying these principles to Elmer Gertz, the Supreme Court concluded he was not a "public figure." Although he had long been active in community affairs, serving as an officer in various civic and professional organizations, and was well known in some circles, "he had achieved no general fame or notoriety in the community." "We would not lightly assume that a citizen's participation in community and professional affairs rendered him a public figure for all purposes. Absent clear evidence of general fame or notoriety in the community, and pervasive involvement in the affairs of society, an individual should not be deemed a public personality for all aspects of his life." Turning to the particular matters which prompted the story about Gertz—the filing of a lawsuit against a police officer—the Court concluded that Gertz's participation in that event did not render him a public figure even in that context: "He plainly did not thrust himself into the vortex of this public issue, nor did he engage the public's attention in an attempt to influence its outcome."[80]

Do any statements about a public figure come within the Times rule?

Not necessarily. Before *Gertz*, courts suggested that the statements must relate to the qualities, characteristics, or conduct which elevated the person to the "public figure" status in the first place.[81] However, once a person has attained that status, it cannot easily be shed, even with the passage of time: "No rule of repose exists to inhibit speech relating to the public career of a public figure so long as newsworthiness and public interest attach to the events in such public career."[82] In one case, an article about Bill Russell, the basketball player, contained a quote describing the way Russell early in his career had "destroyed" an opposing player on the court. That player had retired nine years earlier, although he then went into coaching for several years. He sued over the article, and the court ruled that he was a public figure when the reported episode took place and had not lost that status in the interim. Since the story described him "in relation to a matter of legitimate public interest," the *Times* rule applied.[83] *Gertz* made it clear that there are two kinds of public figures: all-purpose and special-purpose. Those who achieve "pervasive fame or notoriety" become public figures for all purposes, and the actual malice rule applies to anything said about them. But, as to those who are public figures only as to certain matters, defamatory statements about them come within the *Times* rule only if they relate to those matters.

Is the New York Times rule limited to defamation suits brought by public officials or public figures?

It is now. In 1971, the Supreme Court expanded the protection of the press against defamation suits by "extend-

ing constitutional protection to all discussion and communication involving matters of public or general concern,
without regard to whether the persons involved are famous or anonymous."[84] The case involved a distributor of
nudist magazines who was arrested, and his magazines
seized, in connection with a police crackdown on obscenity. A local radio station, in its hourly news broadcast, reported the law enforcement campaign, the plaintiff's arrest, and the police claim that they had "hit the supply of
a main distributor of obscene material" in the city. After
his acquittal on obscenity charges, the distributor sued the
radio station, claiming that the magazines he sold were
perfectly legal. The Supreme Court held that the *Times*
rule applied even though the plaintiff was neither a public
official nor a public figure. "If a matter is a subject of
public or general interest, it cannot suddenly become less
so merely because a private individual is involved, or because in some sense the individual did not 'voluntarily'
choose to become involved. The public's primary interest
is in the event; the public focus is on the conduct of the
participant and the content, effect, and significance of the
conduct, not the participant's prior anonymity or notoriety."[85] Therefore, any reporting of "newsworthy" events
would come within the *Times* rule and require that persons falsely defamed in connection with such reporting
must prove actual malice in order to recover damages.

There were three dissenters who thought that the *Times*
rule had been taken too far.[86] In their view, the considerations present in the public-official or public-figure cases
were inapplicable to defamation suits brought by private
individuals who had not chosen to enter the public arena.
Their interest in reputation should be given more protection, and they should be allowed to recover damages
where the press had acted negligently, a less demanding
standard than "actual malice." The press could be protected in such cases by requiring that damage judgments be
limited to actual financial loss and that punitive damages
either bear some reasonable relationship to actual damages or be eliminated completely.

In *Gertz* these dissenting views became the law. *Gertz*

was an activist lawyer in Chicago who filed a civil lawsuit for the family of a youth killed by a policeman. The John Birch Society magazine subsequently ran an article contending there was a nationwide conspiracy against the police, mentioning the lawsuit and charging Gertz with being a "communist-fronter." Gertz brought suit and lost in the lower courts on the ground that the story involved a matter of public interest and thus the *Times* doctrine covered the case. The Supreme Court disagreed. It found sharp distinctions between public persons and private individuals in terms of the interests in reputation which state libel law protects. First, public figures and public officials have a much greater capacity to respond to defamatory charges since they "usually enjoy significantly greater access to channels of effective communication and hence have a more realistic opportunity to counteract false statements than private individuals enjoy." Second, and conversely, public persons, by entering their particular arena, "have voluntarily exposed themselves to increased risk of injury from defamatory falsehoods concerning them." In short, "private individuals are not only more vulnerable to injury than public officials and public figures; they are also more deserving of recovery." Finally, the majority was troubled by allowing courts and juries to determine what is a matter of public or general interest, i.e., what is newsworthy. Thus, the Court concluded that private individuals could be treated differently and could win libel suits by showing the press defamed them in a negligent or careless manner. But recovery will normally be limited in such cases to the actual damages suffered by such individuals.

What is a "matter of public or general concern"?

Before the *Gertz* decision altered the rule, the lower courts had attempted to identify the kinds of issues which constitute matters of public or general concern. In those decisions, the courts ruled that a wide variety of subjects were matters of public or general concern—for example, virtually all crime reporting about arrests, prosecutions, law enforcement activities, victims of crimes, and members of organized crime and their associates.[87] Similarly, stories about prison conditions which focus on individual inmates came within the old rule,[88] as did reporting about the private use of electronic eavesdropping devices,[89] off-brand religions,[90] policies of hotels,[91] the practices of medical laboratories,[92] efforts to influence the outcome of a foreign election,[93] and a sports article describing a lawsuit arising out of an unusually errant golf shot.[94]

As one court put it, ". . . the right of the public to know, and of the press to tell, is so deeply entrenched in the American conscience that a great deal of latitude must necessarily be afforded the media in its selection and presentation of news."[95]

What is "actual malice"?

So far the discussion has centered on what kinds of reporting about what kind of stories will require a plaintiff to prove that any false, defamatory statements were made with "actual malice." Now the focus shifts to what that term means and what kinds of failures by the reporter will enable a plaintiff to win the lawsuit. It should be noted that, depending on whether the subject of the story is a public or a private individual, reporting deficiencies which do not amount to actual malice under the *Times* rule, may constitute negligence or carelessness under the *Gertz* rule.

"Actual malice" encompasses two elements: (1) knowledge that a defamatory statement was false *or* (2) a reckless disregard of whether or not it was false. The first condition has been simply described as the "known lie," the "calculated falsehood" which is inconsistent with the purposes of the First Amendment.[96] Very few libel cases involve a claim that the reporter deliberately and knowingly published a false, defamatory statement about someone. Most litigation has centered on the "reckless disregard" standard, which the Supreme Court has described as "a high degree of awareness" of the "probable falsity" of the statement.[97] And it must be emphasized that this is not the traditional "reasonable man" standard of negligence law; it requires the plaintiff to prove substantially more than just negligence: "reckless conduct is not measured by whether a reasonably prudent man would have published, or would have investigated before publishing. There must be sufficient evidence to permit the conclusion that the defendant in fact entertained serious doubts as to the truth of his publication."[98] Now, however, negligence under the *Gertz* rule does become a factor, depending on who the plaintiff is.

The burden of proving actual malice is on the plaintiff, and it must be proven with "convincing clarity," a more demanding requirement than in the normal civil lawsuit. However, the reporter cannot automatically prevail simply by testifying that he honestly believed the statements were true:

The finder of fact must determine whether the publication was indeed made in good faith. Professions of good faith will be unlikely to prove persuasive, for example, where a story is fabricated by the defendant, is the product of his imagination, or is based wholly on an unverified anonymous telephone call. Nor will they be likely to prevail when the publisher's allegations are so inherently improbable that only a reckless man would have put them in circulation. Likewise, recklessness may be found where there are obvious reasons to doubt the veracity of the informant or the accuracy of his reports.[99]

In practice, most defamation cases are decided through the procedure of a motion for summary judgment (without a trial). The news organization turns its files over to the plaintiff, makes its reporters and editors available for depositions, and then, when this "discovery" process has concluded, moves for summary judgment on the ground that the plaintiff cannot show enough evidence of actual malice to justify taking the case to trial. And the plaintiff cannot defeat this motion simply by pointing to the possibility that skillful cross-examination at trial might produce favorable evidence. Courts have stressed the importance of the summary judgment procedure as a method of easing press burdens in defamation cases.[100]

Does ill will toward the subject of the story amount to actual malice?

No. While at common law the privilege to comment on public affairs could be defeated if the comment was made with ill will, bad motives, general hostility, or a desire to harm the plaintiff, the constitutional rule is the contrary.[101] Similarly, the fact that a particular reporter or editor has an ideological bias—for example, strident anti-Communism—is no evidence of actual malice.[102]

In short, actual malice involves the reporter's attitude toward the truth, not toward the plaintiff.

However, a publication's conscious effort to embark on a crusade of "sophisticated muckraking" or a reporter's expressed design to do a hatchet job on someone, might be evidence of actual malice.[103]

Does failure to investigate a statement or check the facts automatically make a reporter liable?

No, not under the *Times* rule. While a reasonable man would do so, that's not the standard. In the *New York Times* case, the plaintiff argued that all the paper had to do was check its own news files to see that the statements in the advertisement were false. The Court noted that the *Times* had published the ad without checking its accuracy, but ruled that the omission did not constitute "actual malice" in light of a reasonable reliance on the good reputation of the ad's sponsors.[104] Conversely, of course, extensive research and investigation by the reporter to support the story make it virtually impossible for the plaintiff to prove reckless disregard of the truth.

Under the new negligence standard for reporting about private individuals, the failure to check an obviously defamatory statement may result in liability.

Is a reporter obliged to check first with the subject of the statement in order to avoid liability?

That depends on who the subject is.

In the *Rosenbloom* case, the plaintiff argued that the failure to contact him, learn his side of the story, and examine the magazines he sold constituted a reckless disregard of the truth. The Court disagreed, holding that the failure to take such reasonable steps did not amount to culpability under the *Times* standard.[105] Nor is reckless disregard established because the reporter relies on information provided by people on only one side of the dispute.[106] Under the *Gertz* test, however, the plaintiff in *Rosenbloom* might win today, since the failure to investigate the other side of the story might be deemed unreasonable. Also, where the subject of the story contacts a reporter in advance and claims the story is false, the failure to investigate further might be strong evidence of actual malice or negligence.[107]

If your story is based on information from reasonably trustworthy sources, is that a defense to a charge of actual malice?

Yes, unless there is something inherently improbable about the information or obvious reason to doubt the truth of the report.

In the *Times* case, the advertising personnel "relied upon their knowledge of the good reputation of many of those whose names were listed as sponsors of the advertisement, and upon the letter from A. Phillip Randolph, known to them as a responsible individual, certifying that the use of the names was authorized."[108] Whether or not such reliance was reasonable, the Court held that it disproved the charge of actual malice. Reliance on information provided by law enforcement officials is valid,[109] as is reliance on wire service stories,[110] and on syndicated columnists, even occasionally inaccurate ones.[111] Verification of the information obtained from such sources is usually unnecessary.

If your sources are confidential ones, do you have to reveal them in order to defend the case?

Not necessarily. As indicated in Chapter II, the disclosure-of-sources question in the libel context is a thorny problem. Plaintiffs' attorneys argue: What is to prevent a reporter from making up defamatory statements, claiming they originated with confidential sources, and thus preventing the plaintiff from proving actual malice; or from publishing material which the source stated was of doubtful veracity? The answer, according to one federal appeals court, is not to allow disclosure of sources unless the plaintiff, based upon his access to all non-confidential files and sources, uncovers "substantial evidence tending to show that the [reporter's] published assertions are so inherently improbable that there are strong reasons to doubt the veracity of the defense informant or the accuracy of his reports. . . ."[112] However, the New Jersey courts have ruled, under their shield law, that a refusal to disclose sources requires a surrender of the defense of privilege. [113]

The issue threatens to pose problems for the foreseeable future. One possible solution in situations where the reporter refuses to disclose sources even to his editor is to employ a panel of experts to review the story and determine whether any of the factual assertions are inherently improbable. The Time-Life organization has employed this device in organized-crime stories with some success.[114]

Does reliance on the expertise of the reporter tend to disprove reckless disregard?

Yes. In several cases courts have pointed to editorial reliance on the reporter's experience as a factor rebutting evidence of actual malice. For example, in overturning a verdict against *Time* magazine, an appeals court noted that the reporter had worked for the magazine for four years and that his work was considered reliable by his editors.[115] Another appeals court has ruled that the "mere fact that a publisher fails to verify the accuracy of defamatory statements in an article submitted by an author whom he could reasonably assume to be trustworthy" is not sufficient to establish a reckless disregard for the truth.[116] However, the question of whether reckless disregard by a free-lance author, who is in effect an independent contractor, can be imputed to the publisher is still open.[117]

Does the story have to be reviewed by a lawyer to resist a charge of reckless disregard of the truth?

No. In one case involving a magazine article critical of the Universal Life Church, the magazine's table of contents used the term "Instant Minister Racket." The plaintiff argued that the failure of the magazine's attorneys to review the terms used in the table of contents was evidence of culpability, but the court rejected the contention and ruled for the magazine.[118]

Will minor inaccuracies or embellishments of the truth render you liable?

Probably not. The courts have afforded reporters a substantial amount of room for embellishment, minor inaccuracies or deviations from the truth, and use of rhetorical language. For example, where a reporter embellishes law enforcement characterizations of a criminal defendant, or misstates some minor detail about an arrest, or fictionalizes dialogue slightly, the courts have refused to find reckless disregard.[119] Using the term "hoodlums" is not evidence of culpability.[120] And describing a man as a "vicious criminal" on the basis of FBI reports that he was to be considered "armed and dangerous" was allowed,[121] as was the term "uncaged killer" employed on the basis of inferences from official records and statements.[122] Similarly, where a story described a businessman as a member of the Mafia, even though he only associated with such persons, the inaccuracy did not amount to reckless reporting.[123] But there are limits to this leeway, and the slanted use of materials or the reliance on quotations taken out of context will be deemed as evidence of reckless disregard.[124]

Does the omission of "alleged" in connection with crime reporting always amount to recklessness?

Not necessarily. In the *Rosenbloom* case, the Court ruled that the failure to characterize the confiscated magazines as "reportedly" or "allegedly" obscene did not demonstrate that the radio station in fact "entertained serious doubts" about the accuracy of its news reports of the plaintiff's arrest.[125] But this does not mean that the use of "alleged" is superfluous.

The question was explored at length in a libel case arising out of a *Time* magazine story about the release of a Civil Rights Commission Report of episodes of police brutality.[126] The Report described a Chicago police raid on a private home by quoting from the allegations in a civil lawsuit filed by the victims. The *Time* account described the episode but omitted the word "alleged," thus giving the impression that the description of the raid was the Commission's, not the victims'. The *Time* reporters had researched the story carefully and thought the statements were correct and reflected the Commission's conclusion; but they admitted that they had consciously omitted the word "alleged."

The lower court ruled that this deliberate omission was sufficient evidence of actual malice to send the case to the jury, but the Supreme Court disagreed. In its view there was a difference between reporting what someone has done and describing what a person or agency has said about what someone has done:

A press report of what someone has said about an underlying event of news value can contain an almost infinite variety of shadings. Where the source of the news makes bald assertions of fact—such as that a policeman has arrested a certain man on a criminal charge—there may be no difficulty. But where the source itself has engaged in qualifying the information released, complexities ramify. Any departure from full direct quotation of the words of the source, with all its qualifying language, inevitably confronts the publisher with a set of choices.[127]

Since the Commission Report was itself "extravagantly ambiguous" as to whether the facts stated were only allegations from one side of the controversy, the Court ruled that the reporter's deliberate "adoption of one of a number of possible rational interpretations" of an ambiguous document, "though arguably reflecting a misconception," was not enough to create liability.[128] But the Court added a "final cautionary note," warning reporters that the ruling applied only in the context of news reports of government publications like the Commission Report and that the decision did not make the word "alleged" "a superfluity in published reports of information damaging to reputation."[129]

What if materials in a reporter's files indicate that a statement or implication in a story is false?

If a reporter asserts that something is true even though his files contain contrary information, the court may find actual malice. The Supreme Court made this clear in an invasion-of-privacy case resulting from a magazine story about the opening of a new play. The article characterized the play as a reenactment of a true-life ordeal of a family victimized by three escaped convicts. In fact, the actual events were completely different from the depictions in the play, newsclips in the magazines files made this clear, and the magazine reporters were aware of the discrepancies. The Court ruled that a jury could reasonably find the existence of actual malice, and the case was sent back for a new trial.[130]

The same point was also made in separate lawsuits stemming from a photograph of several men sitting in a restaurant. The photo was part of a story about a meeting of "top Cosa Nostra hoodlums." Two of the men in the picture were lawyers who represented some of the others. But the article did not identify them as attorneys even though that information was in the magazine's "bio" files and had been included in the first draft of the story. The lawyers sued, and in both cases the appeals courts held that this evidence was enough to take the case to the jury.[131]

Is the amount of time available to prepare the story an important factor?

Yes. Where the story involves "hot news," courts are extremely reluctant to second-guess reporting techniques or editorial judgments. But the more time available to prepare the story, the more judicial scrutiny will be given to the investigatory and verification methods employed.[132]

Indeed, the few cases where liability for defamation has been imposed have almost all involved stories written without the pressure of deadlines.

What kinds of reporting deficiencies will result in a finding of actual malice?

Of the very few cases where courts have upheld a finding of "actual malice," two famous ones provide a handy checklist of what *not* to do.

The Wally Butts case is a good example. The *Saturday Evening Post* story described a conspiracy between Butts and another coach to fix a big game. The story was based on the claim by an Atlanta businessman that he had accidentally cut in on the telephone conversation and overheard the plan. Butts did not deny the conversation but contended that it consisted of general football talk. In affirming the judgment against the publisher, the Court pointed to the following factors: (1) the story was not "hot news": (2) the allegations were extremely damaging (indeed, the article concluded with the observation that "careers will be ruined, that is sure"); (3) the *Post* relied solely on the businessman's story, even though the editors knew he had a criminal record; (4) his notes of the conversation were not examined; (5) a person supposedly with him during the overheard conversation was not even interviewed; (6) the films of the "fixed" game were not viewed to determine whether the game followed the contours of the supposed conspiracy; (7) the writer was not a football expert and did not check with any; (8) even though Butts contacted the writers and claimed that the story about to be published was false, no additional inquiries or investigations were made; and (9) the story was part of the magazine's effort to change its image to one of "sophisticated muckraking."[133] By contrast, in the companion case, the jury verdict for General Walker was unanimously overturned because the reporting dealt with "news which required immediate dissemination" and came from a trustworthy correspondent on the scene.[134]

The other case where a libel judgment was upheld involved the effort by *FACT* magazine to demonstrate that Senator Barry Goldwater was psychologically unfit to be elected President.[135] A great deal of research was done, but only those statements derogatory to the Senator were used. A questionnaire was sent out to psychiatrists, under a highly slanted cover letter. The poll was not conducted in a scientific manner; a warning to that effect was ignored; the bulk of the responses were anonymous; and many of the replies were misleadingly reported. Numerous statements about episodes demonstrating mental instability were unsupported, and the conclusions were based on the publisher's non-expert evaluations. Based upon this evidence, the court said, the jury could have reasonably found "a predetermined and preconceived plan to malign the Senator's character."[136] In reaching this conclusion, the court ruled that reliance on and citation of source material does not insulate a reporter from liability where the material is taken out of context, or results in "misplaced emphasis, or exaggeration or distortion."[137] Moreover, as in the Wally Butts case, the article did not contain "hot news"; the charges were extremely serious, yet there was no thorough investigation; the writers were not psychiatric experts and none were consulted; and, despite warnings, improper polling techniques were employed. In short, the evidence showed "a possible pre-conceived plan to attack Senator Goldwater regardless of the facts."[138]

These cases demonstrate that although one or two lapses will rarely lead to a finding of actual malice, if defamatory falsehood has resulted from a combination of aggravating factors, the reporter may very well be held responsible.

What kind of reporting deficiencies will constitute negligence or carelessness?

The answer is unclear. The *Gertz* decision means that where defamatory statements are made about a private individual, and the defamatory nature of the statement is apparent from its content, the person defamed can win the case on a showing that the statements were made negligently. In traditional tort law, negligence is judged by the standard of the hypothetical "reasonable man"—for example, whether a reasonably prudent man would have investigated the statement before publishing it. In its libel decisions, the Supreme Court has indirectly indicated that the following reporting deficiencies may be found unreasonable or careless: failing to verify highly damaging assertions, relying instead on the reputation or credentials of the writer or reporter;[139] failing to check factual statements against materials in the news agency's files, especially where such materials indicate the statements are incorrect;[140] refusing to hear the subject's side of the story.[141]

It is also possible that testimony from comparably situated reporters, editors, and publishers will increasingly be sought out in order to establish what standards of investigation are adhered to by "reasonable" members of the press.[142]

Since much will depend on a particular jury's determination of whether reasonable efforts to investigate were made, there will be a great deal of uncertainty for some time to come.

What is the difference between defamation and invasion of privacy?

The essence of defamation is damage to a person's reputation by virtue of statements which engender a false opinion about him. In invasion of privacy, "the primary damage is the mental distress from having been exposed to public view, although injury to reputation may be an element bearing upon such damages."[143] While efforts to construct an encompassing definition of privacy continue, the original description still remains the best one: "the right to be let alone," to draw a line between one's self and the community.[144]

While redress for damage to reputation occasioned by defamatory statements developed gradually in the old common law, legal protection of the right of privacy is a relatively contemporary phenomenon. Its origin can be directly traced to a famous 1890 law review article co-authored by Louis D. Brandeis.[145] Ironically, the primary impetus for the article was the authors' reaction to excesses by the press:

The press is overstepping in every direction the obvious bounds of propriety and of decency. Gossip is no longer the resource of the idle and of the vicious, but has become a trade, which is pursued with industry as well as effrontery. . . . The intensity and complexities of life, attendant upon advancing civilization, have rendered necessary some retreat from the world, and man . . . has become more sensitive to publicity, so that solitude and privacy have become more essential to the individual. . . .[146]

Since then, the right to privacy has gained increasing recognition and is now protected by statute or judicial decision in most states.

What are the elements of the right to privacy?

Through statutes and judicial decisions, the right of privacy has actually come to encompass at least four identifiable categories which are usually, but not necessarily, distinct:

(1) appropriation of a person's name or likeness for the defendant's advantage (usually commercial);
(2) intrusion upon a person's seclusion or solitude or into his private affairs;
(3) publicity that places a person in a false light in the public eye; and
(4) public disclosure of embarassing private facts about an individual.[147]

"Appropriation," the first form of invasion of privacy to be afforded judicial and statutory recognition, gives the individual in effect "a species of trade name" in his identity or likeness.[148] Since it implies some element of commercial exploitation and usually excludes incidental mention of a person or publication of his photograph, this aspect of privacy is of only marginal concern to reporters.

The other three elements of privacy are extremely relevant. Liability for "intrusion" usually results from the methods of newsgathering which are employed, and publication is not a necessary element of the tort.[149] However, publication is the central feature of "false light" and "disclosure" invasions of privacy, and, by virtue of that fact, First Amendment protections are more available than with regard to "intrusion." Moreover, the three elements are not mutually exclusive, and one story can lead to multiple privacy claims. For example, in one recent case, a reporter and photographer went to the rural home of a widow whose husband had been killed in a bridge disaster, were let in the house by her young children, photographed the

untidy conditions in the home, and then reported the
rather pitiful plight of the family. The family sued for violation of privacy "by the intrusion of the newsman and
photographer, for unreasonable publicity about their private lives and for falsely presenting their condition and
making them objects of pity and ridicule.[150] Also, the
same story can result in both an invasion-of-privacy claim
and a defamation charge, which usually happens when
"false light" invasion of privacy is involved.

Is truth always a defense to invasion of privacy?

No. Truth is a defense only in the case of a "false light"
claim where the crux of the harm depends on the falsity
of the statement. Indeed, the main feature that distinguishes invasion of privacy from defamation is the general
unavailability of truth as a complete defense. In privacy
cases, particularly those involving disclosure of private
facts, the truth of the statement is the very essence of the
harm. Accordingly, under privacy law a reporter can be
found liable for printing a truthful, non-defamatory
story.[151]

If the story is newsworthy, is that a defense?

Usually, but not always. In general, the newsworthiness
of a story, statement, or photograph is a complete defense
to an invasion-of-privacy claim.[152] If the court finds the
item newsworthy, then the invasion of privacy is deemed
to have been justified by the public's right to know. Even
the originators of the right to privacy recognized this defense: "The right of privacy does not prohibit any publication of matter which is of public or general interest."[153] But
there are limits to this privilege, and in some situations
courts have upheld privacy claims even where the story involved truthful reporting of newsworthy events.[154] More
frequently, they have avoided the clash of interests by
concluding that the subject matter of the story in question

was not truly newsworthy and therefore the invasion of privacy was not privileged.[155]

What makes a story or a subject "newsworthy"?

The absence of a precise definition of what is "newsworthy" or "of public or general interest" may cause serious difficulties if that standard becomes the constitutional dividing line between protected reporting and invasion of privacy.[156] Some courts have explained the term as the function of three variables: (1) the social value of the facts communicated; (2) the depth of intrusion on privacy; and (3) the extent of voluntary accession to public notoriety.[157] Under such an approach, reporting about a person who is involuntarily the object of public attention—for example, the victim of a violent crime—probably has to be reasonably related to the event which focused the attention in the first place.[158] By the same token, stories about voluntary public figures can legitimately search out remote corners of the person's life, even where the subject has attempted to "cloak himself in obscurity."[159] However, even the most public person is entitled to protect some area of his private life. The distinction has been described as follows: "Revelations may be so intimate and so unwarranted in view of the victim's position as to outrage the community's notions of decency. But when focused upon public characters, truthful comments upon dress, speech, habits and the ordinary aspects of personality will usually not transgress this line."[160] Finally, all agree that a reporter cannot simply take an obscure individual involved in no event of public interest, and, by focusing attention on him, make that person involuntarily "newsworthy."[161]

In short, as against a claim of privacy, there is a general privilege to report truthfully about newsworthy persons or those involved in newsworthy events. But not everything will be deemed newsworthy, and not everything so characterized can be reported. Finally, overbearing

techniques of newsgathering may also constitute an unpro-
tected intrusion on privacy.

**Can a reporter be held liable for intruding upon some-
one's expectation of privacy while investigating a story?**

Possibly. This branch of the right of privacy protects
against intrusion upon a person's physical solitude or seclusion or his private affairs, usually in a way offensive or objectionable to the reasonable person.[162] Normally it involves
some invasion of private precincts of the home or office,
but occasionally can result from something which occurs
in public. Moreover, this aspect of privacy is available to
public persons no less than ordinary citizens; elements of
the claim have been invoked by Jacqueline Onassis, Ralph
Nader, and the late Senator Thomas Dodd.

A leading case arose out of articles about Senator Dodd
written by Drew Pearson and Jack Anderson. Some of
Dodd's staffers had copied documents from Dodd's files
and made them available to the columnists, who used the
materials in several articles. Since the information published was newsworthy, that was a defense to one aspect
of the privacy claim.[163] But Dodd also claimed an "intrusion" on his privacy by virtue of the rummaging of his
files. In theory, the court agreed:

We approve the extension of the tort of invasion of privacy
to instances of intrusion, whether by physical trespass or not,
into spheres from which an ordinary man in a plaintiff's position could reasonably expect that the particular defendant
should be excluded. Just as the Fourth Amendment has expanded to protect citizens from government intrusion where intrusion is not reasonably expected, so should tort law protect
citizens from other citizens.[164]

However, since the reporters themselves did not instigate
or participate in the intrusion, but only used the information they were given, there would be no liability for invasion of privacy.

In a more recent case, *Life* magazine reporters did not

fare so well. Through subterfuge, and in cooperation with the local district attorney, the reporters gained access to the home of a supposed "quack" healer and surreptitiously photographed and recorded one of the sessions. They were also on hand to photograph the man's arrest on charges of illegal practice of medicine. The whole episode was hardly an example of responsible journalism, and the court's distaste for the methods ("calculated misdeeds") was made apparent:

. . . we have little difficulty in concluding that clandestine photography of the plaintiff in his den and the recordation and transmission of his conversation without his consent resulting in his emotional distress warrants recovery for invasion of privacy in California.[165]

Although the plaintiff took the risk that his guests would repeat what they saw and heard, he should not be required to assume they would record and transmit it "in full living color and hi-fi to the public at large."[166] "The First Amendment is not a license to trespass, to steal or to intrude by electronic means into the precincts of another's home or office."[167] Bad cases make bad law.

Finally, if a reporter gains access to a person's home by misrepresenting the nature of the story being investigated, an intrusion of privacy claim may be sustained. In one case, a magazine cover story entitled "The White Majority" included a picture of the plaintiff standing in front of his typical suburban home complete with American flag. The article described the frequently prejudiced attitudes of Middle America. The man sued for invasion of privacy, claiming that the photographer had asked to take the picture for use in "a patriotic article" and also that his children had been cropped out of the photograph. The court held that the man could recover for invasion of privacy unless the magazine could prove that he had agreed to the use of the photograph in connection with the kind of article which actually ran.[168] However, where a photographer and reporter walked into a home when the mother was out, and were neither asked in by the children nor told to leave, the intrusion claim was rejected.[169] Apparently the absence of misrepresentation is a key factor.

Can a reporter cover, photograph, or interview any subject out in public?

Yes, unless the coverage becomes excessive or overbearing. "On the public street, or in any other public place, the plaintiff has no legal right to be alone; and it is no invasion of his privacy to do no more than follow him about and watch him there."[170]

But the principle has some limits. In a suit brought by Ralph Nader against General Motors, the New York Court of Appeals ruled that interviewing Nader's associates did not constitute an invasion of privacy, but that overzealous and constant surveillance of Nader, even in public places, might allow recovery: "A person does not automatically make public everything he does merely by being in a public place, and the mere fact that Nader was in a bank did not give anyone the right to try to discover the amount of money he was withdrawing."[171] The same point was reaffirmed in the litigation over the harassment of Jacqueline Onassis by "paparazzo" Ron Galella. Mrs. Onassis claimed that Galella's repeated efforts to photograph her and her family when they ventured into public constituted harassment and an invasion of privacy. The courts agreed: "Mrs. Onassis was properly found to be a public figure and thus subject to news coverage. . . . Nonetheless, Galella's action went far beyond the reasonable bounds of news gathering. When weighed against the *de minimus* public importance of the daily activities [of Mrs. Onassis], Galella's constant surveillance, his obtrusive and intruding presence, was unwarranted and unreasonable."[172]

These two cases are extreme, and the results make sense. But a very recent decision demonstrates that reporting techniques which are only mildly enthusiastic may still pose legal problems. The movie *Woodstock* contained a two-minute segment of a conversation with a workman cleaning portable toilets. Claiming that while he was going about his business, he had been drawn into the conversation without warning or consent, the man sued for invasion of privacy. The lower court threw the case out, but a federal appeals court reversed and sent the case back for trial. The majority reasoned that it was one thing to film the man "as he went about his duties at a newsworthy event and to include such photographs in a factual description of the event, but quite another thing to deliberately draw him out in conversation for the purpose of making him an inadvertent performer in a sequence intended to be exploited for its artistic effect."[173] A dissent saw the decision as a distinct threat to reporters:

... [the workman] was simply filmed going about his ordinary occupation and asked a few questions that directly related to his participation in, and opinions on, a clearly newsworthy event. This is a common and important technique of investigative reporting and should enjoy the same constitutional protection as would a written or filmed account of that event.

Can a reporter describe or photograph anything which occurs out in public?

Generally, yes. Anything which occurs in a public place, indoors or outside, can be photographed or written about.[174] Thus, photographs or descriptions of suicides, homicides, and the grisly results of accidents do not invade the privacy of the victims or their families.[175] However, two exceptions have been recognized. First, depiction of highly embarrassing, involuntary occurrences in public may be invasions of privacy.[176] Second, the place must truly be public, as distinct from, for example, a hospital room or a home.[177]

To what extent can a reporter be found liable for publicizing an individual in a false light?

If the subject of the story is a public person, then a reporter can probably defend the case as though it were a defamation action, with the plaintiff obliged to prove the characterization was false and made with actual malice.[178] The traditional situation which plagues reporters is the use of the wrong photograph with a caption or the photograph of a person whose activities or personality have no reasonable connection to the thesis of the story.[179] The false light usually must be substantially objectionable and minor inaccuracies are not covered.

The only Supreme Court decision to date on the conflict between reporting and privacy involved a "false light" claim.[180] In 1952 the Hill family involuntarily became front-page news when held hostage by three escaped convicts. One year later, a novel was published with a plot similar to the Hills' experiences but differing in crucial respects. In the novel the family suffered verbal assaults and physical violence; in the true life event they did not. Two years later, when the novel was made into a play, *Life* magazine ran an article about the opening, described the Hill incident, and indicated that the play was inspired by the true episode.

Hill sued for invasion of privacy on the theory that the article was a false account of what had really happened. The New York courts agreed, and the magazine appealed. First, the Supreme Court approved the New York rule that truth was a defense to a false-light privacy suit: "The factual reporting of newsworthy persons and events is in the public interest and is protected."[181] Since the harm turned on a determination that the statement was false, the principles underlying the *New York Times* doctrine required that in privacy suits "to redress false reports of matters of public interest" the plaintiff must show actual malice.[182]

Although the magazine won the point, it did not win the case. Since the evidence showed that the *Life* writer had some doubts about the relationship between the play and the Hills' experiences, a jury might find knowing or reckless falsity, so the case had to be retried under proper instructions.[183]

The principle in the *Hill* case was decided in favor of the press by a narrow margin of 5 to 4. (The dissenters thought that when reporting on essentially private persons involuntarily thrust into the limelight, the press should be more careful.) The results in lower courts since then have been mixed, although reporters have tended to prevail. For example, in one case, a news story falsely depicted a family, whose husband and father was killed a year earlier in a bridge collapse, as living in impoverished conditions. Although the article could have been more carefully written, there was no proof of actual malice: "Absent a calculated falsehood, the publication or broadcast of material concerning an event of public interest may not result in the imposition of a judgment for damages because of falsehoods or distortions arising from negligence or poor reporting."[184]

In another case, a segment of NBC's "First Tuesday" focused on the different justice meted out to white men and Indians in South Dakota. The report compared one case where an Indian had been convicted for killing a white man with the plaintiff's acquittal two years later of killing an Indian. The reporting contained numerous inaccuracies and omissions, and the plaintiff claimed the story cast him in a false light. Despite the reporting lapses, a jury verdict in favor of the plaintiff was overturned:

However, we hold that the proof that persons did infer that [the plaintiff] was the wrongful beneficiary of a double standard, and the proof of irrelevant inaccuracies, together fall short of establishing the 'malice' needed to sustain a verdict against a broadcaster in light of the dictates of the First Amendment.[185]

However, sometimes the courts have found malice in the false-light situation. In one case the *National Enquirer* ran an article about a woman who killed herself and her two children. In order to heighten the irony, the article portrayed her as the perfect wife and mother, even though the writer knew that her suicide note indicated the contrary. Her husband sued, and the court ruled that the story was "a substantially false and distorted picture of the plaintiff and his relationship with his wife" published with actual malice.[186] Similarly, in the case where *Newsweek* magazine used a photograph of a man standing in front of his house to illustrate a story on the "White Majority," the court ruled that an invasion of privacy claim was possible: ". . . while the subject of the article, to wit: the public concern of troubled Americans, is obviously a matter of public interest, nevertheless there is nothing to show that the plaintiff was ever involved either wilfully or unintentially in these matters."[187]

In light of the *Gertz* decision, which placed emphasis on the privacy interests of private individuals, the courts may follow suit and cut back on press protection in this particular area of privacy law which bears such a strong resemblance to defamation.

Can a reporter be held responsible for digging up and reporting true but embarrassing things about a person?

Theoretically you can be, but the newsworthiness of the story will usually be a valid defense.

The law recognizes the public disclosure of private facts as a distinct form of invasion of privacy.[188] In some respects this is the ultimate invasion since it breaches the individual's right to control information about himself.[189] In general, the facts disclosed have to be private ones, not items that are a matter of public record open to general inspection.[190] And the information made public must be the kind whose revelation would be objectionable to the ordinary person.[191] In general, the cases involve the disclosure of intimate facts about a person, the reporting of embarrassing facts, or the publication of skeletons in a person's closet.

Can you freely report matters involving the intimate details of a person's life?

Not without limits. Courts have generally upheld privacy claims where the matters disclosed involved a person's physical characteristics or peculiarities, details of sexual relations, or descriptions of unusual behavior traits.[192]

Thus, photographs or articles about intimate or deformed portions of the anatomy have resulted in liability.[193]

The problems are illustrated by the legal battles over the film *Titticut Follies*, which depicted life in a state institution for the criminally insane and included scenes of inmates shown nude and engaged in acts which would be highly embarrassing. Employees of the institution sought to enjoin distribution of the film on the ground that it cast them in a false light, but a federal court disagreed.[194] However, the state of Massachusetts brought a separate suit in order to protect the privacy of the inmates and was partially successful. The court compromised between freedom of the press and privacy by allowing distribution of the film only to audiences of professional people concerned with those problems, and not to the general public.[195]

Finally, the Supreme Court has suggested that the private intimacies of even the most public persons are entitled to protection.[196]

What about reporting current, but embarrassing or distressing, facts about a person?

So long as the reporting does not involve intimate matters and the subject is relatively current, almost anything is fair game. Courts have been extremely deferential to editorial judgments about what is newsworthy, especially where "hot news" is concerned: "The scope of privilege thus extends to almost all reporting of recent events, even though it involves the publication of a purely private individual's name or likeness."[197] But, while the "judgment of what is newsworthy must remain primarily a function of the publisher," "in cases where essentially private persons are the subject of publicity because of their involuntary connection with events of widespread interest, this discretion or judgment of the publisher cannot be absolute. The curiosity and voracious appetite of the public for scandal would be too easily exploited by unscrupulous publishers."[198]

Applying these principles, courts have allowed reporting

about the home life of a family whose father was killed in a bridge collapse,[199] a dispute concerning a white merchant in a black community who discontinued selling a black-oriented newspaper,[200] and the tragedy of a family whose two children had been trapped and suffocated in a refrigerator.[201]

By the same token, virtually all crime reporting is protected against privacy claims: "There can be no doubt that reports of current criminal activities are the legitimate province of a free press. The circumstances under which crimes occur, the techniques used by those outside the law, the tragedy that may befall the victims—these are vital bits of information for people coping with the exigencies of modern life."[202] This includes the right to identify the participants—criminal or victim—unless some statute or decision (for example, those shielding the identity of rape victims or juvenile offenders) provides otherwise.

The question of whether the press can constitutionally be barred from reporting the identity of a rape victim is now pending in the Supreme Court. The case involves a Georgia law making it a crime to report such information. The family of a rape victim sued a local television station for identifying their daughter in a newscast about the trial of her assailants. Although the Georgia court ruled that the criminal statute did not provide the basis for a civil suit, it concluded that as a matter of common law there is a right of privacy against public disclosure of such distressing information. The family could recover damages by proving that the publication of such information wilfully or negligently disregarded the fact that a reasonable person would find the revelation highly offensive.[203]

Are there limits on dredging up facts from a person's past?

Yes, but the precise boundaries are unclear.

Where an individual has at one time been a public figure or chosen to become involved in an event of public interest, reporting about him may remain protected for

years. The classic case involved a former child prodigy
who subsequently sought obscurity. Twenty-five years
later, in connection with a story in the *New Yorker* about
another similar person, the former prodigy was located
and made the subject of a "where are they now" sketch
which described his idiosyncratic life style. His suit for invasion of privacy was rejected on the theory that having
once been of great public interest he and his subsequent
career and current mode of living remaihed newsworthy.[204]
Similarly, where a shopkeeper had been involved in a race
riot in 1964, his life remained a matter of public interest
for a book about race relations written seven years later.[205]

On the other hand, where a person's newsworthiness
was essentially involuntarily, there may be a point in time
beyond which that person is entitled to a fresh start and
can no longer be subjected to publicity. The point is made
in two California cases decided forty years apart.

In the first, a woman who had been a prostitute and a
defendant in a sensational murder case changed her life
style, married, and dropped from sight. Several years later
a movie based on the details of her earlier life was released. The courts upheld her claim of invasion of privacy.[206]

More recently the California Supreme Court, in a leading case, reached the same result. A 1967 *Reader's Digest*
article about hijacking mentioned that the plaintiff had
stolen a truck in Kentucky and had a gun battle with police. There was no indication that the events had occurred
eleven years earlier. Since then the plaintiff had moved to
California, started a family, and become a respected member of his community. He sued for invasion of privacy and
won. Though approving complete reporting about current
and past criminal activity, the court ruled that ". . . the
identity of the *actor* in reports of long past crimes usually
has little public purpose."[207] Unless the individual has somehow reattracted public attention, or unless his crime was
such "that he has never left the public arena" (e.g., a political assassin), then the only purpose served by dredging
the matter up is curiosity.[208] And satisfying public curiosity
is insufficient to defeat a privacy claim. Applying a three-

fold test of "newsworthiness" and concluding that privacy and reporting can coexist, the court ruled that the plaintiff could prevail if he proved that his privacy was invaded "with reckless disregard for the fact that reasonable men would find the invasion highly offensive."[209]

This approach adopted by a distinguished court may well become the rule in this privacy area.

Footnotes to Chapter VI

1. The most useful guide to the law of defamation and the invasion of privacy is Dean William L. Prosser's classic *Law of Torts* (4th Ed. 1970) (hereafter referred to as *Prosser*). Equally useful to the reporter is Arthur B. Hanson's two-volume work, *Libel and Related Torts* (ANPA, 1969) (hereafter referred to as *Hanson*). Volume II contains the libel statutes of all 50 states. Volume I is a thorough discussion of the law. It also contains a concluding chapter, "Prognosis in the Newsroom" which sets forth practical pointers.
2. 376 U.S. 254 (1964).
3. 376 U.S. at 279-280.
4. *Gertz* v. *Robert Welch, Inc.*——U.S.——, 42 U.S. Law Week 5123 (June 25, 1974).
5. Thomas I. Emerson, *The System of Freedom of Expression* (1970), p. 543 (hereafter referred to as *Emerson*); Melville B. Nimmer, "The Right to Speak from *Times* to *Time*: First Amendment Theory Applied to Libel and Misapplied to Privacy," 56 Cal. L. Rev. 935 (1968).
6. *Prosser*, p. 739 (footnotes omitted).
7. See, *Prosser*, pp. 757-58; *Hanson*, pp. 26-29.
8. *Goldwater* v. *Ginzburg*, 414 F.2d 324, 338 (2d Cir. 1969), *cert. denied*, 396 U.S. 1049 (1970).
9. *Prosser*, p. 758 (footnotes omitted).
10. Compare, *Remington* v. *Bentley*, 88 F. Supp. 166 (S.D. N.Y. 1949) with *Gurtler* v. *Union Parts Mfg. Co.*, 1 N.Y.2d 5 (1956). See also, *Grant* v. *Reader's Digest Assn.*, 151 F.2d 733 (2d Cir. 1945); see generally, *Hanson*, pp. 26-29.
11. Compare *Raible* v. *Newsweek, Inc.*, 341 F. Supp. 804 (W.D. Pa. 1972) with *Afro-American Publishing Co.* v. *Jaffe*, 366 F.2d 649 (D.C. Cir. 1966).
12. *Greenbelt Cooperative Publishing Ass'n.* v. *Bresler*, 398 U.S. 6, 14 (1970); *Old Dominion Branch No. 496* v.

Austin, ——U.S.——, 42 U.S. Law Week 5102 (June 25, 1974).

13. *Gertz* v. *Robert Welch Inc., supra,* 42 U.S. Law Week at 5131.

14. See *Hanson* pp. 39-40.

15. *Id.* at p. 44.

16. *Braun* v. *Armour and Co.,* 254 N.Y. 514 (1930).

17. See, *e.g., Bon Air Hotel Inc.* v. *Time, Inc.,* 426 F.2d 858 (5th Cir. 1970) (article accusing luxury hotel of charging exhorbitant prices).

18. See, *Garrison* v. *Louisiana,* 379 U.S. 64 (1964); *Rosenblatt* v. *Baer,* 383 U.S. 75 (1966).

19. *Beauharnais* v. *Illinois,* 343 U.S. 250 (1952); See *Emerson,* pp. 391-99.

20. *New York Times Co.* v. *Sullivan,* 376 U.S. 254, 292 (1964).

21. *Rosenblatt* v. *Baer,* 383 U.S. 75, 78-79 (1966).

22. *Id.* at 82.

23. See, *Nieman-Marcus* v. *Lait,* 13 F.R.D. 311 (S.D. N.Y. 1952).

24. *Hanson,* pp. 71-80.

25. *Near* v. *Minnesota,* 283 U.S. 697 (1931).

26. *Pittsburgh Press Co.* v. *Pittsburgh Commission on Human Relations,* 413 U.S. 376, 386 (1973).

27. *Hanson,* p. 232

28. *Goldwater* v. *Ginzburg,* 414 F.2d 324, 337 (2d Cir. 1969), *cert. denied,* 396 U.S. 1049 (1970).

29. See *New York Times Co.* v. *Sullivan,* 376 U.S. 254, 281-83 (1964); *Barr* v. *Mateo,* 360 U.S. 564, 575 (1960).

30. See, *e.g. Gordon* v. *Adcock,* 441 F.2d 261 (9th Cir.), *cert. denied,* 404 U.S. 833 (1971); *Joftes* v. *Kaufman,* 324 F. Supp. 660 (D. D.C. 1971).

31. See *Curtis Publishing Co.* v. *Butts,* 388 U.S. 130, 151-52 (1967).

32. *Hanson,* p. 81.

33. Compare *Goldwater* v. *Ginzburg,* 414 F.2d 324 (2d Cir. 1969), with *Firestone* v. *Time, Inc.,* 460 F.2d 712, 721-23 (5th Cir. 1972) (concurring opinion).

34. See *Hanson,* pp. 81-84.

35. See *Rosenbloom* v. *Metromedia, Inc.* 403 U.S. 29, 37-38 (1971).

36. See, *e.g., Miller* v. *News Syndicate,* 445 F.2d 356 (2d Cir. 1971) (reporting about arrests, charges and prosecution protected as fair and accurate reports of official proceedings and fair comment on matters of public interest).

37. *Prosser*, pp. 830-31; *Hanson*, pp. 100-102.
38. *Hanson*, p. 100.
39. See, *e.g.*, *Campbell* v. *New York Evening Post*, 245 N.Y. 320 (1927).
40. *Danziger* v. *Hearst Corp.*, 304 N.Y. 244 (1952); *Shiles* v. *News Syndicate*, 27 N.Y.2d 9 (1970).
41. *Hanson*, p. 104 (footnotes omitted).
42. See, *e.g.*, *Buckley* v. *Vidal*, 327 F. Supp. 1051 (S.D. N.Y. 1971).
43. See, *New York Times Co.* v. *Sullivan*, 376 U.S. 254, 267, 279-80 (1964).
44. See, *e.g.*, *Coleman* v. *MacLennan*, 78 Kan. 711, 98 P. 281 (1908).
45. *New York Times Co.* v. *Sullivan*, 376 U.S. 254, 279-80 (1964).
46. 376 U.S. at 267-73.
47. *Id.* at 292, n. 30.
48. *Rosenblatt* v. *Baer*, 383 U.S. 75, 92 (1966) (concurring opinion).
49. *Garrison* v. *Louisiana*, 379 U.S. 64, 71-72 (1964).
50. *Rosenblatt* v. *Baer*, 383 U.S. 75, 85 (1966).
51. *Monitor Patriot Co.* v. *Roy*, 401 U.S. 265, 271-72 (1971).
52. *Rosenblatt* v. *Baer*, 383 U.S. 75, 86 (1966); see generally *Pauling* v. *Globe-Democrat Publishing Co.*, 362 F.2d 188, 196-97 (8th Cir. 1966).
53. *Harkaway* v. *Boston Herald Traveler Corp.*, 418 F.2d 56 (1st Cir. 1969).
54. *Rosenblatt* v. *Baer*, 383 U.S. 75, 87, n. 14 (1966).
55. *Garrison* v. *Louisiana*, 379 U.S. 64, 77 (1964).
56. *Monitor Patriot Co.* v. *Roy*, 401 U.S. 265, 277 (1971).
57. *Rosenblatt* v. *Baer*, 383 U.S. 75, 83 (1966).
58. *Ocala Star-Banner Co.* v. *Damron*, 401 U.S. 295, 300, n. 4 (1971).
59. *Garrison* v. *Louisiana*, 379 U.S. 64, 76-77 (1964); see also, *Monitor Patriot Co.* v. *Roy*, 401 U.S. 265, 273-74 (1971).
60. *Garrison* v. *Louisiana*, 379 U.S. 64, 72, n. 8 (1964); *Monitor Patriot Co.* v. *Roy*, 401 U.S. 265, 275 (1971).
61. *Monitor Patriot Co.* v. *Roy*, 401 U.S. 265, 274 (1971).
62. *Rosenbloom* v. *Metromedia, Inc.*, 403 U.S. 29, 48 (1971).
63. See *Curtis Publishing Co.* v. *Butts*, 388 U.S. 130 (1967).
64. *Id.* at 155.
65. *Id.* at 155-56.

66. *Prosser*, p. 823.

67. *Pauling* v. *Globe-Democrat Publishing Co.*, 362 F.2d 188 (8th Cir. 1966).

68. *Prosser*, p. 827.

69. *Cepeda* v. *Cowles Magazines and Broadcasting, Inc.*, 392 F.2d 417, 419 (9th Cir.) *cert. denied*, 393 U.S. 840 (1968).

70. *Greenbelt Coop. Publishing Co.* v. *Bresler*, 398 U.S. 6, 10-11 (1970).

71. See, *Belli* v. *Orlando Daily Newspapers, Inc.*, 389 F.2d 188, 195-97 (8th Cir. 1966).

72. *Pauling* v. *Globe-Democrat Publishing Co.*, 362 F.2d 188, 195-97 (8th Cir. 1966).

73. *Dacey* v. *Florida Bar, Inc.*, 427 F.2d 1292 (5th Cir. 1970).

74. *Waskow* v. *Associated Press*, 462 F.2d 1173 (D.C. Cir. 1972).

75. *Time, Inc.* v. *Johnston*, 448 F.2d 378 (5th Cir. 1971).

76. *Grayson* v. *Curtis Publishing Co.*, 72 Wash. 2nd 999, 436 P.2d 756 (1967).

77. *Maloney* v. *Gibson*, 263 So.2d 632 (Fla. 1st Dist. Ct. of Appeals 1972).

78. 42 U.S. Law Week at 5130.

79. *Id.* at 5132.

80. *Ibid.*

81. See, *e.g.*, *Belli* v. *Orlando Daily Newspapers, Inc.*, 389 F.2d 579, 587-88 (5th Cir. 1967).

82. *Time, Inc.* v. *Johnston*, 448 F.2d 378, 381 (5th Cir. 1971).

83. *Id.* at 380-83.

84. *Rosenbloom* v. *Metromedia, Inc.*, 403 U.S. 29, 43-44 (1971).

85. *Id.* at 43.

86. *Id.* at 62-87.

87. See, *e.g.*, *Miller* v. *News Syndicate*, 445 F.2d 356 (2d Cir. 1971); *Time, Inc.* v. *Ragano*, 427 F.2d 219 (5th Cir. 1970); *Mistrot* v. *True Detective*, 467 F.2d 122 (5th Cir. 1972); *LaBruzzo* v. *Associated Press*, 353 F. Supp. 979 (W.D. Mo. 1973); *Konigsberg.* v. *Time, Inc.*, 312 F. Supp. 848 (S.D. N.Y. 1970).

88. *Kent* v. *Pittsburgh Press Co.*, 349 F. Supp. 622 (W.D. Pa. 1972).

89. *Firestone* v. *Time, Inc.*, 460 F.2d 712 (5th Cir. 1972).

90. *Hensley* v. *Life Magazine, Time, Inc.*, 336 F. Supp. 50 (N.D. Cal. 1971).

91. *Bon Air Hotel, Inc.* v. *Time, Inc.*, 426 F.2d 858 (5th Cir. 1970).

92. *United Medical Lab.* v. *Columbia Broadcasting System*, 404 F.2d 706 (9th Cir. 1968), *cert. denied*, 394 U.S. 921 (1969).

93. *Time, Inc.* v. *McLaney*, 406 F.2d 565 (5th Cir.), *cert. denied*, 394 U.S. 921 (1969).

94. *Sellers* v. *Time, Inc.* 299 F. Supp. 592 (E.D. Pa. 1969), *aff'd*, 423 F. 2d 887 (3rd Cir.), *cert. denied*, 400 U.S. 830 (1970).

95. *Goldman* v. *Time, Inc.*, 336 F. Supp. 133, 318 (N.D. Cal. 1971).

96. *Garrison* v. *Louisiana*, 379 U.S. 64, 75 (1964).

97. *St. Amant* v. *Thompson*, 390 U.S. 727, 721 (1968).

98. *Ibid.*

99. *Id.* at 732.

100. See, *e.g.*, *Wasserman* v. *Time, Inc.*, 424 F.2d 920 (D.C. Cir. 1970) (concurring opinion); *Cervantes* v. *Time, Inc.*, 464 F.2d 986 (8th Cir. 1972), *cert. denied*, 409 U.S. 1125 (1973).

101. *Rosenbloom* v. *Metromedia, Inc.*, 403 U.S. 29, 52, n.18 (1971); see also, *Garrison* v. *Louisiana*, 379 U.S. 64, 71-75 (1964) (defense of truth cannot be conditioned on noble motives); *Greenblatt Coop. Pub. Ass'n.* v. *Bresler*, 398 U.S. 6(1970).

102. *Gertz* v. *Robert Welch, Inc.*, 471 F.2d 801, 807-08, n.15 (7th Cir. 1972); *rev'd on other grounds,——U.S.——* (1974).

103. *Curtis Publishing Co.* v. *Butts*, 388 U.S. 130, 158 (1967); *Goldwater* v. *Ginzburg*, 414 F.2d 324 (2d Cir. 1969), *cert. denied*, 396 U.S. 1049 (1970).

104. *New York Times Co.* v. *Sullivan*, 376 U.S. 254, 287-88 (1964); see also, *Beckley Newspapers Corp.* v. *Hanks*, 389 U.S. 81 (1967); *Kent* v. *Pittsburgh Press Co.*, 349 F. Supp. 622 (W.D. Pa.).

105. *Rosenbloom* v. *Metromedia, Inc.*, 403 U.S. 29, 56-57 (1971).

106. *Firestone* v. *Time, Inc.*, 460 F.2d 725, 718-21 (5th Cir. 1972).

107. *Curtis Publishing Co.* v. *Butts*, 388 U.S. 130, 161, n.23 (1967).

108. 376 U.S. at 287.

109. *Rosenbloom* v. *Metromedia, Inc.*, 403 U.S. 29, 56-57 (1971); *Miller* v. *News Syndicate Co.*, 445 F.2d 356 (2d Cir. 1971).

110. *Ibid.*
111. *Washington Post Co.* v. *Keogh*, 365 F.2d 965 (D.C. Cir. 1966), *cert. denied*, 385 U.S. 1011 (1967).
112. *Cervantes* v. *Time, Inc.*, 464 F.2d 986, 994 (8th Cir. 1972), *cert denied*, 409 U.S. 1125 (1973); see also, *Garland* v. *Torre*, 259 F.2d 545 (2d Cir.), *cert. denied*, 358 U.S. 910 (1958), but cf., *Gialde* v. *Time, Inc.*, 481 F.2d 1295 (8th Cir. 1973).
113. *Brogan* v. *Passaic Daily News*, 22 N.J. 139, 123 A.2d 473, 480 (1956); *Beechcroft* v. *Point Pleasant Printing and Publishing Co.*, 82 N.J. Super. 269. 197 A.2d 416 (1964).
114. See, *e.g.*, *Cerrito* v. *Time, Inc.*, 302 F. Supp. 1071 (N.D. 1972); *aff'd*, 449 F.2d 306 (9th Cir. 1971).
115. *Firestone* v. *Time, Inc.*, 460 F.2d 712, 719, 723 (5th Cir. 1972); see also, *Hensley* v. *Life Magazine, Time, Inc.*, 336 F. Supp.50 (N.D. Cal. 1971) *Cerrito* v. *Time, Inc.*, 302 F. Supp. 1071 (N.D. Cal. 1971); *aff'd* 449 F.2d 306 (9th Cir. 1971).
116. *Gertz* v. *Robert Welch, Inc.*, 471 F.2d 801 (7th Cir. 1972); *rev'd on other grds*, ——U.S.—— (1974).
117. *Gordon*. v. *Random House*, 349 F. Supp. 919 (E.D. Pa. 1972); *rev'd*, 486 F. 2d 1356 (3rd. Cir. 1973).
118. *Hensley* v. *Life Magazine, Time, Inc.*, 336 F. Supp. 50, 54 (N.D. Cal. 1971).
119. See, *e.g.*, *Miller* v. *News Syndicate Co.*, 445 F.2d 356, 358 (2d Cir. 1971); *Porter* v. *Guam Publications, Inc.*, 475 F.2d 744 (9th Cir. 1973); cf. *Varnish* v. *Best Medium Publishing Co.*, 405 F.2d 608 (2d Cir. 1968) (invasion of privacy suit).
120. *Prosser*, p. 821.
121. *McFarland* v. *Hearst Corp.*, 332 F. Supp. 746 (D. Md. 1971).
122. *Konigsberg* v. *Time, Inc.*, 312 F. Supp. 848 (S.D. N.Y. 1970).
123. *LaBruzzo* v. *Associated Press*, 353 F. Supp. 979 (W.D. Mo. 1973).
124. *Goldwater* v. *Ginzburg*, 414 F.2d 324 (2d Cir. 1969), *cert. denied*, 396 U.S. 1049 (1970).
125. 403 U.S. at 56-57.
126. *Time, Inc.* v. *Pape*, 401 U.S. 279 (1971).
127. *Id.* at 286.
128. *Id.* at 289-90.
129. *Id.* at 292.
130. *Time, Inc.* v. *Hill*, 385 U.S. 374 (1967).

131. *Wasserman* v. *Time, Inc.*, 424 F.2d 920 (D.C. Cir. 1970); *Time, Inc.* v. *Ragano*, 427 F.2d 219 (5th Cir. 1970); but compare *LaBruzzo* v. *Associated Press*, 353 F. Supp. 979 (W.D. Mo. 1973).

132. See, *e.g.*, *McFarland* v. *Hearst Corp.*, 332 F. Supp. 746 (D. Md. 1971).

133. *Curtis Publishing Co.* v. *Butts*, 388 U.S. 130, 156-59, 168-70 (1967).

134. *Id.* at 158-59.

135. *Goldwater* v. *Ginzburg*, 414 F.2d 324 (2d Cir. 1969); cert. denied, 396 U.S. 1049 (1970).

136. *Id.* at 337.

137. *Ibid.*

138. *Id.* at 339-40.

139. See, *e.g. Gertz* v. *Robert Welch, Inc; New York Times Co.* v. *Sullivan.*

140. *New York Times Co.* v. *Sullivan; Time, Inc.* v. *Hill.*

141. *Rosenbloom* v. *Metromedia, Inc.*

142. *Curtis Pub. Co.* v. *Butts.*

143. *Time, Inc.* v. *Hill*, 385 U.S. 374, 385, n. 9 (1967); see generally, Melville B. Nimmer, *The Right to Speak from Times to Time: First Amendment Theory Applied to Libel and Misapplied to Privacy*, 56 Cal. L. Rev. 935, 959 (1968).

144. See *Emerson*, pp. 544-48.

145. Samuel D. Warren and Louis D. Brandeis, *The Right to Privacy*, 4 Harv. L. Rev. 193 (1890).

146. *Id.* at 196.

147. See generally, William L. Prosser, *Privacy*, 48 Cal. L. Rev. 383 (1960); *Prosser*, pp. 802-18; Freedom of Information Center Report No. 275, *Privacy: A Chilling Tort* (January 1972).

148. *Prosser*, p. 807.

149. See, *e.g.*, *Diettemann* v. *Time, Inc.*, 449 F.2d 245 (9th Cir. 1971).

150. *Cantrell* v. *Forest City Publishing Co.*, 484 F.2d 150, 153, (6th Cir. 1973).

151. See, *e.g.*, *Briscoe* v. *Reader's Digest Association, Inc.*, 4 Cal.3d 529 (1971) (and cases cited therein).

152. See, *Time Inc.*, v. *Hill*, 385 U.S. 374, 384-86, n. 8-9 (1967).

153. 4 Harv. L. Rev. at 215.

154. Compare, *Commonwealth of Massachusetts* v. *Wiseman*, 356 Mass. 251 249 N.E.2d 610, cert. denied, 398 U.S. (1970) with *Cullen* v. *Grove Press, Inc.*, 276 F. Supp.

(S.D. N.Y. 1967); see *Briscoe* v. *Reader's Digest Association, Inc.*, 4 Cal.3d 529, 535-37 (1971).

155. See, *e.g.*, *Briscoe* v. *Reader's Digest Association, Inc.*, 4 Cal.3d 529 (1971).

156. See *Emerson*, pp. 553-57.

157. *Briscoe* v. *Reader's Digest Association, Inc.*, 4 Cal.3d 529 (1971); *Gallela* v. *Onassis*, 353 F. Supp. 196, 224 (S.D. N.Y. 1972); *aff'd in part, mod. in part*, 487 F.2d 986 (2d Cir. 1973).

158. See *Hanson*, pp. 206-07.

159. *Sidis* v. *F-R Publishing Corp.*, 113 F.2d 806, 809 (2d Cir.), *cert. denied*, 311 U.S. 711 (1940).

160. *Ibid;* see also, *Time, Inc.* v. *Hill.* 385 U.S. 374, 383, n.7 (1967); *Rosenbloom* v. *Metromedia, Inc.*, 403 U.S. 29, 45-49.

161. See, *e.g.*, *Raible* v. *Newsweek*, 341 F. Supp. 804 (W.D. Pa. 1972); see generally, *Prosser*, pp. 824-27.

162. *Prosser*, pp. 807-08.

163. *Pearson* v. *Dodd*, 410 F.2d 701, 703-04 (D.C. Cir.) *cert. denied*, 395 U.S. 947 (1969).

164. *Id.* at 704; see also, *Liberty Lobby, Inc.* v. *Pearson*, 390 F.2d 489 (D.C. Cir. 1968).

165. *Dietteman* v. *Time, Inc.*, 449 F.2d 245, 248 (9th Cir. 1971).

166. *Id.* at 249.

167. *Ibid.*

168. *Raible* v. *Newsweek*, 341 F. Supp. 804 (W.D. Pa. 1972).

169. *Cantrell* v. *Forest City Publishing Co.* 484 F.2d 150 (6th Cir. 1973).

170. *Prosser*, p. 808.

171. *Nader* v. *General Motors, Corp.*, 25 N.Y. 2d 560, 570 (1970).

172. *Galella* v. *Onassis*, 353 F. Supp. 196 (S.D. N.Y. 1972), *aff'd in part, mod. in part*, 487 F.2d 986, (2d Cir. 1973).

173. *Taggart* v. *Wadleigh-Maurice Ltd.* 489 F.2d 434 (3rd Cir. 1973).

174. *Prosser*, pp. 808-09. With the exception of courts and similar places. *But see, e.g.*, *Berg* v. *Minneapolis Star and Tribune, Co.*, 79 F. Supp. 957 (D. Minn. 1948) (photo of divorce litigant in courthouse corridor).

175. See, *e.g.*, *Jenkins* v. *Dell Publishing Co.*, 251 F.2d 447 (3rd. Cir. 1958) (article about murder victim of street gang); *Goldman* v. *Time, Inc.*, 336 F. Supp. 133 (N.D. Cal. 1971) (photo of two Americans living in Crete to illustrate story on young American nomads); *Metter* v.

Los Angeles Examiner, 35 Cal. App.2d 304, 95 P.2d 491 (1939). (suicide leap); *Kelley* v. *Post Publishing Co.*, 327 Mass. 275, 98 N.E.2d 286 (1951) (accident victim).

176. See, *e.g.*, *Daily Times Democrat* v. *Graham*, 276 Ala. 380, 162 So.2d 474 (1964) (photo of woman whose dress was unexpectedly blown up in an amusement park); compare, *Gill* v. *Hearst Publishing Co.*, 40 Cal.2d 224, 253 P.2d 441 (1953) (no invasion of privacy to publish photograph of husband and wife embracing in their place of business since any member of the public happening by could have seen the same thing).

177. *Prosser*, p. 809.

178. See, *Time, Inc.* v. *Hill*, 385 U.S. 374 (1967).

179. See, *Prosser*, pp. 812-13; see, *e.g.*, *Leverton* v. *Curtis Publishing Co.*, 192 F.2d 974 (3rd Cir. 1951) (finding liability where the photograph of a girl almost hit by a car was used to illustrate a story on negligence by pedestrians, entitled "They Ask to Be Killed").

180. *Time, Inc.* v. *Hill*, 385 U.S. 374 (1967).

181. *Id.* at 383, quoting from *Spahn* v. *Julian Messner, Inc.*, 18 N.Y.2d 324, 328 (1966).

182. *Id.* at 387-88.

183. *Id.* at 391-98.

184. *Cantrell* v. *Forest City Publishing Co.*, 484 F.2d 150, 157 (6th Cir. 1973).

185. *Berry* v. *National Broadcasting Co.*, 480 F.2d 428, 433 (9th Cir. 1973); see also, *Goldman* v. *Time, Inc.*, 336 F. Supp. 133 (N.D. Cal. 1971); cf. *Kapellas* v. *Kofman*, 81 Cal. Rptr. 360, 459 P.2d 912 (1969).

186. *Varnish* v. *Best Medium Pub. Co.*, 405 F.2d 608, 613 (2d Cir. 1968); cert. denied, 394 U.S. 987 (1969).

187. *Raible* v. *Newsweek*, 341 F. Supp. 804, 809 (W.D. Pa. 1972).

188. *Prosser*, pp. 809-12.

189. *Briscoe* v. *Reader's Digest Ass'n., Inc.*, 4 Cal.3d 529, 533-34 (1971).

190. *Prosser*, pp. 810-11. However, if they are obtained from confidential records, a privacy action will be possible. *Id.* at 811, n. 92.

191. *Prosser*, 811-12.

192. *Prosser*, 809-12.

193. See, *e.g.*, *Barber* v. *Time, Inc.*, 348 Mo. 1199, 159 S.W.2d 291 (1942) (account of a person's intimate medical history); *Bazemore* v. *Savannah Hospital*, 171 Ga. 257, 155 S.E.2d 194 (1930); *Douglas* v. *Stokes*, 149 Ky. 506,

149 S.W. 849 (1912) (pictures of deformed babies); *Banks* v. *King Features Syndicate*, 30 F. Supp. 352 (S.D. N.Y. 1939) (X-rays of a woman's pelvic region).

194. *Cullen* v. *Grove Press Inc.*, 276 F. Supp. 727 (S.D. N.Y. 1967).

195. *Commonwealth* v. *Wiseman*, 356 Mass. 251, 249 N.E.2d 610 (1970), *cert. denied*, 398 U.S. 960 (1970).

196. *Rosenbloom* v. *Metromedia, Inc.*, 403 U.S. 29, 47-48 (1971).

197. *Briscoe* v. *Reader's Digest Ass'n, Inc.*, 4 Cal.3d 529, 535 (1971).

198. *Cantrell* v. *Forest City Publishing Co.* 484 F.2d 150, 157 (6th Cir. 1973).

199. *Id.*

200. *Afro-American Publishing Co.* v. *Jaffe*, 366 F.2d 649 (D.C. Cir. 1966).

201. *Costlow* v. *Cusimano*, 34 App. Div.2d 196, 311 N.Y.S.2d 92 (4th Dept. 1970). However, publication of matters such as private debts has not been allowed. *Prosser*, p. 810.

202. *Briscoe* v. *Reader's Digest Association, Inc.*, 4 Cal.3d 529, 536 (1971); see also, *Miller* v. *News Syndicate Inc.*, 445 F.2d 356 (2d Cir. 1971).

203. *Cohn* v. *Cox Broadcasting Co.*, 231 Ga. 60 (1973).

204. *Sidis* v. *F-R. Publishing Co.*, 113 F.2d 806 (2d Cir. 1940).

205. *Gordon* v. *Random House*, 349 F. Supp. 919 (E.D. Pa. 1972), *rev'd*, 486 F.2d 1356 (3rd Cir. 1973).

206. *Melvin* v. *Reid*, 112 Cal. App. 285, 297 P. 91 (1931).

207. *Briscoe* v. *Reader's Digest Association, Inc.*, 4 Cal.3d 529, 537 (1971).

208. *Id.* at 537-38.

209. *Id.* at 542-43.

VII

Special Problems of the Underground Press

The last several years have witnessed the emergence—or more properly the re-emergence—of an important segment of the press generally characterized as the underground press. Its components ranged from the relatively staid *Village Voice* to extremely dissident, sporadically mimeographed "street" papers. At its apex the underground press—including student papers, military papers, and even prisoner publications—reached an estimated 18 million people.[1]

Reporters for such publications face most of the same problems shared by journalists in general and covered in the preceding chapters. The purpose of this chapter is to describe those legal issues which are more or less confined to reporters for the underground press.

Are reporters for an underground paper generally protected by the First Amendment?

Yes. The protection of the First Amendment is in no way limited to reporters for the establishment press: "... liberty of the press is the right of the lonely pamphleteer who uses carbon paper or a mimeograph machine just as much as of the large metropolitan publisher who utilizes the latest photo composition methods."[2] "The press in its historic connotation comprehends every sort of publication which affords a vehicle of information and opinion."[3] On at least two occasions, the Supreme Court has applied regular First Amendment principles to invalidate criminal or administrative sanctions imposed against reporters for underground papers.[4]

Moreover, not only have courts afforded First Amendment protection to the underground press, they have also recognized the unique functions that this segment of the press can serve:

The history of this nation and particularly of the development of many of the institutions of our complex federal system of government has been repeatedly jarred and reshaped by the continuing investigation, reporting and advocacy of independent journalists unaffiliated with major institutions and often with no resources except their wit, persistence, and the crudest of mechanisms for placing words on paper.[5]

Can reporters for the underground press be denied privileges afforded to the established media?

No. With one or two exceptions, courts have consistently ruled that the underground press and its reporters cannot be denied privileges granted to the press generally. This is simply an application of the rule that the government must be even-handed in its regulation of First Amendment activity and cannot discriminate on the basis of the content of the expression or the status of those who seek to engage in it.[6]

The problem has usually come up in connection with press credentials or access to news generally, where public officials have attempted to limit those privileges to reporters from "established" or "legitimate" news organizations. (These matters are discussed more fully in the chapter on gathering the news.) In general, courts have held that once the government opens an area or place to the press,[7] or provides credentials or information,[8] or allows papers to be sold or distributed,[9] all reporters and media must be treated the same.

Can an underground reporter be punished for publishing or distributing a paper with sexual content or four-letter words?

No, neither the presence of "dirty words" nor of sexual materials in an underground paper can be punished, unless the material falls into the category of hard-core pornography. There may be some limits on this rule where radio and television are involved.

During the heyday of the underground press, the obscenity laws were a favorite police device for harassment, arrests of street vendors, and raids on places where the paper was produced.[10] If there was any sexual content at all, it served as a pretext for police action. But when the prosecutions got to court the cases were usually or eventually thrown out. The courts ruled that the existence of four-letter words or sexual descriptions did not automatically make the publication legally obscene. Thus, a cartoon of policemen raping the Statue of Liberty, an explicit "love poem," a photograph of a nude couple locked in embrace,[11] a photograph of a nude man masturbating to satirize a magazine ("What Sort of Man Reads *Playboy?*"),[12] and an article about rock-group camp-followers making plaster-of-Paris casts of intimate parts of their hero's anatomy[13]—all have appeared in the underground press and been ruled non-obscene. Moreover, even the existence of some marginally vulgar item will not make the entire paper obscene: "Although several other items besides the picture in question advert to sexual matters, and Anglo-Saxon and colloquial words are used to refer to human organs, bodily functions and sexual relations, the sixteen page newspaper is devoted predominantly to libidinally neutral news reports, poetry, art-work, and discussions of topics generally of interest to the particular community that the newspaper seeks to serve."[14] Thus, so long as the paper "taken as a whole" does not constitute hard-core pornography, preparing or distributing it is not a crime.[15]

Can anything be done in advance about police harassment or arrests for "obscenity"?

Successfully defending an obscenity charge is all well and good, but can anything be done in advance? The answer is unclear.

In the late 1960s, underground papers often went into federal court to get an injunction against a pattern of harassment or arrests made under arguably unconstitutional obscenity statutes.[16] Sometimes they were successful in getting the statute declared invalid and the arrests or prosecutions halted. But in 1971 the Supreme Court limited the power of federal judges to interfere with a pending state prosecution.[17] However, you are still entitled to seek such relief if no criminal charges have been filed, or if the prosecution is being pushed in "bad faith."

In addition, while the Supreme Court has recently reaffirmed the government's power to prohibit hard-core pornography, limits have been placed on the power of the police to confiscate such materials. While a policeman might be able to take one copy of the paper if he arrests you, he cannot seize all the copies you have or raid a paper's offices without a prior judicial determination that the entire paper is legally obscene.[18]

Do you have to get a license or permit to distribute an underground paper on the street?

No. If you are giving the paper away, it is clearly unconstitutional to require a license or permit in order to do so.[19] And even if you are selling the paper, courts have held that the state's power to license the sale of merchandise like vacuum cleaners does not authorize regulation of the sale of newspapers.[20] For that reason, many ordinances which provide for licensing street vendors specifically exclude newspapers from their application.[21]

If a permit is required to sell a paper, do the officials have discretion to refuse to issue one?

No. Assuming a permit can be required, the courts have made it clear that the local officials cannot be granted broad discretion to refuse to give you one.[22] In various cases courts have invalidated attempts to make street vendors of underground papers register, because the ordinance contained no standards for governing the official's decision, or the standards were not written, or they contained impermissibly vague criteria.[23] In one case, an ordinance giving an official the power to issue permits "to such persons as he shall deem proper" was used to harass people selling the Black Panther paper.[24] The court ruled the ordinance unconstitutional. In another case the ordinance was invalidated in part because it did not require a statement of reasons for any denial of a permit.[25]

Can the officials make it burdensome to get a permit to sell the paper?

No. Courts have generally invalidated any requirement that went beyond simply applying for a license. Thus, you cannot be required to register or provide extensive identification,[26] to be fingerprinted or photographed,[27] to demonstrate financial responsibility,[28] to pay a license fee,[29] or to wear a badge.[30] All of these conditions have been held to be invalid burdens on freedom of the press.

(The following three questions are discussed at length in *The Rights of Students*, but a brief description of the law may prove helpful here.)

If you are a student, do you have to clear your paper with school officials before distributing it on or near campus?

At the high-school level the courts have generally split on the question. Some have ruled that students must submit unofficial publications to school officials before attempting to distribute them on campus.[31] But if the officials want to prevent distribution, they must expeditiously afford a hearing on the matter.[32] However, other courts have said that a requirement of prior submission, even as to high school students, is an invalid prior restraint on freedom of the press.[33] These issues are now pending before the Supreme Court.

At the college level, any such prior submission rule would probably be unconstitutional. The Supreme Court has stated that the First Amendment applies with the same force on the college campus as it does in the community generally.[34] Since such a rule could never be imposed on a regular newspaper, then it cannot apply to distribution of newspapers on the college campus.[35]

Can you be punished because of the content of the paper you distribute on campus?

Again, the answer varies with whether a high school or a college is involved. On the college campus, punishment can only be imposed for distributing material which could be punished if sold on the streets of the community, for example, because it contained hard-core pornography or defamatory statements.[36]

On high-school campuses a slightly different situation prevails. Since the Supreme Court has said that secondary-school officials can prevent conduct which might cause "substantial disruption of or material interference with school activities . . .",[37] many schools have tried to ban the distribution of certain kinds of publications on a variety of grounds. For example, schools have tried to ban the sale of unofficial publications, but the courts have frequently invalidated such a prohibition.[38] Efforts to ban papers which advocate illegal activities have also been unsuccessful.[39] Finally, bans on publications which include obscene language have been overturned.[40]

If you are a reporter or editor on an official school publication, can the authorities censor what you write?

Probably not. Schools consistently try to control what appears in official student-run publications; a popular device to accomplish this is to cut off funds. But the courts have pretty consistently prevented such actions. One recent case described the law well:

... if a college has a student newspaper, its publication cannot be suppressed because college officials dislike its editorial comment. ... The principles ... have been extensively applied to strike down every form of censorship of student publications at state-supported institutions. Censorship of constitutionally protected expression cannot be imposed by suspending the editors, suppressing circulation, requiring imprimatur of controversial articles, excising repugnant material, withdrawing financial support, or asserting any other form of censorial oversight based on the institution's power of the purse.[41]

Thus, once a school has chosen to establish and fund a paper or magazine, it cannot use its power of the purse or any disciplinary device in order to impose censorship.

Do you have any remedy if your printer refuses to print the paper because he doesn't like what it contains?

That depends. If the printer is somehow connected with a publicly supported institution—for example, if he is the campus printer—then you might be able to argue that his refusal constituted government censorship.[42] Otherwise, the only probable remedy would be a breach-of-contract lawsuit.

Can the police search an underground paper's office to see if the reporters have any evidence of a particular crime?

One recent case held that the police could not search the offices of a college newspaper in order to look for evidence about a recent campus demonstration.[43] The local police had obtained a search warrant to look for films and pictures taken by reporters of the *Stanford Daily*. The court ruled that where evidence was sought from members of the press not themselves suspected of any crime, the First and Fourth Amendments, read together, prohibited the use of a search warrant. If the police think a reporter has relevant information, then they must proceed by subpoena which the reporter will have an opportunity to challenge in advance. Moreover, the court reasoned, the execution of a warrant improperly allows the police to rifle the entire office to find what they are looking for, while a subpoena allows the reporter to bring only those items requested. Because a search presents an overwhelming threat to the press' ability to gather and disseminate the news, and because less drastic means exist to obtain the same information, third-party searches of a newspaper office are impermissible in all but a very few situations.

Finally, even where a reporter is suspected of having committed a crime, the police cannot search the entire office and seize all the books and files. Indeed, one of the main evils which the Fourth Amendment was designed to prevent was the English practice of searching all homes to find dissident literature.[44] Accordingly, the Supreme Court has ruled that the Fourth Amendment's requirement of particularity in describing what things are to be searched "is to be accorded the most scrupulous exactitude when the 'things' are books and the basis for their seizure is the ideas which they contain."[45]

Can the government compel a reporter from an underground paper to testify about the paper's internal workings and editorial responsibilities?

According to an important recent decision, the government cannot do so without a compelling need for the information.

The case involved the same grand jury investigation into the Black Panthers that resulted in Earl Caldwell's subpoena. The government called two women who worked with the Party newspaper and asked them a long list of questions about the workings of the paper, and about the reprinting of a speech which included threats against the President. For refusing to answer some of the questions the women were cited for contempt of court.

On appeal the citations were reversed. First, the court ruled that the First Amendment was applicable to grand jury inquiries, and that questions about who is responsible for editorial content "cut deeply in to press freedom."[46] Accordingly, where a grand jury's questions infringe on a reporter's rights, the government has the burden of showing that "there is a substantial possibility that the information sought will expose criminal activity within the compelling subject matter of the investigation."[47] Since the decision to print the speech was not a crime, there was no valid reason to inquire into the editorial processes:

If [the reporters] can be required to disclose the identity of all persons who worked on the paper and pamphlets, to describe each of their jobs, to give the details of financing the newspaper, any editor, reporter, typesetter, or cameraman could be compelled to reveal the same information about his paper or television station, if his paper or station carried the story. The First Amendment forbids that result.[48]

Footnotes to Chapter VII

1. Hearings Before the Senate Subcommittee on Constitutional Rights, *Freedom of the Press*, 92nd Cong., 1st and 2d S ss p. 112 (testimony of Lawrence Leamer); see also, Report of the 20th Century Fund, Press Freedoms Under Pressure, (1972) pp. 98-108.

2. *Branzburg* v. *Hayes*, 408 U.S. 665, 704 (1972); see also, *State* v. *Buchanan*, 250 Ore. 244, 436 P.2d 729 (1968). See generally, Comment, *Has Branzburg Buried the Underground Press?* 8 Harv. Civ. R. Civ. L. L. Rev. 181 (1973).

3. *Lovell* v. *Griffin*, 303 U.S. 440, 452 (1938).

4. *Kois* v. *Wisconsin*, 408 U.S. 229 (1972); *Papish* v. *Bd. of Curators of the U. of Missouri*, 410 U.S. 667 (1973).

5. *Quad-City Community News Service Inc.* v. *Jebens*, 334 U.S. 8, 16-17 (S.D. Iowa 1971); see also, *United States* v. *Head*, 317 F. Supp. 1138 (E.D. La. 1970).

6. See, *e.g.*, *Chicago Police Department* v. *Mosley*, 408 U.S. 92 (1972); *Healy* v. *James*, 408 U.S. 169 (1972); see generally, Comment, *Has Branzburg Buried the Underground Press?* 8 Harv. Civ. L. Civ. R. L. Rev. 181 (1973).

7. See, *e.g.*, *Kovach* v. *Maddux*, 238 F. Supp. 835 (M.D. Tenn. 1965) (access to floor of legislature); *Consumer's Union Inc.* v. *Periodical Correspondents' Association*, 365 F. Supp. 18. (D. D.C. 1973) (access to Congressional press galleries).

8. See *Quad-City Community News Service Inc.* v. *Jebens*, 334 F. Supp. 8 (S.D. Iowa 1971); but see, *Los Angeles Free Press, Inc.* v. *Los Angeles*, 9 Cal. App. 3d 448, 88 Cal. Rptr. 605 (1970); *cert. denied*, 401 U.S. 982 (1971).

9. *Overseas Media Corp.* v. *McNamara*, 385 F. 2d 308 (D.C. Cir. 1967) (access to newsstands at military bases overseas).

238

10. See, *e.g. Stein* v. *Batchelor*, 300 F. Supp. 602 (N.D. Tex 1969) (three judge court), *vacated on other grds. sub. nom.; Dyson* v. *Stein*, 401 U.S. 200 (1971).

11. See, *e.g., Papish* v. *Board of Curators of the University of Missouri*, 410 U.S. 667 (1973); *Kois* v. *Wisconsin*, 408 U.S. 229 (1972).

12. *United States* v. *Head*, 317 F. Supp. 1138 (E.D. La. 1970).

13. *Henley* v. *Wise*, 303 F. Supp. 62 (S.D. Ind. 1969).

14. *United States* v. *Head*, 317 F. Supp. 1138 (E.D. La. 1970).

15. *Kois* v. *Wisconsin*, 408 U.S. 229 (1972); *United States* v. *Head*, 317 F. Supp. 1138 (E.D. La. 1970); see generally, *Miller* v. *California*, 413 U.S. 15 (1973); *Paris Adult Theatre* v. *Slaton*, 413 U.S. 49 (1973).

16. See, *e.g., Carpenter* v. *Davis*, 424 F., 2d 257 (5th Cir. 1970); *Great Speckled Bird of Atlanta* v. *Stynchcombe*, 298 F. Supp. 291 (N.D. Ga. 1969); *Kois* v. *Brier*, 312 F. Supp. 19 (E.D. Wis. 1970).

17. *Younger* v. *Harris*, 401 U.S. 37 (1971).

18. See *Roaden* v. *Kentucky*, 413 U.S. 496 (1973); *Heller* v. *New York* 413 U.S. 483 (1973).

19. See *Schneider* v. *State*, 308 U.S. 147 (1939).

20. See, *e.g., Gall* v. *Lawler*, 322 F. Supp. 1223 (E.D. Wis. 1971).

21. See, *e.g., OD* v. *Wilson*, 323 F. Supp. 76 (D. D.C. 1971) (three judge court).

22. See, *e.g., Lovell* v. *Griffin*, 303 U.S. 444 (1938); *Schneider* v. *State*, 308 U.S. 147 (1939).

23. See, *e.g., Hull* v. *Petrillo*, 439 F. 2d 1184 (2d Cir 1971); *OD* v. *Wilson*, 323 F. Supp. 76 (D. D.C. 1971) (three-judge court).

24. *Hull* v. *Petrillo*, 439 F.2d 1184 (2d. Cir. 1971), *cf., Washington Free Community* v. *Wilson*, 426 F.2d 1213 (D.C. Cir. 1969).

25. *OD* v. *Wilson*, 323 F. Supp. 76 (D. D.C. 1971) (three judge court); see also, *Strasser* v. *Doorley*, 309 F. Supp. 716 (D.R.I. 1970) *aff'd*, 432 F.2d 567 (1st Cir. 1970).

26. *Strasser* v. *Doorley*, 432 F.2d 567 (1st Cir. 1970); *Wulp* v. *Corcoran*, 454 F.2d 826 (1st Cir. 1972).

27. *Gall* v. *Lawler*, 322 F. Supp. 1223 (E.D. Wisc. 1971); *OD* v. *Wilson*, 323 F. Supp. 76 (D. D.C. 1971) (three judge court).

28. *Gannet Co.* v. *City of Rochester*, 330 N.Y.S. 2d 648 (Sup. Ct. Monroe County 1972).

29. *Id.*; see also *Murdoch* v. *Pennsylvania*, 319 U.S. 105 (1943); *Hull* v. *Petrillo*, 439 F.2d 1184 (2d Cir. 1971); *Gall* v. *Lawler*, 322 F. Supp. 1223 (E.D. Wisc. 1971).

30. *Strasser* v. *Doorley*, 432 F.2d 567 (1st Cir. 1970); *Wulp* v. *Corcoran*, 454 F.2d 826 (1st Cir. 1972).

31. See, *e.g.*, *Quarterman* v. *Byrd*, 453 F.2d 54 (4th Cir. 1971); *Eisner* v. *Stamford Board of Education*, 440 F.2d 803 (2d Cir. 1971).

32. See *Eisner* v. *Stamford Board of Education*, 440 F.2d 803 (2d Cir. 1971).

33. See, *e.g.*, *Fujishima* v. *Board of Education*, 460 F.2d Cir. 1972).

34. *Healy* v. *James*, 408 U.S. 169 (1972).

35. *Cf.*, *New Left Education Project* v. *University of Texas*, 472 F.2d 218 (5th Cir.) *dismissed as moot*, 414 U.S. 807 (1973).

36. See *Papish* v. *Board of Curators of the University of Missouri*, 410 U.S. 667 (1973).

37. *Tinker* v. *Des Moines Independent Community School District*, 393 U.S. 503, 514 (1969).

38. See, *e.g.*, *Jacobs* v. *Board of Education*, 349 F. Supp. 605 S.D. Ind. 1972); *aff'd*, 490 F.2d 601 (7th Cir. 1974); *cert. granted*, 42 U.S. Law Week 3666 (June 3, 1974).

39. See *Scoville* v. *Board of Education*, 425 F.2d 10 (7th Cir. 1970).

40. See *Fujishima* v. *Board of Education*, 460 F.2d 1355 (7th Cir. 1972); *Koppell* v. *Levine*, 347 F. Supp. 456 (E.D. N.Y. 1972).

41. *Joyner* v. *Whiting*, 477 F.2d 456, 460 (4th Cir. 1973); see also, *Trujillo* v. *Love*, 322 F. Supp. 1266 (D. Colo. 1971); *Korn* v. *Elkins*, 317 F. Supp. 138 (D. Md. 1970) (three judge court).

42. Compare *Korn* v. *Elkins*, 317 F. Supp. 138 (D. Md. 1970) (three judge court).

43. *Stanford Daily* v. *Zurcher*, 353 F. Supp. 124 (N.D. Cal. 1972).

44. See *Stanford* v. *Texas*, 379 U.S. 476 (1965).

45. *Id.* at 485; see also *Stein* v. *Batchelor*, 300 F. Supp. 602 (N.D. Tex. 1969), *vacated on other grds, sub. nom., Dyson* v. *Stein*, 401 U.S. 200 (1971).

46. *Bursey* v. *United States*, 466 F.2d 1059, 1084 (9th Cir. 1972).

47. *Id.* at 1082-83.

48. *Id.* at 1087. A few days after this decision, the Supreme Court decided the *Branzburg* case. The government asked the Ninth Circuit to reconsider its ruling but the court held that *Branzburg* was applicable only to grand jury questions probing confidential sources.

Appendix

What follows is a listing and brief description of the twenty-five press shield laws which were on the books at this writing. In addition, we have included the Department of Justice Guidelines on contacts with the press.

1. Summary of State Shield Laws

Unless otherwise indicated, each of the shield laws applies to news media in general (including newspapers, magazines, radio, and television); many statutes, however, make no specific mention of wire services or press associations.

Whenever a problem arises, the text of the relevant statute must be carefully examined.

Alabama (Ala. Code Recompiled Title 7 Section 370 (1960))
Reporter privilege to protect "the sources of any information procured or obtained" while engaged in newsgathering capacity and published or broadcast in the news medium.

Alaska (Alaska Stat. §09.25.150-220 (1967))
Reporter privilege to protect "the source of information procured or obtained" while engaged in newsgathering. But a court, after hearing, may limit or deny the privilege where its exercise is "contrary to the public interest" or where necessary

to prevent "a miscarriage of justice or the denial of a fair trial." Privilege specifically applicable to ex-reporters.

Arizona (Ariz. Rev. Stat. Ann. §12-2237)
Privilege to protect "the source of information procured or obtained" for publication or broadcasting; specifically applicable to ex-reporters.

Arkansas (Ark. Stat. Ann. §43-917 (1964))
Privilege to protect "the source of information used as the basis for any [written, published or broadcast] article" unless it is shown that article was "written, published or broadcast in bad faith, with malice, and not in the interest of the public welfare."

California (Ann. California Codes, Evidence Code §1070)
Privilege to protect "the source of any information procured" for publication or broadcast while "connected with or employed upon" a newsgathering organization.

Delaware (Del. Code, Title 10, Ch. 43 (1973))
Reporter privilege to protect "the source or content of information that [the reporter] obtained within the scope of his professional activities," except that in an adjudicative proceeding, (1) the reporter must first state under oath that "the disclosure of the information would violate an express or implied understanding with the source" or would hinder maintenance and development of source relationships, and (2) the *content* is not privileged "if the judge determines that the public interest in having the reporter's testimony outweighs the public interest in keeping the information confidential."

Illinois (Smith-Hurd Illinois Ann. Stats., ch. 51, §§111-119 (1971))
Privilege to protect "the source of any information obtained by a reporter during the course of his employment." However, upon application, a court may divest the reporter of this privilege after consideration of "the nature of the proceedings, the merits of the claim or defense, the adequacy of the remedy otherwise available, if any, the relevancy of the source, and the possibility of establishing by other means that which it is alleged the source requested will tend to prove," if the Court finds "that all other available sources of information have been exhausted and disclosure of the information sought is essential to the protection of the public interest involved." The privilege

applies to any person who was a reporter at the time the information sought was procured or obtained.

Indiana (Ind. Code of 1971 §34-3-5-1)
Privilege to protect "the source of any information procured or obtained in the course of [the reporter's] employment" whether published/broadcast or not; privilege specifically extends to ex-reporters.

Kentucky (Ky. Rev. Stat. §421.100 (1969))
Privilege to protect "the source of any information procured or obtained [by the reporter] and published" in the news medium.

Louisiana (La. Stat. Ann. Rev. Stat. 45:1451-54)
Privilege to protect "the identity of any informant or any source of information obtained by [the reporter] from another person while acting as a reporter," except that after a hearing, a court may "find that the disclosure is essential to the public interest."

Maryland (Md. Ann. Code, Art. 35 §2 (1957))
Privilege to protect "the source of any news or information procured or obtained by [the reporter] for and published in the [news medium]."

Michigan (Mich. Stat. Ann. §28.945 (1))
"Communications between reporters of newspapers or other publications and their informants are ... privileged and confidential."

Minnesota (Minn. Stat. Ann. §§595.021-595.025)
Privilege to conceal "the person or means from or through which information was obtained or ... any unpublished information procured by [the reporter] in the course of his work or any of his notes, memoranda, recording tapes, film or other reportorial data which would tend to identify the person or means through which the information was obtained." However, the court may, upon application and after hearing, order disclosure if by "clear and convincing evidence" it finds (1) probable cause to believe that the source has information clearly relevant to a specific violation of law other than a misdemeanor, (2) no alternative or constitutionally less intrusive means to get the information are available, and (3) a "com-

pelling and overriding interest" in disclosure to "prevent injustice."

Montana (Mont. Rev. Codes Ann. §§93-601-2, 93-701-4 (1947))
Privilege to protect "the source of any information procured or obtained by [the reporter] in the course of his employment"; reporter "cannot without his consent be examined as to any communication made to him in confidence for the purpose of proper publication."

Nebraska (Rev. Stat. of Nebraska §§20-144-147 (1943))
Privilege to protect "the source of any published or unpublished, broadcast or non-broadcast information" obtained in the process of newsgathering or any "unpublished or non-broadcast information obtained or prepared for any medium of communication to the public."

Nevada (Nev. Rev. Stat. §§49.275, 49.385, 49.395 (1971))
Privilege to protect "the source of any information procured or obtained" by the reporter; privilege may be waived by voluntary disclosure or consent to disclosure.

New Jersey (N.J. Stat. Ann. Tit. 2A, ch.84A, §§21, 29)
Newspaperman's privilege to refuse to disclose the source of any information published in the newspaper; privilege may be waived by voluntary disclosure, consent to disclosure, or by contract.

New Mexico (New Mexico Stat. Ann. NMSA §§20-1-12.1 (1973))
Privilege to protect "the source of any published or unpublished information . . . [and] . . . any unpublished information obtained or prepared . . . for any medium of communication to the public"; however, a court may, upon application, order disclosure where "essential to prevent injustice."

New York (N.Y. Civ. Rights Law §79-h (McKinney 1973))
Privilege to protect "any news or the source of any news coming into [the professional journalists' or newscasters'] possession in the course of gathering or obtaining news. . . ."

North Dakota (N.D. Century Code §31-01-06.2)
Privilege to protect "any information or the source of any information procured or obtained" in newsgathering capacity, ex-

3. Department of Justice Guidelines

October 1973
[Order No. 544-73]

PART 50—STATEMENTS OF POLICY

Policy Regarding Issuance of Subpoenas to, and Interrogation, Indictment, or Arrest of, Members of News Media

By virtue of the authority vested in me by sections 516 and 519 of Title 28, of the United States Code, Part 50 of Chapter I of Title 28 of the Code of Federal Regulations is amended by inserting immediately after §50.9 a new §50.10 as follows.

§ 50.10 Policy with regard to the issuance of subpoenas to, and the Interrogation, Indictment, or arrest of, members of the news media.

Because freedom of the press can be no broader than the freedom of reporters to investigate and report the news, the prosecutorial power of the government should not be used in such a way that it impairs a reporter's responsibility to cover as broadly as possible controversial public issues. In balancing the concern that the Department of Justice has for the work of the news media and the Department's obligation to the fair administration of justice, the following guidelines shall be adhered to by all members of the Department:

(a) In determining whether to request issuance of a subpoena to the news media, the approach in every case must be to strike the proper balance between the public's interest in the free dissemination of ideas and information and the public's interest in effective law enforcement and the fair administration of justice.

(b) All reasonable attempts should be made to obtain information from nonmedia sources before there is any consideration of subpoenaing a representative of the news media.

(c) Negotiations with the media shall be pursued in all cases in which a subpoena is contemplated. These negotiations should attempt to accommodate the interests of the trial or grand jury with the interests of the media. Where the nature of the investigation permits, the government should make clear what the needs are in a particular case as well as its willingness to respond to particular problems of the media.

(d) If negotiations fail, no Justice Department official shall request, or make arrangements for, a subpoena to any member of the news media without the express authorization of the Attorney General. If a subpoena is obtained without authorization, the Department will—as a matter of course—move to quash the subpoena without prejudice to its rights subsequently to request the subpoena upon the proper authorization.

(e) In requesting the Attorney General's authorization for a subpoena, the following principles will apply:

(1) There should be reasonable ground based on information obtained from nonmedia sources that a crime has occurred.

(2) There should be reasonable ground to believe that the information sought is essential to a successful investigation —particularly with reference to directly establishing guilt or innocence. The subpoena should not be used to obtain peripheral, nonessential or speculative information.

(3) The government should have unsuccessfully attempted to obtain the information from alternative nonmedia sources.

(4) The use of subpoenas to members of the news media should, except under exigent circumstances, be limited to the verification of published information and to such surrounding circumstances as relate to the accuracy of the published information.

(5) Even subpoena authorization requests for publicly disclosed information should be treated with care to avoid claims of harassment.

(6) Subpoenas should, wherever possible, be directed at material information regarding a limited subject matter, should cover a reasonably limited period of time, and should avoid requiring production of a large volume of unpublished material. They should give reasonable and timely notice of the demand for documents.

(f) No member of the Department shall subject a member of the news media to questioning as to any offense which he is suspected of having committed in the course of, or arising out of, the coverage or investigation of a news story, or while engaged in the performance of his official duties as a member of the news media, without the express authority of the Attorney General: *Provided, however,* That where exigent circumstances preclude prior approval, the requirements of paragraph (j) of this section shall be observed.

(g) A member of the Department shall secure the express authority of the Attorney General before a warrant for an arrest is sought, and whenever possible before an arrest not requiring a warrant, of a member of the news media for any offense which he is suspected of having committed in the course of, or arising out of, the coverage or investigation of a news story, or while engaged in the performance of his official duties as a member of the news media.

(h) No member of the Department shall present information to a grand jury seeking a bill of indictment, or file an information, against a member of the news media for any offense which he is suspected of having committed in the course of, or arising out of, the coverage or investigation of a news story, or while engaged as a member of the news media, without the express authority of the Attorney General.

(i) In requesting the Attorney General's authorization to question, to arrest or to seek an arrest warrant for, or to present information to a grand jury seeking a bill of indictment or to file an information against, a member of the news media for an offense which he is suspected of having committed during the course of, or arising out of, the coverage or investigation of a news story, or committed while engaged in the performance of his official duties as a member of the news media, a member of the Department shall state all facts necessary for determination of the issues by the Attorney General.

A copy of the request will be sent to the Director of Public Information.

(j) When an arrest or questioning of a member of the news media is necessary before prior authorization of the Attorney General can be obtained, notification of the arrest or questioning, the circumstances demonstrating that an exception to the requirement of prior authorization existed, and a statement containing the information that would have been given in requesting prior authorization, shall be communicated immediately to the Attorney General and to the Director of Public Information.

(k) Failure to obtain the prior approval of the Attorney General may constitute grounds for an administrative reprimand or other appropriate disciplinary action.

Dated October 16, 1973.

ELLIOT RICHARDSON
Attorney General

[FR Doc.73-22773 Filed 10-25-73: 8:45 a.m.]

FEDERAL REGISTER, VOL. 38, NO. 206—Friday, October 26, 1973
(pp. 29588-29589) [28 C.F.R. §50.10]

ACLU HANDBOOKS